The Recurring Dark Ages

TRILOGY ON WORLD ECOLOGICAL DEGRADATION
by
Sing C. Chew

World Ecological Degradation: Accumulation, Urbanization, and Deforestation, 3000 B.C.–A.D. 2000

The Recurring Dark Ages: Ecological Stress, Climate Changes, and System Transformation

Ecological Futures: What History Can Teach Us

The Recurring Dark Ages

Ecological Stress, Climate Changes, and System Transformation

Sing C. Chew

ALTAMIRA
PRESS

A division of
ROWMAN & LITTLEFIELD PUBLISHERS, INC.
Lanham • New York • Toronto • Plymouth, UK

ALTAMIRA PRESS

A division of Rowman & Littlefield Publishers, Inc.
A wholly owned subsidary of The Rowman & Littlefield Publishing Group, Inc.
4501 Forbes Boulevard, Suite 200
Lanham, MD 20706
www.altamirapress.com

Estover Road, Plymouth PL6 7PY, United Kingdom

British Library Cataloguing in Publication Information Available

Library of Congress Cataloging-in-Publication Data

Chew, Sing C.
    The Recurring Dark Ages : ecological stress, climate changes, and system
transformation / Sing C. Chew.
        p.   cm. — (World ecological degradation)
    Includes bibliographical references.
    ISBN-13: 978-0-7591-0451-8 (cloth : alk. paper)
    ISBN-10: 0-7591-0451-4 (cloth : alk. paper)
    ISBN-13: 978-0-7591-0452-5 (pbk. : alk. paper)
    ISBN-10: 0-7591-0452-2 (pbk. : alk. paper)
    1. Environmental degradation. 2. Global environmental change. 3. Ecological
disturbances. 4. Climatic changes. 5. Environmental responsibility. I. Title.
    GE149.C54 2007
    304.2—dc22

                                                                2006018851

Printed in the United States of America

∞™ The paper used in this publication meets the minimum requirements of
American National Standard for Information Sciences—Permanence of Paper for
Printed Library Materials, ANSI/NISO Z39.48-1992.

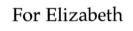

For Elizabeth

Contents

Figures and Tables

FIGURES

TABLES

APPENDIX 1: ARBOREAL POLLEN INFLUXES

Western Europe Pollen Counts

Central and Eastern Europe, Russia Pollen Counts

Northern Europe Plantago Pollen Counts

Mediterranean Plantago Pollen Counts

APPENDIX 3: ARBOREAL/NONARBOREAL POLLEN INFLUXES PERCENTAGES

Western Europe Arboreal/Nonarboreal Pollen Percentages

Central and Eastern Europe, Russia Arboreal/Nonarboreal Pollen Percentages

Northern Europe Arboreal/Nonarboreal Pollen Percentages

Mediterranean Arboreal/Nonarboreal Pollen Percentages

Preface

The reader will find in this book, the second of a three-volume series, my continuing journey to understand the structural conditions and processes that determine the relationship between Nature and Culture. In particular, I am focusing on a specific conjuncture in world history known as the Dark Ages to elucidate further the structural processes of the Nature-Culture relations, and the structural transformation of the world system.

In the first volume, *World Ecological Degradation*, I indicated that Dark Ages were critical phases in system reproduction, and that a comparative understanding of them was necessary to understand the evolution of the world system. Particularly in this book, I wish to clarify further the Nature-Culture relations via an examination of the Dark Ages in order to have a clearer understanding of system crisis and system transformations from an ecological world system history perspective—an approach I proposed some ten years ago (Chew 1997b). This attempt on my part to scrutinize the issue of system crisis and transformation is to propose that perhaps it is "ecology in command" that might be the key that will offer a more robust explanation of system crisis and transformation than what has been attempted to date as the "economy in command" approach in world-systems analysis (Chew 2002b). In an era of global environmental crisis, I hope that my approach will become more convincing as the crisis deepens, and that we will shift our way of thinking and analysis so that we can have a clearer view of what has occurred and what will happen.

To delve further into an understanding of system transformation, I propose in this book to consider Dark Ages in world history not only as a historical period for study, but also as a *historical-theoretical* concept to understand the historical moments of social system crisis and transition. By doing this in a historical-comparative manner over time-space boundaries, I believe, we can have a better grasp of system crisis and transition. This effort on my part is to try to convince the reader that we need to consider that *theory is history*, and that *history is theory*. In this sense, a comparative-historical examination of the Dark Ages over world history and our understanding of these phases are informed by our ecological world system history perspective, and pari passu, our analysis of the historical events and processes of Dark Ages informs and modifies our theoretical view of Dark Ages over world history.

Given the above, my investigation of Dark Ages over world history has convinced me, and hopefully the reader, that these periods are significant moments in human world history, for they are transitional phases of system transformation. It is my belief that Dark Ages (as historical events and as a theoretical concept) are critical crisis periods in world history over the course of the last five thousand years when environmental conditions have played a significant part in determining how societies, kingdoms, empires, and civilizations are reorganized and organized. Therefore, Dark Ages are significant moments for human history. They are periods of devolution of human communities, and as such from the perspective of human progress, a period of socioeconomic and political decay and retrogression. However, Dark Ages are periods of the restoration of the landscape, which are a consequence of the slowdown of human activities. In short, Dark Ages rejuvenate Nature but are bad for Humans.

To view it in such light would be in my view limiting by pitting one position against the other. Dark Ages, if we examine the historical events, conditions, and circumstances, are also historical phases of innovations, learning, and reorganizations. Being so, they are periods whereby the human communities that are impacted by these Dark Age conditions are forced by circumstances, and not perhaps by choice, to reorganize in a different manner to meet the contingencies of ecological scarcity and climate changes. It is my belief that this forms the basis for system transformation and the evolution of the world system. This theme of system transition is discussed briefly in the concluding chapter of this book. I have reserved the full treatment of this theme, which I have termed *ecological futures*, for the final volume of this three-volume study of world ecological degradation over five thousand years of world history.

It is always a pleasure to thank friends and colleagues who have supported this project. Matthias Gross always provided pertinent and supportive comments when I finished each chapter and constant encouragement to finish the manuscript. Bill Devall read each chapter carefully and gave me his advice. Gunder Frank, despite his illness, commented extensively on a partially completed manuscript. Regrettably, he passed away before I could complete the book. Besides reading over the chapters, Kristian Kristiansen invited me to present chapters of this book in four research seminars at Gothenburg University, where I obtained very valuable feedback from him, Jarl Nordbladh, and the participants of these meetings. Don Hughes and Bill Thompson also read the manuscript and provided pertinent comments and suggestions. At the invitation of Mats Widgren, some of the themes of this book were presented to the Royal Swedish Academy of Sciences and to the Human Geography Department at Stockholm University. Jonathan Friedman also invited me for a seminar at Lund University. These encounters provided valuable feedback on the manuscript. Despite his retirement, Bjorn Berglund has always been helpful in answering my questions on the pollen analysis. Others, such as Mitch Allen, Bob Denemark, Nick Kardulias, Baohong Mao, and George Modelski, have read specific chapters. Besides pointing out my errors and omissions, I would like to thank them all for their input. Earlier versions of the chapters of this book were also presented to various invited lectures and conferences in Sweden, Germany, Canada, People's Republic of China, and various places in America over the years, and I have benefited from comments and questions offered by the various audiences.

The research for this book, especially the pollen analysis, could not have been done without the help of Greg Gibson and Renee Benson. Both of them have been a tremendous help in this project, especially Greg, who went beyond the call of duty for supervising the pollen analysis profiles. The research for this book has been assisted by the California State University System Faculty Research and Creative Grants Program and the Humboldt State University Foundation.

I wish to thank my former editor, Mitch Allen, who saw the promise of this topic being an archaeologist himself and continued to do so even though he is no longer with AltaMira Press. My current editor, Rosalie Robertson, has filled wonderfully the vacuum left by Mitch. I wish to thank Annie Thomsen, who has done a remarkable job on the illustrations and maps.

My family has been very supportive of this long-term project. Even with their busy schedules, Ben and Siang have often asked about how the book is going. My "boys" (Beau, Billy, and Zeus) through their nudges and barks often reminded me that it was time to switch off the laptop and go for our daily walks on the beach. In view of my administrative responsibilities as chairperson and the difficult work environment at Humboldt when this book was being written, my wife Elizabeth offered constant encouragement throughout the writing of this book when at times completion seemed so far away. At her suggestion, this book was finalized at our other home in Stockholm in peace and quiet. For this, I am forever grateful.

Sing Chew
Gamla Stan, Stockholm

I

THE DARK AGES
OVER WORLD HISTORY

1

System Crisis

PROLOGUE: SYSTEM CRISIS

The basis for the reproduction of material life over world history has been the wide-scale utilization of the resources of the natural environment. In *World Ecological Degradation,* the history of this utilization process was traced over geographic space spanning five thousand years of world history (Chew 2001). The recurring outcome of this process—based on the human communities' efforts to reproduce social life according to the social organizational patterns that have evolved—appears to be ecological degradation. Nonetheless, the motions of history do also suggest periods of ecological recovery of the degraded areas, and the penetration of new areas for the extraction of fresh natural resources to sustain further system/economic expansions. Therefore, viewed from the perspective of *la longue durée,* ecological degradation and recovery appear to recur in phases.[1]

As *World Ecological Degradation* has revealed, excessive ecological degradation leads to environmental collapse, and along these lines, there are certain phases of environmental collapses that occur mutatis mutandis with civilization demises. This relationship between environmental collapses and civilization demises suggests that when societal relations with the natural environment become exploitative and unsustainable over time, a social system crisis is triggered. As the natural environment plays a part in social system reproduction, we need therefore to widen our gaze for other factors that engender a social system crisis/transition beyond those that are social, political, and economic in nature.

In this subsequent volume to *World Ecological Degradation,* given the above set of sequences, the focus will be to deliberate on other nonanthropogenic factors conditioning a social system crisis by continuing our historical examination of the Culture-Nature relationship that was started in _World Ecological Degradation._ What calls for further exploration is the dimension of the natural environment and the part it has within the overall matrix that produces a social system crisis, and in the process, long-term and large-scale social change. By this consideration, the orthodox manner of explaining social system crisis along social, political, and/or economic factors can then be recalibrated. No doubt, there will be concerns, especially from positions that have considered anthropogenic factors as the only "primordial" elements for engendering a social system crisis and long-term social change. However, such stringent adherence to human factors needs to be reconsidered in view of recent studies focusing on other elements conditioning social system crises (Chew 2001, Kristiansen 1993, N. Brown 2001, Baillie 1994, Weiss 2000, Hughes 2001, Burroughs 2005).[2]

The way forward requires a redrawing of the baseline for our understanding of long-term social change and social system crisis. Nonanthropogenic elements need to be brought into play, of which besides the natural environment, the other crucial factors are climate and natural events such as tectonic shifts and volcanicity. Such an inclusion of the natural environment, climate, and natural disturbances as factors assumes an intimate interaction between natural systems dynamics and social systems dynamics that produces a series of tendencies that determine the parameters of social (world) systems reproduction. These tendencies are determined by the intensity of the Culture-Nature relationship in the reproduction of life, that is, the relationship between the social system and the natural systems. When the intensity of this relationship reaches critical limits over the long term, we have the appearance of a world (social) system crisis as well as a natural system crisis.

Social (world) system crisis means that the continued evolution of the system faces obstacles, and that necessary structural changes or adjustments have to be made for systems reproduction to continue. These crisis phases become the key periods for our understanding of the dynamics of world-system evolution and transition (long-term social change). Over world history, these crisis moments are rare. Historically, when they do occur, these phases are extremely impactful in terms of geographic coverage, and they extend over a long period in terms of socioeconomic and ecological recovery. In world history, these phases are known as the _Dark Ages._

SYSTEM CRISIS AND ECOLOGY

Much scholarly attention has been directed to analyzing the socioeconomic and political processes such as capital accumulation, political hegemonic rivalries, technological changes (or the lack thereof), trade system collapses, social-political unrest, and border incursions to explain the basis for system crisis and long-term change (e.g., see Gills and Frank 1992, Wilkinson 1995, Goldstone 1991, Abu-Lughod 1989, Wolf 1982, Wallerstein 1974, Modelski and Thompson 1999, Amin 1982, Anderson 1974, Tilly 1992, Mann 1986). What perhaps needs more attention is the interaction between world (social) system and the natural system to flesh out further the conditions for system crisis. Along such lines, various studies have intimated the relationship between climatological and ecological changes with human organizations and activities (e.g., see Ladurie 1971, Berglund 2003, N. Brown 2001, Chew 2001, Kristiansen 1998a, Thompson 2000, Burroughs 2005). Some like Fernand Braudel (1972, 1981, 1982, 1984, 1989) have couched the social, political, and economic factors in concert with the natural environment and the climatological patterns as determinants of long-term and large-scale transformations.[3] However, what is still lacking is an exploration in greater depth and, on a longer-term basis, the impacts of climate and ecological changes on the generation of system crisis. After all, in the material reproduction of the world (social) system, we still rely on the natural system.

Given the above parameters, we need to *abstract historically* the several processes at work. The natural occurrences and shifts in terms of climate changes and natural disturbances, such as volcanic eruptions and earthquakes, independently condition the reproduction and evolution of the world system. Just considering only these elements would be myopic on our part, for we know through world history that social and organizational factors (urbanization, accumulation, wars, technological innovations, and population) also impact on world-system reproduction. Thus, human-induced changes to the ecology and the climate in turn form barriers to the reproduction of the world system.

Most models that attempt to explain long-term system change concentrate overwhelmingly on anthropogenic causes as I have suggested in the previous pages. If we consider the parameters at work in engendering a system crisis (see previous paragraph), the explanation requires the inclusion of the natural environment and other nonsocial factors, for they also form the basis for the reproduction of the world system. Moving a step forward, what needs also to be considered is the degree of weight these latter factors have in precipitating a system crisis. The answer cannot be sought theoretically, but rather within a framework of historical structures and processes and via an analysis of the historical dynamics of Nature-Culture relations and climatological trends.

Our task ahead is to sketch out a *theoretically generalized history* of Dark Ages or system crisis and, within the limits of available historical information, identify contingent factors and agents that could have engendered each specific Dark Age phase or system crisis from the Bronze Age to the Iron Age of world history. *However, our overall effort in this exercise is to move away from just a history understood and interpreted within a geospatial-dependent and time-contingent framework. The aim is to abstract a theoretically generalized account of the dynamics and structures of world-system evolution from historical events.* Methodologically, we are considering Dark Ages in world history not only as a historical period of study, but also as a *historical-theoretical* concept to understand the historical moments of social system crisis and transition over world history. In this regard, we want to have an understanding of system crisis and long-term social change that is theoretically generalizable, albeit with *some conjunctural elements that are different.* The end point would be a social science history of long-term change, that is, a theoretically informed history of the evolution of the world system.

Such a theoretical-methodological attempt discussed above, and employed previously (Chew 2001), has been met with concerns and even skepticism by some specialists whose works have focused on a specific nation-state, local area, or region, and who are guided mostly by the naturalistic-scientific methodological conception of knowledge generation or subjectivistic-phenomenological interpretations (e.g., see Butzer 2005). "Find the data/interpretation and let the data/interpretation inductively inform us about what happened ecologically" seems to be the basis of such critiques of my approach, and thereby dismissing my attempt to provide coherence and structure to micro- or regional-level analyses so that the motions of world history can be understood. Without attempting to generalize and perform theoretically informed comparative analysis of various ecological transformative-structural outcomes across time and geographic space juxtaposing different archaeological, palynological, and historical sources, in my view, prevents us from seeing the big picture, and thus, world history.

A THEORETICALLY GENERALIZED HISTORY OF DARK AGES: DARK AGES AS A WORLD-SYSTEM PROCESS

Nature and Geographic Scope of Dark Ages

System crises are moments when system reproduction experiences obstacles and difficulties. The historical dynamics of Nature-Culture relations exhibiting system crisis moments appears in the form of Dark Ages. Over world history, such Dark Ages, or prolonged periods of widespread social and economic distress and ecological crisis lasting for centuries, are rare. Between 3000 B.C. to A.D. 1000, there have been identifications of only two or three such periods impacting Northwestern India, west Asia, the Mediterranean, and Europe. V. R. Desborough in *The Greek Dark Ages* identified such a phase of distress for prehistoric Greece:

> during these generations the changes that came about are little short of fantastic. The craftsmen and artists seem to vanish almost without a trace: there is very little new stone construction of any sort, far less any massive edifices; the metal-worker's technique reverts to primitive, and the potter, except in early stages, loses his purpose and inspiration; and the art of writing is forgotten. But the outstanding feature is that by the end of the twelfth century the population appears to have dwindled to about one-tenth of what it had been little over a century before.

A. M. Snodgrass' characterization of such a period in *The Dark Age of Greece* complements the conditions and extends it further to cover the collapse of trade and commerce across geographic boundaries beyond those of prehistoric Greece. Here is how he described it:

> the modern doctrine would hold that the following characteristics were present in the post-Mycenaean period: first, a fall in population that is certainly detectable and may have been devastating; secondly, a decline or loss of certain material skills; thirdly, a similar decline or loss in respect of some of the more elevated arts, of which the apparent loss of the art of writing is most striking to us . . . ; fourthly, a fall in living standards and perhaps in the sum of wealth; fifthly, a general severance of contacts, commercial and otherwise, with most peoples beyond the Aegean area and even with some of those within it.

Recently, John Bintliff (2004, 312) has again reiterated similar types of socioeconomic characterizations for prehistoric Greece:

> many other striking signs of "de-skilling" characterize this period: the disappearance of elaborate architectural complexes; impoverished assemblages of metal; the virtual absence of human representations; a dramatic decline in the number of dated occupation sites; very reduced evidence for foreign exchange compared with the preceding period; and no sign of political centers of regional control. Whatever the reasons for the end of the palace states, the reduction in social, economic, and artistic complexity was severe and persisted for many generations.

In *Memory and the Mediterranean*, Fernand Braudel identified these types of disruptions at the end of the twelfth century for the Mediterranean region:

> the move back into the past seems to have been most marked for Greece. Along with writing, the jewel amongst achievements, all the luxury arts

vanished too: jewelry, mural paintings, engraved precious stones and seals, sculpted ivory and so on. Only pottery turned on the wheel seems to survive, with the last relic of the Mycenaean style vanishing during the eleventh century to be replaced by the first proto-geometrical ceramics. At the same time, all links with the Middle East seem to have been severed after the Dorian invasion and would only be restored much later when Greece and the Aegean in the full flush of expansion began to trade once more with the Syrian ports and Egypt, establishing outposts on the coast of Asia Minor.

These socioeconomically and politically determined excerpts describe for us the social and economic conditions of the times, but there are no references to ecological and climatological changes. However, if we read Thascius Cyprianus' (cited in Toynbee 1939, 8) depiction of the period, he gives us an account of these latter conditions that were not addressed by the previous scholars:

> This truth is proclaimed, even if we keep silence . . . , by the World itself, which testifies to its own decline by giving manifold concrete evidences of the process of decay. There is diminution in the winter rains that give nourishment to the seeds in the earth, and in the summer heats that ripen the harvests. The springs have less freshness and the autumns less fecundity. The mountains, disemboweled and worn out, yield a lower output of marble; the mines, exhausted, furnish a smaller stock of the precious metals: the veins are impoverished, and they shrink daily.

Recently, Marc Van De Mieroop in *A History of the Ancient Near East* has also wondered whether the recurrence of long periods of drought in the Ancient Near East could have serious consequences for the Near East leading to Dark Ages. However, with the paucity of records on the ancient climate of the Near East as he has noticed, he veered toward the side of caution by refraining from deriving a conclusion from such an association. Instead, he juxtaposed this issue by acknowledging the commonly accepted theme that emergence of the Dark Ages was a consequence of human factors. Listen to his thinking:

> Long periods of drought could easily have occurred in the time span we study here, however. While we can assume that over the last 10,000 years the climate of the Near East has not substantially changed, it is certain that even marginal variations could have had serious consequences for the inhabitants. The question arises as to whether the so-called Dark Ages resulted from a drying of the climate which made rainfed agriculture impossible in zones usually relying on it, and which lowered the rivers to such an extent that irrigated areas were substantially reduced. Or should we focus on human factors in trying to explain such periods? So far, insufficient data on ancient climate are available to serve as historical explanation for the drastic political and economic changes we observe.

The above combination of excerpts from various scholars does provide a glimpse of what political, socioeconomic, and ecological conditions were like during a Dark Age. They provide us with the historical-theoretical contours of the ecological, socioeconomic, and political landscape of Dark Ages, and thus are our map for interpreting and understanding Dark Ages.

From a growth and social progress model, the above descriptions of widespread distress indicate that a significant crisis in social reproduction whereby production/appropriation, exchange/distribution, and consumption as interlocked processes were not maintaining comparable reproduction levels to the period prior to the phase of darkness.[4] Instead of social growth and development, we see stagnation and devolution. Viewed from a long-term perspective, these distressed phases suggest that system transformation is not just a process that propels forward in a linear or geometric fashion, but also one that constitutes processes of evolution (growth) and devolution (stagnation) as the periods of Dark Ages reveal.

The dynamics producing Dark Ages or crisis (devolution) in reproduction—assuming that the social reproduction processes have no priority of one over the other—should not be attributed to just *local* constraints hindering a region (such as prehistoric Greece) from reproducing itself within its social and ecological parameters. With the different levels and manner of interconnectedness of social formations in a world system, the roots of the crisis of reproduction are not solely limited to local or regional conditions, but to world-systemic dimensions as well, depending on the state of the evolution of the world system.[5] It involves, therefore, multiple levels of conditions and factors on a large geographic scale.[6]

Given the above, the constraints to system reproduction can arise because of different relations and interactions over time and space, and Dark Ages are the periods when these constraints manifest themselves. There are a variety of reasons and factors at different levels that could engender social reproduction constraints and hence crisis. For example, constraints can emerge as a consequence of a social formation's intensive relation with its ecological environment within and without. They can also be the result of the contradictions between inter- and intrasocial groups or the outcome of the incommensurability of different functions of the social formation giving rise to contradictions (e.g., a chosen social strategy that cannot be supported by the existing economy). Beyond this, reproduction limitations can also emerge because of unintended consequences from the social strategies chosen.

The numerous constraints and factors, such as contradictions between inter- and intrasocial groups or the incommensurability of different functions of the social formation giving rise to contradictions triggering crises of reproduction, identified have been mostly derived from social, political, and economic roots. What is seldom discussed during these phases of Dark Ages is the social formation's relation with its ecological environment within and without. This neglect frames our perception that Dark Ages are characterized *only* by social, political, and economic depressive conditions. They exhibit conditions of acute social, economic, and political disruptions exhibited by trends such as:

- economic slowdowns and trade disruptions
- political unrest and breakdowns
- reduced social stratification and social simplification of lifestyles
- deurbanization
- increased migration
- population losses[7]

The above trends do not reveal to us the scale of ecological degradation. If explanations of crisis sequences are limited to only those of socioeconomic and political origins—Dark Ages therefore are not understood as periods circumscribed by ecological crisis and climatological changes—we will accordingly miss other factors and dimensions that might be determinative[8] or contingent in terms of explanatory power. Widening and deepening our gaze through the inclusion of the ecological landscape, the natural processes, and the climatological cycles that circumscribe our material lives would compensate for the deficit.

However, such an adjustment would mean a different line of reasoning and presentation of historical data (from the ecological landscape) that will lead to an explanation for sequences (Dark Ages) in world history from a different angle than what has been proposed to date. It would reveal that there are costs associated with the reproduction of socioeconomic life, and the consequence being a trajectory of numerous collisions with the natural environment as civilizations, empires, kingdoms, and nation-states seek to expand and grow (Chew 1999, 2001; Ponting 1991; Hughes 2001). Such collisions have a number of outcomes such as natural resource depletion, loss of species diversity, polluted oceans and rivers, siltation, population losses due to flooding, etc. (Chew 1999, 2001; Ponting 1991; Hughes 2001).

Examining the Dark Ages in greater detail reveals that the Culture-Nature relations during such a period exhibit trends and tendencies that are significantly different from expansionary phases (e.g., see Renfrew 1982). The socioeconomic patterns that emerged during these Dark Ages veered away from the usual intensive exploitation of Nature that normally characterizes the trends and dynamics of human societal reproduction. During such phases of world history, all expansionary trends that are typical reproductive features of human communities display negative trajectories and tendencies, especially in the core areas of the world system.[9] In view of this, Dark Ages also represent ecological long phases reflecting the outcomes of the relations between Culture and Nature.[10]

With reduced socioeconomic activities, Dark Ages are perhaps periods of restoration of the ecological balance that has been disrupted by centuries of intensive human utilization of Nature. Several studies have indicated how the relations between human communities and the natural environment have impacted the former's economic reproduction and have also caused socioeconomic organizational changes and perhaps even their collapse (Kristiansen 1993, 1998a; Chew 1995a, 1997a, 1999, 2001, 2002a).

If this is the case, ecological limits become also the limits of the socioeconomic processes of the world system, and the interplay between ecological limits and the dynamics of the system define the historical tendencies and trajectories of the human enterprise (Kristiansen 1998b; Chew 1999, 2001). Therefore, perhaps the usual dictum that "economy in command" is the sole force underlying global transformation in the long term needs to be reconsidered. We need to file down further the key for understanding and explaining world-system dynamics and transformation (Chew 1999, 2001). It is the interpellation between "ecology in command" and "economy in command" that accounts for system transformation. Perhaps even more of the former than the latter is the underlying condition prompting a system crisis or transition.

World history has shown that the impacts of Dark Ages do not extend necessarily and evenly across geospatial boundaries of the system. As we have seen in *World Ecological Degradation,* ecological degradative shadows are cast by the dominant core over wide areas of the world system. These shadows thus are a consequence of core-periphery relations beyond those ecologically degradative effects that might be generated by the periphery itself. The articulations of the connections between and within regions during periods of world history between the core and the periphery determine the impact and spread of Dark Age conditions. Depending on the systemic connections of the world economy at a particular point in time, and the level of intensity of the Culture-Nature relations experienced by a given region, the extent of impact of a Dark Age period is uneven. The state of crisis and/or transition appears to have its greatest impact on the regions of the world system that are considered the core(s) of the system at the specific point in time. No doubt, this is related to the fact that it is in the core region(s) where Culture-Nature relations are at their most heightened levels. This does not imply that the periphery does not experience any crisis conditions. The connections that the core has with the periphery via several economic and political processes ensure that at least some (if not all) crisis conditions will be felt. The extent is based on how incorporated the periphery is in the productive processes of the core(s).

At the nascent stage of world-system connections, it is very clear that during the *early stages* of the evolution of the world system, Dark Age conditions encountered in one part of the world system might not be felt as catastrophically and simultaneously as the part (both core and periphery) encountering these conditions. Over time, the lack of simultaneity of impact will develop to a synchronicity of impact of Dark Age conditions as the evolution of the world system continues, and as available areas of natural resources get reduced and the landscape becomes more and more degraded, thus increasing the vulnerability exposure level and leaving very little room for ecological recovery. In short, the ecological circumstances circumscribe the tendency of the synchronicity of Dark Age conditions being experienced across the world system. To some extent, Dark Ages also offer opportunities for some in the periphery to rearticulate themselves within the hierarchical matrix of the zonal production and reproduction processes.

Climatological changes are also associated with Dark Ages. Climatological changes and natural calamities when they occur during Dark Ages generate further challenges to social system reproduction. Their occurrences and impacts on social systems have been noted during periods of the Dark Ages (e.g., see Keys 1999, Chew 1999, Weiss et al. 1993, Weiss 2000, Weiss and Bradley 2001, Burroughs 2005). Higher-than-normal temperatures can generate salinization problems for agricultural cultivation, especially in areas where irrigation is extensively used. It could also lower harvest yields. The aridity that commonly occurs with high temperatures has often generated severe problems for pastoral herds because of the loss of foliage and grasses that have led to nomadic migrations, thus causing further social pressures on core centers.

If Dark Ages are prolonged crisis periods, then crisis provides opportunities. In other words, crisis conditions, though perhaps restricting continuous unrestricted expansion, provide the opportunities for the resolution of contradictions that have developed to such a state that inhibits the reproduction of the system. Such opportunities are presented timewise during the period toward the end of the Dark Ages when the socioeconomic conditions of deterioration are receding and the natural environment has started to rejuvenate. Thus, crisis enables the necessary adjustments to be made. It leads to pathways and processes that would mean system reorganization and perhaps even transition. Given this, Dark Ages provide the opportunity for systemic reorganization, perhaps also engendering systemic transition followed with redistribution of resources, political power, and economic concentration.

Duration of Dark Ages

Dark Ages therefore depict very specific moments in world history when system reproduction is in a state of crisis and/or transition. Resolution of the crisis requires an extended period (historically at least five hundred years) as the length of occurrence of specific Dark Ages have revealed. Such an expanse of time (ecological time) provides the window of opportunity for the ecological landscape to be restored and to enable economic productive capacities to continue. Especially with resource depletion, the need arises for innovations in social organization and technology.

If it is not possible for the ecological environment and trade networks to be restored, new geographic areas of ecological assets have to be located and/or the replacements of much-depleted natural resources for productions are adopted. Furthermore, technological innovations could also occur to address the issue of depleted natural resources so that some level of economic production can continue. Besides this, it warrants us to consider the different time durations (ecological time) for understanding the interaction between Culture and the natural environment compared to political and economic activities that necessarily are gauged along social time.

In certain circumstances, resolution of a system crisis might not necessarily lead to a system transition. In this case, the crisis is resolved because the ecological balance has been restored, thereby allowing for social reproduction on the extended scale to occur and because the state of the socioeconomic organizations and political hegemonies in place have the capacity to meet the contingencies of the restored ecological balance. If, however, these conditions are not in place, a new set of organizing and learning principles will need to be engendered to meet the contingencies of the transformed terrain generated by the crisis conditions of the Dark Age. In such a context, qualitative changes ensue and a system transition occurs. In this regard, perhaps what has been identified as long economic cycles or *conjonctures* might not reveal the long-term trends of the world system and thus might not be as valuable or insightful for our understanding of the long-term processes of the evolution of the world system. Instead, we suspect that perhaps these long ecological phases might be *the* system transition moments leading to structural changes of the system as a whole. These long ecological phases or Dark Ages ultimately reveal specific conjunctural elements and factors that come into play conducing a system transformation. The outcome is a transformed world system with a number of qualitatively socioeconomic and political structures. The transition from the Bronze Age world system to the Iron Age system (1200 B.C.–700 B.C.) was one such moment in world system history. What this means is that world system history is not a flattened history just accounting for networks of trading links and economic cycles of expansion and contraction with little or no distinguishing differences between periods, rather it is a history that is one with ruptures through time leading to system reorganization and social evolutionary changes.[11]

Hence, Dark Ages are important moments in world history for they provide opportunities for the ecological balance to be restored, political and economic opportunities for some peripheral groups to advance up the zonal power matrix, and for reconfiguration of the hierarchical division of political economic power of the world system at specific conjunctures of world history. The rarity of such occurrences in the last five thousand years of world history suggests the resiliency of the ecological landscape to human assault. Besides this, it underscores further the different time duration for our understanding of the interaction between Culture and the natural environment measured along ecological time rather than social time, which is the gauge for political and economic activities. Given this, Dark Ages is a world system process that occurs in phases in world system evolution.

TIME, LANDSCAPES, ECOLOGICAL PHASES, AND CYCLES

Landscapes harbor histories of human activities. They reflect the outcomes of human impact and mask what had happened in the past. They are historical records of natural processes (wind, tectonic shifts), climate, human activities, and the growth cycles of animals, plants, trees, and other living things. On this basis, ecological recovery and restoration over the *longue durée,* if they occur, keep the histories of human exploitative activities hidden from the present. Our preoccupation with social, economic, and political events and the actions of historical agents is limited often to short time sequences established via the calendar or the clock. Nature's injuries caused by centuries of human excesses take much longer to reveal themselves in ways that impact the reproduction of human communities. When they do appear, the eruptions occur at the most extreme point of the cycle of the degradation process. As a result, we often fail to recognize the deeper swells of world-systemic connections underlying devolution of the system that are conditioned by ecological stress and climatological changes that need to be measured, analyzed, and considered not in decades but in centuries and/or millennia. Timescales of change thus are different in terms of length.

The longer duration is of importance when we are considering outcomes arising from the relationship between Culture and Nature. The impact of socioeconomic activity on the natural environment and hence the length of ecological crisis, I believe, is of a longer duration than, for example, the three-hundred-year economic cycles of boom and bust believed to be pulsations of the world system (e.g., see Frank and Gills 1993). Neither the duration nor the frequency of the occurrences cycle rhythmically over three-hundred- or fifty-year periods, as would be characteristic of economic cycles. We should view these long periods of crisis as phases. The succession of phases is not necessarily evidence of a cyclical theory. The ecological crisis phases (Dark Ages) reflect the rhythms of natural and biological processes with their own distinct pulsations; however, these rhythms *do not necessarily correlate* with anthropogenic-induced social, political, and economic cycles nor have the same duration.

The disruption of natural rhythms of the ecological landscape via the process of the degradation of the environment extends over a longer term, at least as long as five hundred years or perhaps even more. Given this, whatever socioeconomic and political changes are triggered by the Culture-Nature relations appear only after very long periods of ecological stress when the degradation is most extreme. The same consideration should be given to those political and economic circumstances induced by natural processes and climatological changes. In other words, there is a long-term lapse between cause and outcome. We might therefore have time lags of unspecified durations depending on the state of the ecological degradation.

The harmonizing of social time measuring, for example, each fifty-to-three-hundred-year political economic cycle with ecological time that is based on natural processes and mechanisms, and hence of a longer duration (though measured on socially constructed time scale), is complicated by this long-term time lapse. What should be noted is that every political economic shift periodized along the social time continuum *cannot always be correlated* with signs of ecological stress and/or climatological changes because the latter changes operate on much longer time duration. As we have stated above, at times it *is difficult to link* ecologically degradative and climatological changes with political economic changes. The sparse information available on ecological stress caused by specific social systems, and the limited data on climatological and ecological changes during the early eras, further complicate our attempt. At best, the socioeconomic and political cycles can serve as *markers* for our efforts to demarcate the ecological crisis phases that are determined by natural and ecological processes.

Given the above, the natural processes, having their own ecological time rhythms, when placed within a social time continuum would extend over a longer duration. What this means is that attempts to use social, political, and economic cycles to demarcate and characterize specific periods of expansion and efflorescence of human-induced activities such as urbanization would have to be reassessed if ecological conditions are considered as part of the explanation for such transformations. The time durations are necessarily longer than the fifty-to-three-hundred-year cycles that have been assumed to be the time parameters of world-system pulsations that are anthropogenically induced (e.g., see Frank and Gills 1992). Placed within the social time frame, these shorter social, political, and economic cycles nest within the longer ecological phases that last at least five hundred years or more.[12] What then does this long duration of Dark Ages signify in terms of world history? Do they demarcate for us the phases of the human socioevolutionary processes besides marking for us the phases of ecological degradation? The following chapters will examine the world-systemic nature of Dark Ages and their effects on the evolution of the world system in an attempt to address these questions.

NOTES

1. For an exposition of this long-term time duration, see Braudel (1980, 25–54).

2. In the early parts of the twentieth century, there were also other studies emphasizing nonhuman factors in engendering social system crisis, see for example, Huntington (1917).

3. For a fuller explication of Braudel's analytical levels of long-term change see Chew (1997b).

4. If a growth developmental model is assumed, the reproduction levels should be progressively higher rather than lower, hence instead of developmental evolution, stagnation or devolution would be the more appropriate concepts to describe these changes.

5. See, for example, Kristiansen's *Europe before History* for an elaborate articulation of the different levels of interaction and connectedness occurring in European transformation over one millennium.

6. Such a multiplicity of levels has been confirmed in the depictions of Dark Age conditions in prehistoric Greece by Snodgrass (1971).

7. The socioeconomic and political evaluations of Dark Ages in terms of conditions and factors leading to the onset of these periods are found quite commonly among the historical literature, especially for the Dark Age that occurred in the second millennium B.C. They ranged from cultural decadence, invasions and conquests by "barbarians" and nomadic tribes, internal conflicts, overcentralization of authority, famine and diseases, climate changes and tectonic shifts (Toynbee 1939, Childe 1942, Snodgrass 1989, Renfrew 1979, O'Connor 1983, Desborough 1972, Carpenter 1968, Bryson et al. 1974, Weiss 1982, Neumann and Parpola 1987, Bintliff 1982, Harding 1982, Schaeffer 1948, Van De Mieroop 2004, Bintliff 2004).

8. By "determinative," I mean constraints that do not allow the system to reproduce itself within its social and ecological parameters (see also Kristiansen 1998a).

9. For example, in the case of Mycenaean Greece during that Dark Age, we find several Culture-Nature trends and patterns that are subdued: fall in popula-

tion levels, decline or loss in certain material skills, decay in the cultural aspects of life, fall in living standards and thus wealth, and loss of trading contacts within and without Greece (Snodgrass 1971, Desborough 1972).

10. See, for example, Snodgrass (1971) and Desborough (1972) for conditions of Greece during the second millennium B.C. Dark Age.

11. This conception of world system history is different from that proposed by Frank (1998).

12. Recent works by Modelski and Thompson (2001) have indicated longer phases of urbanization and deurbanization processes over world history. They have projected these phases to be at least one thousand years in duration.

II

THE CRISIS OF
THE BRONZE AGE

2

Nature and Culture

Following the Neolithic Revolution, the Urban Revolution as a world historical process further framed the course of human history (e.g., see Childe 1950). One of the earliest signs of this urbanization process appeared in the riverine valleys of southern Mesopotamia, Egypt, and northwestern India over five thousand years ago and continued the transformation of the landscape by human communities that started with the advent of agriculture. The process of urbanization encompassed trade linkages and accumulation, cultural exchanges, and a specialized and differentiated division of labor across the system. This type of architecture of physical structures, social institutions, and commerce further heightened the hierarchical distribution of surplus within and between regions. Coupled with the population increases, the process of urbanization framed the level of extensive resources required to reproduce the system that emerged (Chew 2001).

Viewed from the perspective of the human community, underlying this world historical process was the expansion of production and trade, followed by cultural transformation and the growth of cities. Trade, production, and urbanization processes interacted with demographic increases to construct a human world of exuberance. Innovations in metallurgical processes and in the fabrication of commodities such as textiles and ceramics established the search for and removal of natural resources and forests. During the early Bronze Age, in the Mesopotamian valleys, ziggurats, public buildings, canals, granaries, and other facilities that depicted economic growth were erected coupled with extensive trading across the Arabian Sea and Red Sea through to Egypt in the West and the Harappan civilization in the East (Chew 2001). For this period, the latter two centers had levels of urbanization and human specialization (division of labor) that were of the same scale. Temples, pyramids, grain storage areas, and citadels were constructed from burnt bricks, granite, and other materials that can be secured locally or imported.

Out of this urban and demographic transformation was the further development of a set of urbanized enclaves that specialized in resource extraction, trade exchanges, and commodity production in a systemic context extending initially from West Asia and the eastern Mediterranean to northwestern India (Chew 2001). Further expansion from the second millennium onward brought Europe and central Asia into this expanding network of urbanization, commerce, and trade exchanges.

Viewed from the perspective of Nature, such world historical processes induced a continuous and, perhaps over time, a degradative transformation of the landscape. Trees were removed for agriculture and to meet the energy and material needs of urbanizing communities. The valleys were excavated for canals to provide irrigation for crops and for the transportation of people and goods. Other lands were dug up for their natural resources and building materials. Rivers were dammed. Such wide-scale human activities such as deforestation led to soil erosion in the mountains and hills including the river valleys and the continuous impact of human activities further heightened the process. In all, socioeconomic activities along with wars were transforming the landscape with scars revealing the scale of such acts.

Notwithstanding periods of economic stagnation, such efflorescence of the human communities would ultimately lead to ecological distress. These periods emerged over very long durations. Associated with these long phases of ecological crisis are climatological shifts and eruptions of natural processes that also impacted the social, political, and economic landscapes. The combination of all these conditions induces a *systemic* crisis of the social system. Such systemic crises are what we have come to know as the Dark Ages. One such systemic crisis or Dark Age began about 2200 B.C., initially impacting northwestern India, the Gulf, Mesopotamia, and West Asia and had repercussions for the urbanized core areas such as Mesopotamia and the Indus (Chew 2001, Childe 1942). It marked the start of the system crisis of the Bronze Age.

Following the end of this phase of the crisis about 1700 B.C., new power centers emerged in the Near East, northern Mesopotamia, and the eastern Mediterranean. This systemic crisis emerged again about 1200 B.C. at the social system level and continued until 700 B.C., depending on the region, and impacted the main areas of Near Asia, Egypt, eastern Mediterranean, and central Europe (from 800 B.C. onward). These periods of crises not only were characterized by socioeconomic distress, regime transitions, and center or hinterland conflicts, but they were also riddled with population losses, deurbanization, natural resource depletion, environmental degradation, and climatological changes. Negative ecological trends (such as deforestation) were observed from 2200 B.C. onward (Chew 2001). Temperature increases and aridity pulsated from approximately 2200 B.C. with warm periods and dryness alternating with cool conditions and moistness (Fairbridge et al. 1997, 603–6). Such ecological and climatological circumstances impacted the reproduction capacities of some parts of the system and reverberated throughout the system as the Bronze Age proceeded.

NATURAL AND SOCIAL SYSTEM CONNECTIONS

By the third millennium B.C., urbanized communities had emerged in the riverine valleys of Egypt, Mesopotamia, and northwestern India (and probably China as well). The areas of domestication were small for Egypt and Mesopotamia in comparison to the Harappan civilization in northwestern India. Upper Egypt covered only about 12,000 km² while Lower Egypt was about 11,000 km². Mesopotamia stretched for about 20,000 to 25,000 km². The Harappan civilization was about forty times larger in terms of area—almost close to one million square kilometers. In a semiarid environment dependent on seasonal rainfall, the utilization of the Nile, Tigris, Euphrates, and Indus rivers to satisfy the reproductive needs of these urban complexes structured the linkage of these communities to the rhythms of the landscape and the climate. Hence, changes in climate and wind patterns impacted the harvests and the associated economic activities.

Mesopotamia, located in a vast land mass geographically distinguished as the Ancient Near East, and Egypt to its northwest, are both circumscribed within a natural environment defined by geological phenomena (earthquakes and volcanic eruptions), wind, rain, and water courses. The topography of this land mass is defined by three tectonic plates with the Arabian plate pressing to the North underneath the Iranian plate, forming a long depression when the two plates connect stretching from the Persian Gulf to the Mediterranean Sea. In this depression, the Euphrates and the Tigris flow and discharge into the Gulf. The African plate meets the Arabian plate on the western part of the Near East, creating a valley lined by mountain ranges such as the Taurus, Amanus, and the Lebanon Mountains.

To the east of Mesopotamia, in northwestern India, bordered by a mountainous plateau on the west and the Thar Desert to the east lay the Harappan civilization. To the north and northwest of the Harappans stretched the Jammu ranges and the Great Himalayas. The Harappan urban complexes were located mostly in the lower Indus River, near the minor rivers of Sind west of the Indus, close to Lake Manchhar, in south-western Punjab, and in Bahawalpur and the Sarasvati Valley. The urban concentrations were primarily in the districts of Sind and Bahawalpur.

Variations in the natural environment are quite distinguishable. For example, several ecological zones exist between the Gulf and northern Mesopotamia. A desert plateau borders the North with agricultural cultivation occurring only in river valleys. South of the urban centers of Ur and Lagash are marshes where fishing predominates, interspersed with irrigated agriculture. The landscape structures the human economic practices in the North, which because of its more arid condition, undertakes animal husbandry and irrigated agriculture. The South, closer to the Persian Gulf, leans toward marine resources. Dry farming forms the agricultural practice with a requirement of at least 200 mm of water on an annual basis. Areas within the Near East that have the 200 mm isohyet stretch from the southern Levant to the Gulf. With that moisture level, great reliance on the river systems for irrigation is needed, especially when southern Mesopotamia received no more than 125 mm of winter rainfall per annum. The importance of the Euphrates, Tigris, Nile, and Indus rivers comes into sharper focus within the context of the character of the natural environment. The Euphrates and Tigris rivers originate in the mountains of modern day Turkey and Iran, and the Nile's headwaters were located in the highlands of Nubia. The Indus and the Sarasvati (now known as the Ghaggar) watered the Harappan civilization.

The perennial nature of these rivers afforded the opportunity to tap them for crop irrigation. However, this delicate balance, that is, the reliance on the rivers for irrigation, could be disrupted by changing wind patterns and climate. Changing weather conditions resulted in lowered levels of river flows, hence impacting further on an irrigation system that was gravity-driven such as that in Mesopotamia. The situation was even more precarious for the Harappans. Winter rain (November to April) and a weak summer monsoon delivered moisture areas for Harappan agriculture with the crops sown after the summer monsoon rain (July to August) and harvested before the rivers rise in April (Ratnagar 1981). Therefore, with lower river levels, only the fields closest to the river systems could be assured of receiving irrigated water. In all, this reliance on irrigation water for agriculture defined the delicate balance of the relationship between social and natural systems in the growing of agricultural products for consumption and exchange and hence the accumulation of surplus from this sector of the economies of Mesopotamia, Egypt, and the Harappans.

By no means was agriculture the only source for surplus accumulation. Like modern urban complexes, the manufacture of commodities and luxuries was another avenue for generating surplus. Urbanized areas had immediate needs for salt, wood for buildings, gold, silver, copper, tin, oil, wine, precious stones, ivory, and other luxuries, and these goods were secured locally or traded for in the other areas where they were produced. Economic circuits emerged with caravans, wheeled vehicles, and cargo vessels powered by oars and sails circumscribing the waterways of rivers, gulfs, and oceans. The domestication of animals, such as the camel and the donkey, facilitated the movement of goods (A. Sheratt 1981). By the late third millennium B.C., sailors from the Aegean were able to sail to the Syro-Palestinian coast linking the Aegean and Central Europe by sea with the Near East. Such connections foster the beginnings of a "global" division of labor, from northwestern India to the eastern Mediterranean, and of long-distance trade articulated within a single interacting whole: the Bronze Age world system (see figure 2.1).[1]

Innovations, Production, and Materialistic Consumption

Human achievements and advances in several areas facilitated the development of the urbanized communities located in the valleys of the Nile, Euphrates-Tigris, and Indus. Following the Neolithic Revolution, the "secondary products revolution" led to intensification of agricultural production, transportation, and trade (A. Sheratt 1981). The introduction of the plow brought lands that were of lower quality soil into cultivation. What followed was the extension of larger geographic areas for human cultivation that would not have been undertaken in the past. The adoption of the oxcart, the horse, the donkey, and the camel enabled large distances to be covered, trade to flourish, and natural resources to be sought for and obtained. The domestication of animals for milk and wool provided the nutrition and raw products for exchange. All such transformations facilitated trade between urban environments. From these adoptions, other economic activities followed (pottery making, metallurgy, textile production, etc.) that promoted manufacturing and production, which in turn stimulated consumption in these communities and their hinterlands where they conducted their trading relations.

The introduction of the potter's wheel in the fourth millennium B.C. in Lower Mesopotamia provided the opportunity to undertake large-scale production of pottery, requiring less experienced potters. The mass-manufactured pottery items (Uruk design) were plain and devoid of beauty and usually painted in a one-tone hue of beige or yellow. Later on, a red or purple glaze was added. By 3400 B.C., we begin to see a shift to this style of pottery design replacing the delicate painted ceramics of the past throughout Mesopotamia. Painted pottery such as the red and black pottery of the Jemdet Nasr period (3200 B.C.) or the Ninevite V style (3000

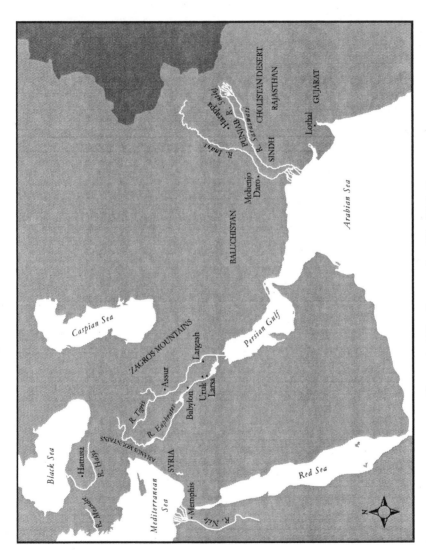

Figure 2.1 The Bronze Age World System

B.C.) were *only* available in parts of Mesopotamia (such as Diyala Valley) that were in contact with hinterland areas like Iran.

In Egypt, by the fourth millennium B.C., handmade pottery items were quite refined in terms of colors and designs. However, by 3200 B.C., the quality of pottery in design and glaze similarly declined. This shift paralleled the one in Mesopotamia, where painted pottery was replaced by the Uruk design that was plain and utilitarian. The potter's wheel came only into use in Egypt about 2600 B.C. This parallel transition from a rich, colorful design to one that is plain and utilitarian for both Mesopotamia and Egypt is interesting and warrants an explanation. Some scholars like Braudel (2001) have suggested that mass production with less skilled labor precipitated the development of this type of pottery: monotone color, poor quality glaze, plain and utilitarian in design. If we accept Braudel's (2001) assertion that the adoption of the potter's wheel in Mesopotamia enabled mass production and lessened the need for skilled labor to manufacture the pottery, which led to the decline in pottery design, glaze, and quality, then Egypt's shift to plain pottery design about 3200 B.C. onward, which paralleled Mesopotamia's changeover, needs another explanation because they adopted the potter's wheel much later—about 2600 B.C.

The simultaneous change in pottery design for both civilizations is intriguing. Perhaps instead of seeking an anthropogenic answer, let us suggest an ecological explanation. There has been no explanation that attributes natural resource scarcity and degraded natural environment during a Dark Age for the shift in the pottery design for Mesopotamia and Egypt about 3200 B.C.[2] Another plausible reason could be that trade disruption with natural resource–producing hinterland areas during a Dark Age (caused by depressed ecological conditions and climatic conditions) forced the shift in pottery design rather than the introduction of the potter's wheel and the need for less skilled labor that caused the lowering of quality, as Braudel (2001) has explained along anthropogenic grounds.

Weaving is another innovation adopted by the Mesopotamians, Egyptians, and the Harappans. As an ancient craft, weaving cloth was practiced at least as early as the sixth millennium B.C. The evidence of woolen fabrics and linen can be found in Anatolia, the Fertile Crescent, and Egypt (A. Sherratt 1981). Woolen fabric appeared much later (about the third millennium B.C.) than linen. Egypt concentrated only on linen, and Mesopotamia specialized in both. Weaving cotton textiles was undertaken in the Indus Valley only to be adopted later in Mesopotamia about the first millennium B.C.

Cultural patterns and changes generated the need for more textile production that subsequently led to a boom in this area. In Egypt, higher status meant the wearing of different costumes that in turn engendered further cloth production. The richer elites wore several loincloths and tunics on top of each other, whereas those at the bottom rung of the social hierarchy could only afford a single loincloth. Egyptian women of higher rank wore long flowing robes instead of being clad in a long tunic of the past. Such patterns of consumption would naturally also influence elites in the hinterland areas where Egypt had political influence or traded. It appeared also in the case of Mesopotamia as well; woolen textiles were a major source of export from the third millennium B.C. onward (Chew 2001, Braudel 2001).

Manufacturing of textiles was undertaken in the temples as directed by the royal palace. The scale of production from records suggests large quantities of textiles were produced; for example, 6,400 tons of wool were purchased for garment manufacturing by the temple workshops as inscribed (Ratnagar 1981, Leemans 1960). The Harappans, however, concentrated on cotton textile production, according to the records, and perhaps importing woolen and linen textiles from the Gulf and southern Mesopotamia through intermediaries in Dilmun.

The working of copper and iron (from meteorites) with hammers and chisels had been in place since very early times. The smelting of these metals utilizing a furnace began about the fifth millennium B.C. in Iran and Cilicia. By the fourth millennium B.C., besides the use of copper, two types of bronzes (tin bronze and arsenic bronze) were in production, with different communities adopting different techniques of manufacturing bronzes. In Egypt, for example, arsenic bronze was preferred appearing about 2000 B.C., while in areas like Mesopotamia and Crete, tin bronze was produced much earlier, about 2800 B.C. (Muhly 1980, Braudel 2001). Developments in metallurgical techniques in Mesopotamia stimulated Aegean metallurgy via Syria, Cyprus, and Anatolia. With the exception of alluvial cassiterite in the eastern desert of Egypt, the utilization of tin in the manufacture of bronze underlined an international trading exchange relationship because there are no known sources of tin in Mesopotamia, the Aegean, Cyprus, and the Eastern Mediterranean (Childe 1957, Muhly 1980). Thus, the early source for tin in the manufacture of bronze in 3000 B.C. remains a mystery. Later, about 1800 B.C., the tin source was probably from Iran. Whether Iran was the source or it was a transshipment point is unclear (Muhly 1980).

In the Harappan context, copper and bronze were also in use by 2600 B.C. Harappan metallurgy at that time was considered of a lower standard than the Mesopotamia (Ratnagar 1981). Copper was used and arsenic bronze was also in production in the major urban centers of Harappa and Mohenjodaro. It has been suggested that the copper for manufacturing came from local sources, and the most likely areas were in Afghanistan, such as Nadir Shah and Safed Kuh, and northwestern India, such as in

Rajasthan and Gujerat (Ratnagar 1981). When tin bronze was produced, the alluvial tin was imported from Anatolia, Afghanistan, or Iran.

The production of bronze generated a luxury trade and afforded the opportunity for blades and other implements to be utilized in the economic and military activities. The adoption and fabrication of these metallic substances spurred the economic transformation of these communities and fostered the continuation of the urbanization process and the division of labor.

Innovations, commercial activities, and cultural processes are facilitated and reproduced by writing and language. Writing is an innovation that enables communication, orders to be dispatched, contracts to be consummated, and the political administration to be carried out. The art of writing appeared in all three communities of the Egyptians, Mesopotamians, and the Harappans, and progressively we discover this art in later civilizations as well.

With this symbolic communication, commerce and contracts could be consummated, thus facilitating the growth of business and trade exchange within the Bronze Age world system. In turn, we have the facilitation of the urbanization process with its structured division of labor and its complex set of occupational groups. Coupled with manufacturing innovations, writing spurred the economic production processes and along with innovations in agricultural techniques surplus was generated. Such surplus fostered exuberant living that distinguished a class of elites in the urbanized areas of Mesopotamia, Egypt, and the Indus. In turn, another set of elites also emerged in the hinterland areas that had political and trading relations with the core (Algaze 1993a, Stein 1999).

All these innovations and transformations ultimately lead to the further tightening of the relationship between the social system and the natural system with the latter being utilized to meet the propensities of the dynamics of surplus accumulation and consumption. At this point, we have the structured relationship between Culture (social system) and Nature (natural system) that over the next five thousand years determined the reproduction of Nature.

Natural Resources

Several key materials are needed in the reproduction of economic, social, and political life in these riverine civilizations. Copper, wood, and other precious materials such as lapis lazuli had to be obtained because the alluvial soil in these river valleys was devoid of these materials and, in the case of timber, in sufficient quantities to meet the demand. In *World Ecological Degradation*, I have outlined the various ways wood has been utilized in human civilizations over the course of five thousand years of world history. As such, it is an excellent proxy for understanding the relationship between the social system and natural system in terms of the state of the ecological environment. Excessive deforestation of anthropogenic origins would indicate pressure on the part of the social system (Culture) over the natural system (Nature). Coupled with climatological changes, tectonic shifts, and other deteriorating ecological circumstances, the reproduction of the social system and the evolution of the system becomes an issue.

With the absence of these key natural resources, trade exchanges and military expeditions were the logistical avenues by which these civilizations ensured a constant uninterrupted supply. A division of labor resulted whereby core goods were exchanged for peripheral natural resources. In the context of the natural environment, we find the removal of trees and the mining of metallic substances and precious stones in peripheral areas that were stimulated in production by the consumptive needs of the core. The dimension of ecological shadow cast by these core civilizations in the peripheral areas is added to the overall equation of world ecological degradation, and thus the historical process of anthropogenic ecological degradation cannot be assessed without the consideration of the ecological consequences that the peripheral areas encounter in their efforts to meet the natural resource needs of the core. Hence, anthropogenic ecological degradation of the Bronze Age is one that occurs within a world system and is world historical in nature in terms of consequences and effects.

Following the above line of thinking, wood as a natural resource material was imported into these civilizations. Egypt and Mesopotamia were aware of the cedar forests in Lebanon and the Amanus Mountains. These forests as sources of wood are depicted by the flotilla of ships sailing between Byblos and the Nile Delta and rafts of timber being transported on the Syrian coast to the ports for transfer overland to Mesopotamia. In the Mesopotamian case, wood was also imported from Magan, Dilmun, and as far as northwestern India. A similar situation also occurred for the Harappan civilization. The Jammu ranges, the Punjab piedmont, the western Ghats, the Sahyadris, and the Great Himalayas to the northeast of the Indus provided the wood needs of the urban centers of the Indus. Given this circuit whereby wood was secured or procured, disruption in supply would necessarily impact the reproductive capacities of these civilizations besides the ecological degradation and its consequences (e.g., soil erosion) that resulted, which are experienced by them and the hinterland areas.

The same goes for the metals and precious stones that are imported to meet their economic needs and production processes. Disruption in trade and natural resource scarcity as a result of excessive utilization exerts pressure on the production processes of these civilizations. All these circumstances underscore the close and dependent connection that the social system (Culture) has with the natural system (Nature). This connection begins to unravel during the Dark Ages when centuries of intense and unremitting exploitation of this relationship by the social system (Culture) exhibit signs of ecological distress.

THE TRADING WORLD OF THE CORE CENTERS IN THE ANCIENT NEAR EAST: EARLY BRONZE AGE

Mesopotamia

Given the structure and processes of the trading network, Mesopotamia's scale of economic production (of textiles, oils, leather, and other manufactured objects) with its high generation of agricultural surplus facilitated the trade exchange with other areas of the economic system. From the fourth millennium B.C. onward, Mesopotamia traded essentially in three directions utilizing both land and water. The Euphrates River served the trade routes to the West and Northwest (such as Syria and Anatolia), linking the eastern parts of the Mediterranean with the Gulf. To the East and Northeast, the land and water transport via the Tigris tributaries linked Mesopotamia to the Iranian plateau and beyond. The southern trade routes were connected via the Gulf to Dilmun, Magan, and Meluhha.

Imports from the Northwest and from the eastern parts such as metals, timber, and other items, including ivory and beads, were for both mass and elite consumption. High-quality timber from the Zagros and Taurus Mountains, the Caspian Sea area, and the eastern Mediterranean was obtained via trade and military expeditions. Natural resources and agricultural products, such as timber, copper, ivory, lapis lazuli, dates, and other metals from the Gulf, the southeastern parts of the Arabian peninsula (Dilmun and Magan), and as far away as the northwestern part of the Indian subcontinent arrived at the docks of southern Mesopotamia. In return, grains such as barley, wool, textiles, and other manufactured items provided the exchange products. Silver obtained through trade (from Elam and east-central Anatolia), plunder, or tribute provided another capital source to pay for the imports (Leemans 1960, 132).

Trade exchanges were facilitated by political expansion/imperialism from as early as the Uruk period (Algaze 1993a, Diakonoff 1991b).[3] Outposts and settlements were established in the hinterland areas to control crucial nodes of trading routes along the Syro-Mesopotamian plains and in Iran. They were planted among native polities controlling communication and trade in the northern plains of the Zagros and Iran (see figure 2.2). During the early Uruk period, colonization of the Susiana plain of

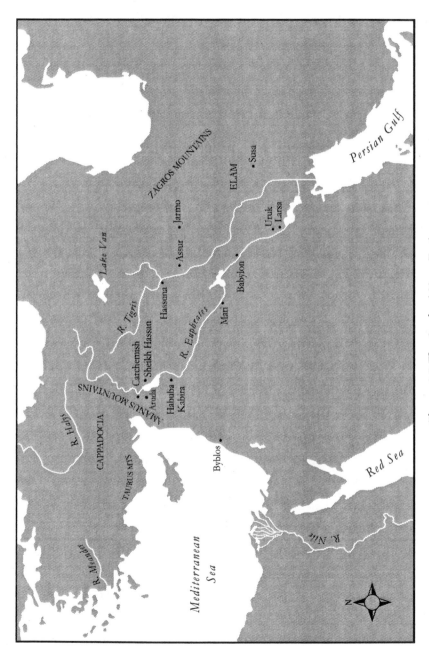

Figure 2.2 The Ancient Near East

southwestern Iran started, and by the Middle and Late Uruk period, the area had become "part and parcel of the Mesopotamian world, an extension eastward of the culture and institutions prevalent in the lowlands of southern Iraq" (Algaze 1993a, 13).

Settlement areas focused on Susa located on the Shaur River and Choga Mish watered by the Shureh River. Both centers dominated the Susiana Plain with subsidiary villages being linked to them. The scale of such colonization can be seen in terms of acreage sizes of these two settlements that were about 18 hectare (ha). Later on with economic growth, between the Middle and Late Uruk phases, the villages ranged from approximately 1 to 2 ha to 5 to 7 ha, and the smaller towns below the urban centers of Susa and Choga Mish were approximately 10 to 12 ha (Algaze 1993a). The historical origins of these settlements led to similar cultural outcomes, accounting practices, and iconography. Algaze (1993a) has noted for us the parallels between these communities and southern Mesopotamia. The relationship continued well into the later part of the Uruk period with the local elites reflecting Sumerian practices.

By no means was settlement expansion concentrated only in Iran; to the North, we find Uruk communities located in northern Mesopotamia, northern Syria, and southwestern Anatolia. These settlements were established for strategic reasons and located primarily on trading routes that crisscrossed the northern plains. Enclaves such as Habuba Kabira-sud/ Tell Qannas on the upper Euphrates was a well-planned urban settlement with streets and differentiated areas of residential, administrative, and production quarters. At Carchemish, several sites also reflected an organized set of settlements such as at Sadi Tepe, estimated to be about 8 ha in size, and seemed to be an administrative center (Algaze 1993a, Stein 1999). Tiladir Tepe near Carchemish and Sadi Tepe were larger, 12 ha in acreage. In the upper Khabur River region, Uruk settlements have also been discovered. Tell Brak is one such enclave. Uruk settlements, such as Nineveh, have also been excavated on the upper Tigris.

Similar to enclaves established in the Susiana plains, these settlements to the north of southern Mesopotamia possessed iconography, architectural techniques, accounting and administrative systems, ceramics, and small objects similar to the cultural and material lifestyles of southern Mesopotamia. They were transplanted communities from southern Mesopotamia located among indigenous Late Chalcolithic communities (Schwartz 1988, Sürenhagen 1986). These indigenous communities were relatively small and less developed socially and politically. They revealed a simpler economic structure with agriculture as a basic form of socioeconomic activity. In terms of the relationship between the Uruk settlers and the local communities, unlike the colonization in the Susiana plain, it was more of one where trade was determinant. There might have been some coercion at first, but the settlements were established to tap into the pre-existing trade network controlled by the local communities. Such a settlement process enabled the southern Mesopotamians to insert themselves into the trade routes.

These settlement communities presumably were in some peaceful co-existence with the indigenous populations as the former relied on the latter for grains and other foodstuffs. In return, we assume that manufactured objects, such as ceramics and oils, were exchanged. Besides foodstuffs, the mineral resources in the highlands were also sought. Copper from the Taurus Mountains was procured from the highland communities. This was also the case for the southeastern settlements. With important copper deposits in the Iranian plateau, we find similar exchanges occurring. Tepe Sialk is one such case in point. Besides copper, gold, silver, and lapis lazuli were the other minerals and precious stones obtained. In addition to this exchange of minerals and precious stones, the Uruk communities also engaged in the trading of other natural resources such as timber from the northern highlands, bitumen from southwestern Iran, gypsum from the Taurus/Zagros foothills, and other materials for building construction.

Beyond the establishment of settlements, military expeditions and wars were also part of the process to secure natural resources to meet the manufacturing and consumptive needs of the Mesopotamian populace. Prior to 2200 B.C., besides regular trading relations exchanging wool, barley, tin, and silver for Elam's timber, precious metals, and stone, Mesopotamia also undertook warlike incursions into Elam. At times, however, according to Lamberg-Karlovsky (1986), Elam held sway over southern Mesopotamia about 2250 B.C. Such moments also coincide with the period of the systemic Dark Age crisis of 2200 B.C. when southern Mesopotamia was in a period of political economic decline.

The Indus Civilization

Similar to the Mesopotamians, the Harappan civilization also had a highly evolved and extensive trading network.[4] This is evident by the mechanics of ensuring a constant supply of natural resources and a market for the manufactured products in the hinterland and in other parts of the economic system. Besides the evidence of direct trading relations between the Harappans and the Mesopotamians, Kulli communities located in the hills between Liari and Bela bordered the western edge of the Indus civilization. These communities provided metals such as copper for Harappan manufacturing and trade (Ratnagar 1981).

The diversity of economic production and trade underlines the varied linkages that the Harappans sought, exchanged, and dominated within this region of the economic system of the Bronze Age. Harappan linkages extended to Baluchistan, Afghanistan, Iran, Central Asia, peninsular India, and the Persian Gulf right to southern Mesopotamia (Asthana 1982). Semiprecious stones such as lapis lazuli and turquoise were obtained from Afghanistan, Iran, peninsular India, and Central Asia for export to areas as far away as southern Mesopotamia. Besides Afghanistan and Oman, northwestern India (Rajasthan and Gujerat) also provided copper to the Harappans (Asthana 1982, Lal 1997). The Harappans incorporated Gujerat into its political and economic sphere to ensure the constant flow of natural resources. Steatite or chlorite for the making of vases, seals, beads, and figurines was obtained from Rajasthan and northern Baluchistan (Asthana 1982) (see figure 2.3). Carnelian, which was used in the manufacture of beads and pendants, was sought in peninsular India. Timber, besides being a major export of the Harappans to Mesopotamia and its utilization for building and home construction, was harvested in the Western Ghats, the Jammu ranges, and the Punjab piedmont. Teak came from the Gir forests or from Panch Mahals, Surat, and the Dangs (Lal 1997). The Harappans even sought timber from as far away as the Himalayas for wood, such as the deodar. Collection centers on the western part of Gujerat were established to facilitate the flow of timber for consumption in the Indus valley and for export via the Harappan coastal ports to the Gulf and beyond.

Securing these semiprecious stones along with gold, lead, silver, copper, and tin was sealed with the establishment of specialized Harrapan outposts in these areas. Like Mesopotamia, gateway settlements or outposts were embedded in a wide periphery to facilitate the flow of goods and natural resources (Asthana 1982, Algaze 1993b, Possehl and Raval 1989). These settlements were established at locations near strategic trade routes/passes (e.g., Nausharo), located in hinterland areas close to the natural resources/commodities (e.g., Shortugai), or near to coastal areas to facilitate the maritime trade (e.g., Lothal). The settlements, some of which were fortified (such as Sutkagen-dor and Sutka-koh), provided the access points for the flow of natural resources much needed by the manufacturing economy of the Harappans (see figure 2.3). In addition to settlements, there were trading posts for the exchange of Harappan manufactured goods and some agricultural products.

Such was the trading and production mechanisms circumscribing the exchange between the Harappans and its vast hinterland. Besides these center-hinterland exchanges that extended as far as perhaps Southeast Asia and East Africa as Tosi (1993) has alluded, there were also center-center exchanges during third and second millennium B.C.[5]

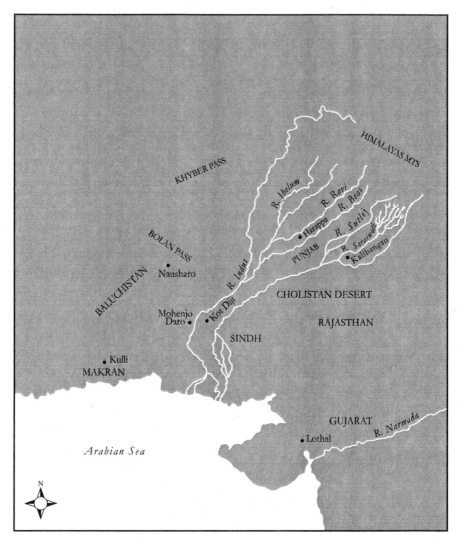

Figure 2.3 The Harappan Civilization

Egypt

Egypt's trading partners were determined in most parts by their geographic locations. Surrounded mostly by desert in the West and East, like other riverine civilizations, Egypt relied on its immediate hinterland for various metals, timber, and other natural resources to sustain the reproduction of its economy (see figure 2.4). The annual flooding of the Nile provided it with the basis for agricultural production and animal husbandry, generating the necessary surplus for expansion and trade. Wool and linen production was undertaken along with porcelain and glass manufacturing and the production of luxuries such as jewelry. Precious metals and natural resources were sought in distant lands. Timber (cedar) was obtained from Lebanon and parts of the Syrian coast via Byblos, and this necessary natural resource connected Egypt with this hinterland. Copper and lapis lazuli were traded for in the Sinai and Syria, and gold was obtained from Nubia in the South. The gold of Nubia provided the exchange medium for Egyptian imports, and as Braudel (2001) has remarked, this gold and the silver of Mesopotamia were the underlining exchange medium of the eastern Mediterranean.

Egypt like Mesopotamia and Harappa traded extensively for the natural resources that it needed. It exported manufactured products such as linen cloth, porcelain, multicolored glass, precious gems, jewelry, and furniture in exchange for the metals and timber that it was devoid of (Shaw 2000). In addition, it was also the transshipment center for ivory, animals, alabaster, and semiprecious stones to the Aegean region and beyond from Africa and the Sinai by the third millennium B.C.

By this economic exchange, the Aegean and western and central Europe were drawn into the evolving nascent world economic system. Egypt's hinterland regions such as the Sinai, the Syrian coast, Cyprus, the Aegean, and central Europe were areas in which it traded directly or indirectly, or at times, in the case of the former areas, military expeditions were also dispatched to secure the needed resources. Regular ass caravan trade was established between the eastern Delta, the Sinai, and Palestine by the fourth millennium B.C. (Moorey 1987, Marfoe 1987, I. Shaw 2000). Pitch was imported from the Dead Sea, and from the Red Sea area, Egypt obtained coral (for its jewelry manufacturing), ivory, and ebony. Feathers, gold, and skins came from Nubia for export North and beyond. The eastern desert areas such as Palestine provided the granite, sandstone, schist, limestone, or basalt and other precious stones for its building construction and the manufacture of luxuries (Braudel 2001).

Like Mesopotamia and Harappa, Egyptian trading posts and commercial settlements were also established in the hinterland areas such as the Sinai and Palestine (Moorey 1987, Braudel 2001, Stager 1992, Kantor 1992, I. Shaw 2000) to facilitate natural resource transfers. Early contact with Mesopotamia came as early as the fourth millennium B.C. with signs of mercantile activity in the Nile Delta (Stager 1992, Moorey 1987, Marfoe 1987). Syrian intermediaries at settlements like Habuba Kabira also participated as contact points between Egypt and southern Mesopotamia (Moorey 1987, I. Shaw 2000). The extent of Egyptian direct and indirect trading contacts in the eastern Mediterranean reached northward to Crete and beyond. Trade was facilitated by the appearance of sailing ships,

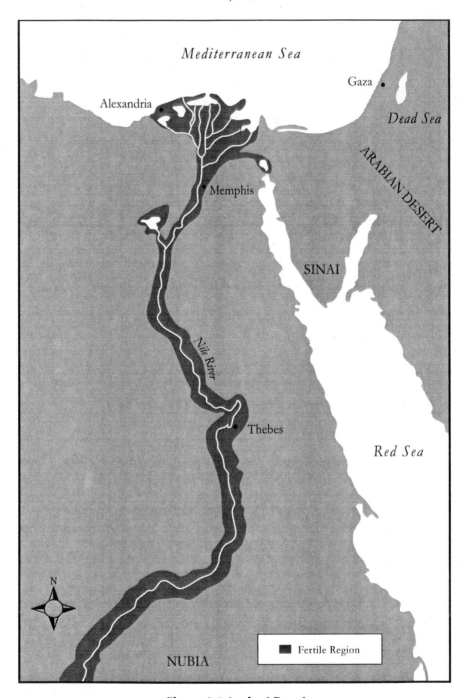

Figure 2.4 Ancient Egypt

which meant cheaper transportation costs in comparison to animal and human porterage. We know of ships constructed from coniferous trees sailing along the Lebanon coast to Byblos (Faulkner 1940).

These main polities—Mesopotamia, Harappa, and Egypt—at this conjuncture were cores of the early Bronze Age world system with their associated peripheries as we have discussed in this chapter. They traded with each other directly or via go-betweens as we have indicated above. Economically and culturally, they dominated the system in the regions where they are geographically located. With the nascent development of communication and transportation at this early period of world history and world system development, there were no indications that each of these cores operated beyond their located geographic areas of influence. In other words, at this conjuncture of world history, we do not find evidence of direct relations between Egypt and the Harappans. This does not mean that there were not products that were exchanged through trading intermediaries. In this sense, there is not the level of globalization that we encounter today in terms of trade and political-social relations. What is clear, however, is the development of a Bronze Age world system with its cores and interconnected region of trade networks. This trading system's vitality and concentration changed over time and were conditioned by the pulsations of ecological, climatological, socioeconomic, and political changes. Especially during Dark Ages, these trading networks come under severe stresses and strains.[6]

At this nascent stage of world system connections, it is very clear that during these *early stages* of the evolution of the world system, Dark Age conditions encountered in one part of the Bronze Age world system might not be encountered simultaneously in other parts of the system. As we move through the history of the evolution of the world system, we will witness this structural difference. For example, while Egypt was experiencing a phase of prosperity and social development during its Middle Kingdom period, southern Mesopotamia and the Harappans were encountering Dark Age conditions.

NOTES

1. McNeill and McNeill (2003, 43) have identified this as the Nile-Indus corridor and the first metropolitan web.

2. There is an indication of a downturn during this period (see Thompson 2001).

3. Stein (1999), however, suggests that some of the communities in the periphery were just as economically, socially, and politically transformed as southern Mesopotamia. Thus, the Uruk settlements coexisted with these other communities in the periphery in Anatolia, for example.

4. Our position differs from that of Shaffer (1982), who has indicated that the Harappan civilization was primarily dependent on internal exchange.

5. Harappan goods were exchanged throughout the Bronze Age economic system as far West as southern Mesopotamia. Dales (1977) has periodized that there was a shift in trading routes of the Bronze Age economic system away from the Central Asian land trade routes to a maritime route by the mid–third millennium B.C. connecting the Indus valley via the Gulf to southern Mesopotamia. The trade on this maritime route started to decline between Mesopotamia, the Gulf, and the Indus Valley by the mid–second millennium.

6. Thompson (2001) has periodized the pulsations of the expansion and contraction of this trading world of the Near East.

3

Ecological Crisis
and System Transformation

DARK AGES ARE ECOLOGICAL CRISIS PHASES

Social historians and archaeologists have noted the various phases in world history when Dark Ages have occurred. These periods cover centuries with perhaps the very earliest starting at 2200 B.C. to 1700 B.C., which Barbara Bell (1971) and Gordon Childe (1942) have defined as the first Dark Age of ancient history. This eclipse was followed by another sequence from 1200B.C. to 700 B.C., and a further phase starting from A.D. 300/400 (depending on the geographic locale) to A.D. 900. Between the fourth and the fifth centuries A.D., changed ecological, climate, and socio-economic and political conditions emerged in the world system. Downturn socioeconomic conditions emerged earlier in the third century A.D. for the Roman Empire, and these conditions were prevalent through to the fifth century. Instead of demarcating the third century as the initiating century of the Dark Age of Antiquity, the fourth and the fifth centuries have been used as the prevalence of changed conditions were widespread.

If we periodize these Dark Age phases on a *social time* continuum, I wish to suggest that this first-known social/natural system crisis of the Bronze Age world system (there is an indication that there was an earlier crisis of the Bronze Age world system about 3800/3400 B.C.) started from 2200 B.C. and continued to 1700 B.C. At 1200 B.C., the social system crisis emerged again and lasted until 700 B.C., when it was finally resolved with the transition to the Iron Age. With the arrival of the Iron Age, system expansion continued through the early Iron Age. However, by A.D. 300/400, system crisis returned resulting in another prolonged period of ecological and socioeconomic distress that lasted until A.D. 900.

41

The extent of the impact of the Dark Age conditions in terms of geographic limits of the system is difficult to map completely, especially with the limited amount of available data to consider, and our present understanding of the level of the connectivity of the system at that time. Therefore a comprehensive coverage is beyond the means of existing available data; instead, the exercise will be to identify selectively the simultaneity and connectivity of the different areas of the world system that were impacted by the Dark Age conditions. As we have indicated previously, it should be noted that not all regions/zones of the world system were impacted simultaneously, for this is dependent on the state of connectivity between the regions of the system.

The above identified periods for the Dark Ages were dated from archaeological finds and literary accounts of social, economic, and political trends and activities. However, if we examine the pollen profiles of deforestation and reforestation, the periodization for the first Dark Age is much longer (see table 3.1). In fact, in *most* cases, continuous from 2200 B.C. to 700 B.C., there are no breaks indicating recovery after 1700 B.C., as the archaeological and literary accounts have indicated (see appendix 1 for arboreal pollen profiles for specified areas, and appendix 2 for *plantago* pollen profiles for specific areas).

Underneath the swell of socioeconomic expansion beginning about 1700 B.C., the structural conditions of ecological distress *continue*.[1] Through time, crisis conditions emerge again at the social system level before a needed reorganization of a social system can occur in order to resolve the system crisis that arose from contradictions in Culture-Nature relations. This continuous period of *uninterrupted* ecological distress from 2200 B.C.–700 B.C. means that natural or even human-induced regeneration takes longer, and has its own rhythm (ecological time), even though an expansion has started at the level of the social system with increasing social systems complexity noted.

Ecological distress in terms of landscape vulnerability is conditioned by the state of the forests and socioeconomic activities of the human communities. Pristine forests were removed during the Neolithic Revolution for agriculture initially, and with the formation of grasslands, pastoralism was practiced. Landscapes that have not suffered continuous deforestation and have forest reserves juxtaposed with agricultural or pastoral lands continue to be productive for the human communities. These landscapes are not as vulnerable to climatological and natural disturbance changes. In this case, we continue to see economic expansion in spite of a drop in pollen count indicating a deforested landscape.

From table 3.1, we get a view of the deforestation phases for the various parts of the world system starting from about 3800 B.C. onward. We

Table 3.1. Arboreal Pollen Profiles—Deforestation Periods

Area	Phase 1	Phase 2	Phase 3	Phase 4
Western Europe				
1) Belgium (Moerzeke)	3093 B.C.–2600 B.C.	2002 B.C.–1274 B.C.	A.D. 180–A.D. 544	
2) Germany 1 (Lake Constance)		2850 B.C.–2050 B.C.	1240 B.C.–230 B.C.	A.D. 600–A.D. 1480
3) Germany 2 (Lake Steisslingen)		2175 B.C.–144 B.C.	A.D. 348–A.D. 1594	
4) Germany 3 (Ahlenmoor)		2200 B.C.–1700 B.C.	A.D. 169–A.D. 664	
5) Switzerland (Lobsigensee)	3920 B.C.–2170 B.C.	1253 B.C.–A.D. 767		A.D. 1055–
6) France (Le Marais St. Boetien)	3520 B.C.–585 B.C.		A.D. 327–A.D. 936	
7) Ireland (Arts Lough)	3726 B.C.–1653 B.C.		A.D. 352–A.D. 1094	
Central and Eastern Europe, Russia				
8) Bulgaria 1 (Besbog 2)		1730 B.C.–A.D. 1160		A.D. 1500–A.D. 1832
9) Bulgaria 2 (Mire Garvan)	3901 B.C.–2123 B.C.	1235 B.C.–A.D. 882		A.D. 1162–A.D. 1628
10) Hungary (Lake Balaton SW)		2683 B.C.–816 B.C.	A.D. 381–A.D. 1296	
11) Poland 1 (Bledowo Lake)	3633 B.C.–2518 B.C.	724 B.C.–A.D. 967		A.D. 1533–
12) Poland 2 (Puscizna Rekowianska)	3638 B.C.–1331 B.C.		A.D. 402–A.D. 881	
13) Poland 3 (Kluki)	3803 B.C.–665 B.C.		A.D. 452–A.D. 884	
14) Byelorussia 1 (Dolgoe)	4800 B.C.–3850 B.C.	3400 B.C.–750 B.C.	A.D. 380–A.D. 1460	A.D. 1000–A.D. 1573
15) Byelorussia 2 (Osvea)	3600 B.C.–330 B.C.			A.D. 1334–A.D. 1778
16) Ukraine 1 (Kardashinski Swamp)	3673 B.C.–2170 B.C.	1338 B.C.–A.D. 300		A.D. 1229–
17) Ukraine 2 (Starniki)		2600 B.C.–727 B.C.	A.D. 93–A.D. 1400	
18) Ukraine 3 (Stoyanov 2)	3900 B.C.–2020 B.C.		A.D. 300–A.D. 1660	
19) Ukraine 4 (Ivano-Frankovskoye)	3937 B.C.–500 B.C.			
20) Ukraine 5 (Dovjok Swamp)		2700 B.C.–224 B.C.	A.D. 40–A.D. 800	A.D. 1200–A.D. 1700
21) Russia (Chabada Lake)	3800 B.C.–1737 B.C.	1400 B.C.–306 B.C.		A.D. 1405–
Northern Europe				
22) Sweden 1 (Ageröds Mosse)	3004 B.C.–256 B.C.		A.D. 435–A.D. 1682	

Table 3.1. *Continued*

Area	Phase 1	Phase 2	Phase 3	Phase 4
23) Sweden 2 (Kansjon)	3752 B.C.–A.D. 978			A.D. 1647–
24) Norway (Grasvatn)	4064 B.C.–3032 B.C.	1612 B.C.–A.D. 323		A.D. 1097–A.D. 1700
25) Latvia (Rudushskoe Lake)	3955 B.C.–1700 B.C.	627 B.C.–A.D. 837		A.D. 1300–
26) Greenland (Lake 31)	2864 B.C.–2178 B.C.	1700 B.C.–121 B.C.		A.D. 1139–
27) Finland 1 (Kirkkosaari)	3022 B.C.–A.D. 1537			
28) Finland 2 (Mukkavaara)	3618 B.C.–A.D. 1757			
29) Finland 3 (Hirvilampi)	4283 B.C.–3540 B.C.	2611 B.C.–696 B.C.	A.D. 389–A.D. 1040	
Mediterranean				
30) Greece (Edessa)	3998 B.C.–2852 B.C.	1941 B.C.–292 B.C.		A.D. 1026–A.D. 1800
31) Greece 2 (Khimaditis 1B)		1641 B.C.–A.D. 1700		
32) Italy (Selle di Carnino)	4539 B.C.–3000 B.C.		A.D. 436–A.D. 1220	A.D. 1529–A.D. 1634
33) Spain 1 (Saldropo)		2202 B.C.–774 B.C.	A.D. 300–A.D. 948	A.D. 1266–
34) Spain 2 (Sanabria Marsh)	3500 B.C.–1700 B.C.		A.D. 856–A.D. 1850	
35) Spain 3 (Lago de Ajo)		1884 B.C.–552 B.C.	A.D. 309–A.D. 1170	
36) Spain 4 (Puerto de Los Tornos)	4200 B.C.–A.D. 395			A.D. 1200–A.D. 1750
37) Spain 5 (Laguna de la Roya)	4500 B.C.–2728 B.C.	968 B.C.–A.D. 848		A.D. 1600
38) Syria (Ghab)		3592 B.C.–1505 B.C.	983 B.C.–A.D. 500	
39) Turkey 1 (Köycegiz Gölü)		2306 B.C.–616 B.C.	180 B.C.–A.D. 916	A.D. 1700–A.D. 1941
40) Turkey 2 (Beysehir Gölü)	3500 B.C.–2527 B.C.		243 B.C.–A.D. 1100	

Source: Based on data from van Zeist et al. (1980); Rankama and Vuorela (1988); Bottema (1974); Eronen and Hyvrinen (1982); Lazarova (1995); Stefanova (1995); Verbruggen et al. (1997); Bezusko (1987); Bezusko et al. (1985); Amman (1985); Watts et al. (1996); Penalba (1994); Binka et al. (1988); Khomutova et al. (1994); Bradshaw et al. (1988); Eisner (1995); Behre and Kucan (1986).

Note: The above pollen profiles were computed using counts of arboreal pollen grains as determined by stratified layers that were distinguished by years that were carbon-dated and calibrated. The number of arboreal pollen grains for each layer specific to each carbon-dated calibrated year were then analyzed in a time series using a polynomial function to determine the trend line. The trend line provided the increases and decreases of total arboreal pollen grains over the time duration specified by the specific palynological analysis from which the data of count of arboreal pollen grains were derived. The same analytical procedures were also used for the plantago pollen grains.

assume that during this early period of world history, the vulnerability of the landscape as a consequence of excessive deforestation was not at a crisis threshold in comparison to a millennium later, whereby following a long period of continuous removal of the forests by humans led to a landscape where the forests disappeared, and by this point in time, grasslands predominated.

For the reproduction of human communities, grasslands are naturally more vulnerable to climate changes without forest resources. Therefore, such a transformed landscape elevated the vulnerability of the human communities, and certain adaptations had to be made resulting in a changed economy. A situation of this nature emerged during the third millennium B.C. leading to technological and cultural adaptations or what A. Sherratt (1981) has termed the "secondary products" revolution. In such a case, from the second millennium B.C. onward, economic adaptation to a very open deforested landscape took place and conditioned the shift from agriculture to pastoralism proceeded incorporating the breakthroughs in technologies and animal husbandry. Coupled with the urban revolution and its set of accumulation and population dynamics, transformations continued. Such adaptations and development occurred in the Fertile Crescent to central and southern Europe including central Eurasia.

As history proceeded with intense land use to meet the structural socioeconomic dynamics that have evolved, by the end of the third millennium B.C., the vulnerability threshold of the landscape became more precipitous. Crisis emerged and social system reproduction was in peril. The Bronze Dark Ages were such periods, punctuated by climate changes and natural disturbances; crisis of social reproduction was at stake. The crisis emerged in those landscapes that were denuded following the above progression of landscape transformations. At the end of the third millennium B.C., these areas were around southern Mesopotamia, northwestern India, and to some extent Egypt (before the Middle Kingdom period), where Culture-Nature relations were at quite heightened levels to meet the needs of the densely populated hierarchical urbanized communities. Their associated hinterlands were also under stress as well.

Given the above, Dark Ages are periods of ecological crises—besides being characterized by anthropologists, historians, and archaeologists as commonly having declining population, trade and economic disruptions, deurbanization, and changes of political regimes. If this were the case, we would expect to find some proxy indicators of ecological degradation, such as deforestation levels, in those devastated landscapes, soil erosion, and endangered species underlining these periods. Along with these ecological indicators, climatological changes such as temperature, rainfall, and natural disturbances also punctuate these periods as well.

Besides natural processes of loss and regeneration, ecological stress levels are outcomes of Culture-Nature relations. These relations are determined by the expansionary dynamics of the process of accumulation in the world system, urbanization processes, and population levels. With *conjonctures* of economic expansion and its other related processes, we would expect to find extreme signs of ecological stress such as deforestation reflecting and *following* these economic expansionary phases. These *conjonctures* of economic expansion serve as markers identifying the periods of extreme exploitation of ecological resources. The scale and scope of ecological degradation is determined by the connectivity of the world system, as well as by the nature of core-periphery relations for the period in question. What this means is that ecological degradation can be quite overarching because of the relations between regions of the world system and the global division of labor existing during the particular period in question. Coupled with these dynamics of accumulation, urbanization, and population circumscribing and underlining the pace of ecological degradation, conflicts and wars further exacerbate the degree of ecological degradation.

THE FIRST PHASE OF THE CRISIS

The ancient world of the Near East and northwestern Indian subcontinent during the third millennium was characterized by a system of overlapping core regions instead of a single dominant core as we have mapped above (e.g., see Gills and Frank 1992, Chew 2001, Kohl 1987a). Within such a political economic matrix, each core interacted with its immediate hinterland as well as with other cores, leading to certain core regions attempting to shape their adjacent hinterlands and at times trying to control them. Given such political incursions and trading initiatives, systemic connections were established (as indicated previously), and during moments of systemic crisis, crisislike conditions reverberated throughout the system, providing opportunities and constraints depending on the circumstances. Such were the conditions that permeated the late third millennium Bronze Age during the Dark Age crisis period starting about 2200 B.C.

As stated previously, the accumulation of surplus, urbanization, and population growth are the prime drivers of the processes of the social system, which in turn define the social system's interactions with the natural system. The collapse of the natural world results from the excessiveness of the accumulation of surplus, urbanization, and population growth—the dynamics of the social world. These dynamics are played out in an interacting fashion. For example, whether the growth in urbanization and population spurs trade or whether trade furthers urbanization and population growth is difficult to delineate.[2] We know that with the formation and development of cities and urban areas, there is also the deepening of the division of labor. This, in turn, fosters the emergence of a variety of technical skills. With the evolution of a specialized division of labor coupled with trade exchanges, new goods are produced, and combined with the agricultural surpluses derived from the rural areas, the trajectory of urban transformation and growth propels forward. Furthermore, the agglomeration of people in urban environments leads also to innovations and ideas being exchanged and adopted. In turn, trade, while injecting resources into the urban areas, is also enhanced.

The interacting relationships between urbanization, population, and production/trade mean that resources from the natural system are utilized so that the social systems can be reproduced. In *World Ecological Degradation*, the level and scale of resource use by the core centers from near and afar in the third millennium B.C. were traced. This history started on an intense trajectory from the fourth millennium onward and by the third millennium B.C., after one millennium of drawdown of the natural capital, the natural and social systems were exhibiting signs of stress-type conditions. Coupled with these signs, there were climatological changes and tectonic shifts during this Dark Age period.

Deforestation

With its many uses, wood has been an important commodity in the reproduction of social life since the Neolithic Revolution (Chew 2001). Over world history from at least 3000 B.C. onward, the available forests have been intensively exploited to meet the needs of an evolving world system, starting from the core centers such as Egypt, Mesopotamia, and Harappa (Chew 2001, Perlin 1989, Williams 2003, Yasuda et al. 2000). As such, deforestation was the order of the day. More than 4,500 years ago, we find the Mesopotamians and the Harappans deforesting their own hills and mountains and conducting military campaigns and trade relations with their peripheries to seek a constant wood supply to reproduce their urbanization and accumulation processes. In the Mesopotamian case, high-quality timber was sought through either military expeditions or trade in the Zagros and Taurus mountains, the Caspian Sea area, and the eastern Mediterranean (Rowton 1967, Willcox 1992, Yasuda et al. 2000). In the Harappan case, northeastern Punjab (on the Siwaliks and the foothills) and the western Ghats were the immediate areas of deforestation. Teak came from the Gir forests or from the Panch Mahals, Surat, and the Dangs (Lal 1997). Timber was also sought as far away as the Himalayas. By no means were the Harappans and the Mesopotamians the exception—the Egyptians sought their wood in neighboring areas of Lebanon and parts of the Syrian coast. For northwestern Europe, Kristiansen (1998a, 281–92) and Berglund (1969) have reported extreme deforestation caused by extensive land use and animal husbandry from early third millennium B.C. onward.

From an empirical analysis of the trend lines of arboreal pollen, table 3.2 presents forty arboreal pollen profiles of deforestation and reforestation starting from as early as 3854 B.C. These profiles cover four geographic regions of the world: western Europe, central and eastern Europe including Russia, northern Europe, and the Mediterranean. With the exception of Byelorussia (Dolgoe), Hungary (Lake Balaton), Latvia (Lake Rudushskoe), and Russia (Chabada Lake) pollen profiles, all dates are ^{14}C calibrated. (Appendix A contains individual graphs of trend lines of arboreal pollen by country).

If we examine table 3.2, despite the fact that historians and archaeologists specializing in the Ancient World did not identify a Dark Age period in the fourth millennium B.C., it seems that twenty-nine of the pollen profiles indicate that there was a phase of deforestation during the fourth millennium B.C. Not only do the pollen profiles exhibit such a period of deforestation, they also reveal the widespread geographic coverage of the degradation of areas in Russia and the Ukraine through to Spain and Syria. It should not be assumed that this was the first phase of deforestation in world history, as the available data are quite limiting. It might perhaps be the first phase of anthropogenically induced deforestation following the advent of the Neolithic Revolution.

Following this first phase of deforestation, from 3854 B.C. to 2400 B.C., there were three or four subsequent phases of deforestation followed by reforestation that occurred toward the latter part of a Dark Age. Table 3.3 exhibits the phase periods based on the *mean* of the dating periods for the thirty-six arboreal pollen trend lines. If Dark Age phase 1 started about 3854 B.C., Dark Age phase 2 followed about approximately 2400/2200 B.C. The latter is the start of the Bronze Age crisis—the early phase of the Dark Ages during the Bronze Age. It should be noted that nested within this phase 2 Dark Age, there was another phase 2A that began about 1200 B.C.—the commonly accepted period for the start of the crisis that witnessed the final demise of the Bronze Age world system. Dark Age phase 2A was followed by Dark Age phase 3 at about A.D. 300, and Dark Age phase 4 at A.D. 1300.

We should not consider these time phasings from only thirty-six available arboreal pollen profiles from different parts of Europe and the Mediterranean as providing the definitive periodizations of Dark Ages. These arboreal pollen profile periodizations provide support to Dark Age periods that have been identified by historians and archaeologists. They

Table 3.2. Arboreal Deforestation Pollen Profiles and Plantago Growth Pollen Profiles

Area	Phase 1	Phase 2	Phase 3	Phase 4
Western Europe				
1) Belgium (Moerzeke)				
Arboreal	3093 B.C.–2600 B.C.	2002 B.C.–1274 B.C.	A.D. 180–A.D. 544	
Plantago	3093 B.C.–2800 B.C.	2002 B.C.–1400 B.C.	A.D. 183–A.D. 362	
2) Germany 1 (Lake Constance)				
Arboreal	2800 B.C.–2050 B.C.	1240 B.C.–230 B.C.	A.D. 600–A.D. 1480	
3) Germany 2 (Lake Steisslingen)				
Arboreal		2175 B.C.–144 B.C.	A.D. 348–A.D. 1594	
4) Germany 3 (Ahlenmoor)				
Arboreal		2200 B.C.–1700 B.C.	A.D. 169–A.D. 664	
Plantago		1514 B.C.–722 B.C.	A.D. 128–A.D. 466	A.D. 763–A.D. 961
5) Switzerland (Lobsigensee)				
Arboreal	3920 B.C.–2170 B.C.	1253 B.C.–A.D. 767		A.D. 1055–
Plantago	3920 B.C.–3200 B.C.	1253 B.C.–242 B.C.		A.D. 616–A.D. 1206
6) France (Le Marais St. Boetien)				
Arboreal	3520 B.C.–585 B.C.		A.D. 327–A.D. 936	
Plantago	4810 B.C.–3815 B.C.	1897 B.C.–853 B.C.		A.D. 631–A.D. 1240
7) Ireland (Arts Lough)				
Arboreal	3726 B.C.–1653 B.C.		A.D. 352–A.D. 1094	
Plantago	4417 B.C.–3104 B.C.		A.D. 681–A.D. 1176	
Central and Eastern Europe, Russia				
8) Bulgaria 1 (Besbog 2)				
Arboreal		1730 B.C.–A.D. 1160		A.D. 1500–A.D. 1832

Table 3.2. *Continued*

Area	Phase 1	Phase 2	Phase 3	Phase 4
9) Bulgaria 2 (Mire Garvan)				
Arboreal	3901 B.C.–2123 B.C.	1235 B.C.–A.D. 882		A.D. 1162–A.D. 1628
Plantago	3605 B.C.–1827 B.C.			
10) Hungary (Lake Balaton SW)				
Arboreal	4338 B.C.–2923 B.C.	2683 B.C.–816 B.C.	A.D. 381–A.D. 1296	
Plantago		1274 B.C.–112 B.C.		A.D. 1296–A.D. 1824
11) Poland 1 (Bledowo Lake)				
Arboreal	3633 B.C.–2518 B.C.	724 B.C.–A.D. 967		A.D. 1533–
Plantago	3280 B.C.–1531 B.C.	257 B.C.–A.D. 967		A.D. 1533–
12) Poland 2 (Puscizna Rekowianska)				
Arboreal	3638 B.C.–1331 B.C.		A.D. 402–A.D. 881	
Plantago	3638 B.C.–2604 B.C.	1331 B.C.–86 B.C.		A.D. 1349–1800
13) Poland 3 (Kluki)				
Arboreal	3803 B.C.–665 B.C.		A.D. 452–A.D. 884	A.D. 1000–A.D. 1573
Plantago	3082 B.C.–1277 B.C.		A.D. 597–A.D. 1703	
14) Byelorussia 1 (Dolgoe)				
Arboreal	4800 B.C.–3850 B.C.	3400 B.C.–750 B.C.	A.D. 380–A.D. 1460	
Plantago	4030 B.C.–2500 B.C.	1150 B.C.–A.D. 380		
15) Byelorussia 2 (Osvea)				
Arboreal	3600 B.C.–330 B.C.			A.D. 1334–A.D. 1778
Plantago	4277 B.C.–3153 B.C.	1579 B.C.–A.D. 1100		A.D. 1889–
16) Ukraine 1 (Kardashinski Swamp)				
Arboreal	3673 B.C.–2170 B.C.	1338 B.C.–A.D. 300		A.D. 1229–
Plantago	3316 B.C.–2170 B.C.		A.D. 448–A.D. 1482	
17) Ukraine 2 (Starniki)				
Arboreal	2600 B.C.–727 B.C.		A.D. 93–A.D. 1400	

Site	Taxon				
18) Ukraine 3 (Stoyanov 2)	**Arboreal**	3900 B.C.–2020 B.C.		A.D. 300–A.D. 1660	A.D. 863–A.D. 1528
	Plantago		2020 B.C.–600 B.C.		
19) Ukraine 4 (Ivano-Frankovskoye)	**Arboreal**	3937 B.C.–500 B.C.			
	Plantago		2062 B.C.–500 B.C.	A.D. 125–A.D. 1063	
20) Ukraine 5 (Dovjok Swamp)	**Arboreal**		2700 B.C.–224 B.C.	A.D. 40–A.D. 800	A.D. 1200–A.D. 1700
	Plantago		956 B.C.–122 B.C.	A.D. 395–A.D. 900	A.D. 1600–A.D. 1872
21) Russia (Chabada Lake)	**Arboreal**	3800 B.C.–1737 B.C.	1400 B.C.–306 B.C.		A.D. 1405–
Northern Europe					
22) Sweden 1 (Ageröds Mosse)	**Arboreal**	3004 B.C.–256 B.C.		A.D. 435–A.D. 1682	A.D. 1856–
	Plantago	3266 B.C.–2485 B.C.		A.D. 208–A.D. 1294	
23) Sweden 2 (Kansjon)	**Arboreal**	3752 B.C.–A.D. 978			A.D. 1647–
24) Norway (Grasvatn)	**Arboreal**	4064 B.C.–3032 B.C.	1612 B.C.–A.D. 323		A.D. 1097–A.D. 1700
25) Latvia (Rudushskoe Lake)	**Arboreal**	3955 B.C.–1700 B.C.	627 B.C.–A.D. 837		A.D. 1300–
26) Greenland (Lake 31)	**Arboreal**	2864 B.C.–2178 B.C.	1700 B.C.–121 B.C.		A.D. 1139–
	Plantago	3030 B.C.–2656 B.C.	1898 B.C.–500 B.C.		A.D. 1065–A.D. 1213

Table 3.2. *Continued*

Area	Phase 1	Phase 2	Phase 3	Phase 4
27) Finland 1 (Kirkkosaari)				
Arboreal	3022 B.C.–A.D. 1537			
Plantago	3852 B.C.–87 B.C.			A.D. 1384–A.D. 1743
28) Finland 2 (Mukkavaara)				
Arboreal	3618 B.C.–A.D. 1757			
29) Finland 3 (Hirvilampi)				
Arboreal	4283 B.C.–3540 B.C.	2611 B.C.–696 B.C.	A.D. 389–A.D. 1040	
Plantago	3726 B.C.–2797 B.C.	696 B.C.–A.D. 400		A.D. 823–
Mediterranean				
30) Greece (Edessa)				
Arboreal	3998 B.C.–2852 B.C.	1941 B.C.–292 B.C.	A.D. 1026–A.D. 1800	
Plantago	3500 B.C.–2852 B.C.	739 B.C.–292 B.C.		A.D. 1595–
31) Greece 2 (Khimaditis 1B)				
Arboreal		1641 B.C.–A.D. 1700		
Plantago			A.D. 400–A.D. 1639	
32) Italy (Selle di Carnino)				
Arboreal	4539 B.C.–3000 B.C.		A.D. 436–A.D. 1220	A.D. 1529–A.D. 1634
Plantago	3774 B.C.–2626 B.C.		A.D. 1070–A.D. 1270	A.D. 1581–
33) Spain 1 (Saldropo)				
Arboreal	3630 B.C.–1431 B.C.	2202 B.C.–774 B.C.	A.D. 300–A.D. 948	A.D. 1266–
Plantago			3 B.C.–A.D. 684	
34) Spain 2 (Sanabria Marsh)				
Arboreal	3500 B.C.–1700 B.C.	2192 B.C.–110 B.C.		A.D. 856–A.D. 1850
Plantago				

35) Spain 3 (Lago de Ajo)				
Arboreal	4963 B.C.–2059 B.C.	1884 B.C.–552 B.C.	A.D. 309–A.D. 1170	
Plantago		768 B.C.–A.D. 94		A.D. 1600–A.D. 1900
36) Spain 4 (Puerto de Los Tornos)				
Arboreal	4200 B.C.–A.D. 395			A.D. 1200–A.D. 1750
Plantago	3965 B.C.–756 B.C.			A.D. 1101–A.D. 1767
37) Spain 5 (Laguna de la Roya)				
Arboreal	4500 B.C.–2728 B.C.	968 B.C.–A.D. 848		A.D. 1600
Plantago	4431 B.C.–2728 B.C.	1594 B.C.–A.D. 700		A.D. 1762–
38) Syria (Ghab)				
Arboreal	3592 B.C.–1505 B.C.	983 B.C.–A.D. 500		
Plantago	4636 B.C.–4000 B.C.	1505 B.C.–1000 B.C.	A.D. 269–A.D. 1000	
39) Turkey 1 (Köycegiz Gölü)				
Arboreal		2306 B.C.–616 B.C.	180 B.C.–A.D. 916	A.D. 1700–A.D. 1941
Plantago	3694 B.C.–2990 B.C.	1278 B.C.–419 B.C.		A.D. 1223–1852
40) Turkey 2 (Beysehir Gölü)				
Arboreal	3500 B.C.–2527 B.C.	243 B.C.–A.D. 1100		
Plantago	4451 B.C.–3489 B.C.	1556 B.C.–724 B.C.		A.D. 1560–

Source: Based on data from van Zeist et al. (1980); Rankama and Vuorela (1988); Bottema (1974); Eronen and Hyvärinen (1982); Lazarova (1995); Stefanova (1995); Verbruggen et al. (1997); Bezusko (1987); Bezusko et al. (1985); Amman (1985); Watts et al. (1996); Penalba (1994); Binka et al. (1988); Khomutova et al. (1994); Bradshaw et al. (1988); Eisner (1995); Behre and Kucan (1986).

Table 3.3. Periodization of Dark Ages*

Phase 1:	3854 B.C.–2400 B.C.
Phase 2:	2402 B.C.–594 B.C.
Phase 2A:	1188 B.C.–A.D. 689
Phase 3:	A.D. 296–A.D. 1171
Phase 4:	A.D. 1311–A.D. 1733

*Mean of thirty-six pollen profiles of deforestation phases.

could also be considered as supportive proxy evidence for our thesis that Dark Ages are also periods of ecological degradation (deforestation) in these selected areas. It is also likely that with a reduced arboreal pollen count it might not necessarily indicate ecological degradation, because the landscape might not be as ecologically stressed, showing evidence of devastating deforestation followed by the formation of grasslands. This will be discussed in the following pages with the presentation of profiles analyzing the percentage of arboreal to nonarboreal pollen count for a specific geographic area.

The lengthy periods of deforestation and reforestation of these arboreal pollen profiles, which are longer than the Dark Age periods identified by historians and archaeologists as exhibited in table 3.3, might indicate the ecological time of recovery measured on a social timescale. Hence, we should not expect these periodizations to fall precisely within the social time phasing of Dark Ages in world history as demarcated by historians and archaeologists.

The Dark Age phase 2 deforestation period is the most pertinent time point for our discussion of the ecological degradation of the early Bronze Age crisis. With one deforestation period starting about approximately 2200 B.C., this dating from the arboreal pollen profiles corresponds approximately with Barbara Bell's (1971) identification of the first Dark Age of the Ancient World. In western Europe, arboreal pollen from areas in Belgium, Germany, and France exhibit the deforestation period starting around 2200/2000 B.C. In central and eastern Europe, trend lines of arboreal pollen show deforestation levels in areas of Hungary and Ukraine. In northern Europe, the trend line of arboreal pollen in an area in Finland also supports this deforestation pattern. Finally, in the Mediterranean, we find areas of Greece, Spain, and Turkey exhibiting such trends. The latter area of Turkey is most pertinent for the present discussion because it is where the southern Mesopotamians sought their natural resources.

Agriculture, animal husbandry, and other anthropogenic-induced changes naturally lead to forest fragmentation and deforestation, and the rise in the pollen record of indicator plants and ground weeds such as *Plantago lanceolata* (Behre 1990, 224; Williams 2003, 12–25). Table 3.2 provides time phases of the *rise* in the amount of *Plantago* pollen when there was a *decline* in the amount of arboreal pollen. Appendix B contains the trend lines of the rise and fall of *Plantago* pollen. It seems that the most widespread pattern of the spread of *Plantago* with deforestation occurred during Dark Age phase 1.

The identification of phases in table 3.2 does not imply that deforestation follows a cycle. Rather, I am suggesting that there is a length of time when the ecological threshold is reached as a consequence of natural system and social system connections that require a period (ecological time) for ecological recovery or social system adaptation (such as reorganization, learning processes, technological adaptation, etc.) to take place. This necessitates a time period. For ecological recovery, timewise it is ecological time that is the underlying basis. For social system adaptation, social time is the case. In this sense, the duration is of different length. We are assuming that ecological recovery will take a much longer period measured on a social time scale because Nature has its own intrinsic rhythm driven by such factors such as generation time, disturbance frequencies, and age of reproduction, and other spatial scales such as topography, interaction lengths, etc. (Redman and Kinzig 2003). Similarly, social system adaptation and recovery has its own rhythm and is dependent on the internal intrinsic factors of the social organizations and social institutions. From what we have been able to surmise from tables 3.2 and 3.3, and the periodization of Dark Ages by historians, archaeologists, and anthropologists, the period of social adaptation, that is, the duration of a Dark Age based on social distress and recovery, is nested within the long duration of ecological time. The latter suggests that deforestation phases (or ecological recovery) are (is) naturally longer, and that ecological stress continues despite the fact that social adaptation and recovery have been completed.

Deforestation and the vulnerability of the landscape in terms of its inability to support existing human land use becomes crucial when grasslands predominate the landscapes and climate changes and volcanicity with tectonic shifts occur. The shift from predominantly forests to grasslands in terms of proportion occurred during periods of Dark Ages. Trend analysis of the arboreal pollen (see appendix 3—Arboreal and Nonarboreal Percentage Pollen Profiles) as a percentage of nonarboreal pollen for pollen profiles that were identified in tables 3.1 and 3.2 shows that nonarboreal pollen having higher percentages than arboreal pollen are specific for certain Dark Age periods and for specific geographic areas. What these specific trend analyses of arboreal and nonarboreal percentages show is that there is reforestation. However, in some cases over several Dark Ages, the landscape has turned to grassland and pastures with fewer trees: for example, Germany (Lake Steisslingen), Switzerland (Lobsigensee), Bulgaria (Besbog 2), Bulgaria (Mire Girvan), Poland (Kulki), Byleorussia (Osvea), Ukraine (Starniki), Ukraine (Ilvano-Frankovskoye),

Russia (Chabada Lake), Latvia (Rudushskoe Lake), Greenland (Lake 31), Finland (Kirkkosaari), Finland (Mukkavarra), Finland (Hirvilampi), Greece (Edessa), Greece (Khimaditis 1B), Italy (Selle Di Carnino), Spain (Puerto de Los Tornos), Spain (Laguna de la Roya), and Turkey (Köycegiz Gölü). In all, this suggests a landscape that is more vulnerable to changes in climate conditions and hence more susceptible to ecological collapses.

It should also be realized that extreme landscape modification, and hence its vulnerability to exogenous changes such as climate and natural disturbances, is the highest during periods of Dark Ages where evidence shows the formation of grasslands and pastures on the landscape in a higher proportion to the number of trees on it. Without specific studies of land use, urbanization, and population density in each geographic area, it is difficult to predict the vulnerability threshold for crisis in social system reproduction. In certain cases, such as the Dark Age of Antiquity (see chapter 4), the existence of pastures and grasslands with the absence of trees in northern Scandinavia along with cool and moist climate conditions did not in any manner heighten the vulnerability of social system crisis so long as there were sources of grazing for a pastoral economy. Social system crisis emerged only when the weather changed to warmer and drier conditions.

With deforestation, there are also other consequences such as soil erosion. The lack of vegetative cover increases the amount of erosion. The amount of erosion is about fifty times higher on a landscape devoid of cover than one that is under a well-developed forest (Redman 1999). It has been estimated that about 146 t/ha of soil are lost per year (Goldsmith 1990). Besides this, the rate of rainfall runoff is five times higher on a landscape that is bare. This rate of runoff thus has two impacts. First, it acts as a transport medium for small soil particles such as clay, thereby increasing the soil sediment carried by the rivers and streams. Second, the increased rate of runoff means that there is less contribution to the moisture of the remaining soil from the rainfall. All these factors generate significant issues for social systems dependent on irrigation-fed agriculture. The loss of moisture means that with climate changes such as an increase in temperature and shifts of wind patterns carrying rain, these latter changes further heighten the distressed conditions.

There is ample evidence even as early as 2200 B.C., during Dark Age phase 2 (2200 B.C.–1700 B.C.), in Mesopotamia, Harappa, and Egypt that soil erosion resulting from deforestation had tremendous consequences for the agricultural economies of these early civilizations (Chew 2001, Butzer 1976). It led to severe economic stress on these social systems and, coupled with climatological changes and natural disturbances, led to crises in the social and natural systems (Chew 1997a, 2001; Redman 1999). Grove and Rockham (2001) have also indicated evidence of soil erosion in the later period of the Bronze Age from 1900 B.C. to 1700 B.C. in the Mediterranean area, for example, Crete.

Climate Changes and Natural Disturbances

Considerations of climate changes, natural disturbances, and catastrophes impacting the reproduction of the social (world) system have not warranted much attention in the social and historical sciences in comparison to capital accumulation issues, class and elite dynamics, technological adaptation, and ideological/cultural processes.[3] Thus innovations in sword manufacturing, invasions by foreign armies, internal corruption, and economic disintegration as possible explanations are proffered and preferred to those that consider climate change, tectonic effects, or even comets impacting on earth as possible vectors for the widespread destruction and demise of communities. This line of thinking is followed closely by explanations that have been provided for the widespread collapse of cities and civilizations in the later phase of the crisis of the Bronze Age (e.g., see K. Friedman 2003, Drews 1993, Yoffee 1988).

Such adherence to anthropogenic-induced explanations for political-economic declines and even collapse of social systems is limiting, for there are some indications linking climate changes and tectonic shifts affecting social (world) system reproduction during the Bronze Age crisis. Throughout world history, socioeconomic and political changes (such as trade collapses and political changes), including large-scale migrations, have occurred during periods of climate change; therefore, this correlative relationship is quite clear. What needs to be presented is the clustering of these climate changes, natural disturbances, and the occurrence of catastrophes during phases of Dark Ages.

Changes in the climate such as temperature increases by no means only started in the first millennium A.D., nor can it be claimed (Crutzen and Stoermer 2000) that it began around A.D. 1800 as is normally assumed (Ruddiman 2003, 2005). Recent studies have indicated that increases in methane gas five thousand years ago can be attributed to have anthropogenic origin, and the calculations indicated that it could not be the result of natural forcing (Ruddiman and Thomson 2001; Ruddiman 2003, 2005). The origin of this, according to Ruddiman (2003, 2005), is from north tropical sources and has been attributed to early rice irrigation and innovations in agriculture in civilizations such as China and India. If increases in methane gas have an anthropogenic origin, so too do the increases in carbon dioxide.

Carbon dioxide, a more abundant gas, would have a larger climatic impact. According to calculations, its increase as a consequence of human activity started almost eight thousand years ago, and not as what is commonly accepted as a feature of the late twentieth century, though the increase is more gradual than the late twentieth-century elevations (Ruddiman 2003, 2005). Largely, this increase in carbon dioxide is a consequence of deforestation, as we have stated previously.

Climatewise, there is evidence of temperature changes (higher temperatures) and increasing droughtlike conditions persisting in the eastern Mediterranean, Egypt, west Asia, Mesopotamia, northwestern India, central Asia, Africa, and parts of the New World starting from 2200 B.C. onward during the onset of the Dark Age of the third millennium (Neumann and Parpola 1987, Chew 2001, Weiss and Bradley 2001, Bentaleb 1997, Enzel et al. 1999, Ratnagar 1981, Fagan 2004, Issar 1998, Burroughs 2005). The start of this warming phase was by no means a phase that followed the Mini Ice Age of 6200 B.C. to 5800 B.C. An earlier phase began about 3800 B.C. and lasted for over one thousand years (commensurate with our phase 1 of deforestation or Dark Age phase 1; see tables 3.1 and 3.2) when the climate began to be drier, which affected southwestern Asia and the eastern Mediterranean.

If we follow the argument of Ruddiman (2003, 2005), this climate change was a consequence of human actions, or if we consider other explanations, it could be a result of the alterations in the earth's angle to the sun, thus affecting the amount of radiation reaching the surface of the earth. Such a difference in radiation levels shifted the southwest monsoons, which normally carry the summer rainfall to the region, further south, thus leading to lowered rain and snowfall in the Anatolian and Ethiopian highlands. The lowered rainfall meant that the waters from the Ethiopian highlands that fed the Nile were also reduced, thus impacting agriculture that was dependent on irrigation or annual flooding. By 3500 B.C., the drought intensified engendering a climatic crisis (Fagan 2004). This crisis deepened further between 3200 B.C. and 3000 B.C. After this period, the climatic cycle changed and swung back to conditions prior to 3800 B.C.

Eight hundred years later, another warming trend started in about 2200 B.C. According to Fagan (2004), who has argued on the impact of climate change on civilizations, this start of a warming trend again was a global event. Affected areas covered Egypt, northern Africa, Greece, Indus, the Fertile Crescent, Crete, Russia, west Asia, and Palestine (Chew 2001, Weiss and Bradley 2001, Bell 1971, Bottema 1997, Krementski 1997, Hassan 1997, Fagan 2004, Hole 1997, Issar 1998, Burroughs 2005). The summer monsoon rainfall that brings moisture to the Ethiopian highlands feeding the waters of the Nile was reduced. Annually, a low-pressure system over India and the Arabian Sea brings southwest winds to the Indian Ocean region and rainfall to the highlands of east Africa. However, should pressure fall in the Pacific Ocean, leading to a weaker low-pressure system in the Indian Ocean, the southwest monsoon winds would blow weaker, leading to less rain falling on India and the Ethiopian highlands. This was the case in about 2200 B.C. and resulted in drought conditions in northwestern India along with lowered flood levels from the Nile flow in Egypt.

Table 3.4 shows temperature changes in terms of warm and cool periods during the third millennium B.C. in Anatolia and the surrounding regions. Warm periods were followed by drought conditions. Between 2710 B.C. and 2345 B.C., Anatolia and the northern Fertile Crescent had arid conditions; however, the Nile floodings continued to be high (Fairbridge et al. 1997). However, by 2205 B.C., the starting time point initializing the start of the Bronze Age crisis, the Nile floods had weakened. From 2205 B.C. to 1650 B.C., a period that covered phase 2 of the Bronze Age crisis, there was widespread aridity in Anatolia and the northern part of the Fertile Crescent including northern Africa (Fairbridge et al. 1997).

For social systems with agricultural practices that are reliant on irrigation waters or from annual floods, this loss of moisture would place tremendous stress on the agricultural systems and, hence, the economy and social-political stability (Neumann and Parpola 1987).[4] Such was the case for the core centers of Mesopotamia, Egypt, the Harappan civilization, and communities in Palestine and Syria. Each responded differently to such stressed conditions depending on what they were facing.

Mesopotamia

Between 2200 B.C. and 1700 B.C., southern Mesopotamia faced a crisis in agricultural productivity. The stratified society pursued intensive socio-economic activities to produce surplus for domestic consumption as well as for exports (in the form of grains and woolen textiles) to west Asia, the

Table 3.4. Cool and Warm Periods: Anatolia and Adjacent Regions

3385 B.C.–3250 B.C.	Cool
3250 B.C.–2900 B.C.	Warm
2900 B.C.–2710 B.C.	Cool
2710 B.C.–2345 B.C.	Warm
2345 B.C.–2205 B.C.	Cool
2205 B.C.–1650 B.C.	Warm (Dark Age)
1670 B.C.–1655 B.C.	Cool
1650 B.C.–1410 B.C.	Warm
1410 B.C.–1205 B.C.	Cool
1205 B.C.–815 B.C.	Warm (Dark Age)
815 B.C.–685 B.C.	Cold
685 B.C.–406 B.C.	Warm

Source: Based on data from Fairbridge et al. 1997.

Gulf, and beyond. The scale of intensity required extensive deforestation, maximal utilization of agriculture, and animal husbandry. Furthermore, with a state structure requiring tax payments, military service, and so on, the farmers were required to have an increasing surplus to meet the reproductive needs of the system (Jacobsen and Adams 1958). Besides requiring surplus production, state direction during the Third Dynasty of Ur (2150 B.C.–2000 B.C.) also concentrated on certain economic activities such as the production of wool and the development of a large-scale textile industry. This further pushed the need to increase agricultural productivity in the form of feed grains such as barley for sheep (Adams 1981). Population increases and state initiatives to establish new towns peopled by conquered populations for the purpose of pursuing agricultural and textile manufacturing added to the range of economic practices that required heightened resource utilization (Gelb 1973). The result of these political and economic initiatives was an intensification of agricultural production that pushed agricultural lands to the limit.

The ability of the natural system to provide for the needs of the social system was disrupted with the increasing salinization of the agricultural lands in southern Mesopotamia.[5] From the third millennium onward, this became an issue when crop yields were being reduced due to the salt content in the soils. Wheat and barley that were grown in the mid-fourth millennium in equal portions had shifted to more barley cultivation by the end of the third millennium. With the salinity problem, after 1700 B.C., the cultivation of wheat was completely given up as barley was a more salt-tolerant grain and more resistant to temperature changes. Besides this, barley was also the preeminent feed for sheep, whose end product, wool, was a commodity required for the long-distance trade. However, this change in grain cultivation did not solve the issue of soil salinity, which is reflected in crop yields. Between 3000 B.C. and 2350 B.C. (Early Dynastic period), crop yields were 2,030 l/ha. By 2150–2000 B.C. (Third Dynasty of Ur), the yield had fallen to 1,134 l/ha. By 1700 B.C., crop yields had slipped to 718 l/ha (Jacobsen and Adams 1958). The agricultural productivity crisis reached its nadir when cultivable land was kept in production with yields of only 370 l/ha (Adams 1981). With such yields, the "burden on the cultivator became a crushing one" (Adams 1981, 152).

How did the social system react to the natural system crisis? Seeding rates were increased in the hope of increasing yield. Between 2150 B.C. and 2000 B.C., 55.5 l of seed were planted per hectare. This volume doubled in comparison to the previous period between 3000 B.C. and 2350 B.C. Furthermore, with no consideration for the repercussions, alternate year fallowing was also violated in order to maintain the maximum amount of land available for cultivation (Gelb 1973). For land where the natural water table comes to within 2 m of the soil surface, and with irrigation bringing the water table within 46 cm, salt concentration would be disastrous for crop yields (Gelburd 1985). Fallowing is the traditional method of handling salinization. In southern Mesopotamia, by leaving the land to fallow, wild plants such as *shok* and *agul* drew moisture from the water table and dried up the subsoil. This prevented the water from rising and bringing the salts to the surface. When the land was cultivated again, the dryness of the subsoil allowed the irrigation water to leach salt from the surface and drain it below the root level. Fallowing therefore returned the land to its cultivation potential. By reducing or violating fallow times, the productivity of the land was endangered.

This salinization problem causing reduced yields coincided with arid conditions and temperature increases. Confirmation of these climate changes via decreased pollen count, Tigris-Euphrates stream flow, dust spikes, and decreases in lake levels has been made in recent years (Weiss and Bradley 2001). The Dead Sea area reported a 20–30 percent drop in precipitation from the previous period of 610 mm (Bar-Mathews and Avalon 1997, 155–68; Bar-Mathews et al. 1998, 203–14; Bar-Mathews et al. 1999, 85–95). Bookman et al. (2004) reported on lower lake levels resulting from low rainfall departing from a previous high that occurred during the Middle Holocene. The Lake Van cores document a dust spike in about 2290–2000 B.C., a decrease in lake levels, and a rapid increase in aridity (Lemcke and Sturm 1997, 653–78). The Lake Van proxies provide a climate record for the Tigris and Euphrates headwaters region. Such a configuration of climate changes impacted reproduction of the social system. The increasing temperatures led to a rise in evapotranspiration. For irrigated agriculture, which is the basis of southern Mesopotamian agricultural practices, this would mean more demand for more water. With the drop in rainfall, intensive use of irrigated water had a deleterious effect on agricultural land that already possessed a salinity problem that southern Mesopotamia was experiencing then.

In northern Mesopotamia, in the Habur plains such climatic conditions also impacted towns such as Tell Brak and Tell Leilan, which were under Akkadian imperial rule and shared the same fate as the urbanized areas in the south (Weiss 2000). Reduced water flow was handled through channelizing and repeated clearing of the silt from soil erosion due to deforestation. Abandonment of towns and settlements on the Habur plains followed about 2200 B.C. onward (Weiss et al. 1993). Such desperate conditions were exacerbated by a major volcanic eruption. Tell Leilan and Tell Brak were affected by this from the end of the third millennium onward. A dust veil persisted for several decades. All this reduced moisture and affected the conditions of agricultural productivity (Weiss et al. 1993). Desertification also followed.

Egypt

With this temperature increase that impacted on the whole region, Egypt by no means escaped from this climatological transformation. During this period, about 2200 B.C., such temperature changes led to a reduced flow of the Nile, thus lowering its level and inducing drought conditions that had a systemic impact on the overall economy of Egypt and its surrounding lands (Bell 1971, Hassan 1997). The growth and expansion of Egypt have to be understood within the context of the Nile River. It is this drainage system that is the backbone of the agricultural economy of Egypt. The annual flooding of the Nile Valley provides rejuvenation of the agricultural landscape. On this basis, lower Nile flows would mean falling Nile flood levels. Such occurrences would severely impact agricultural production, especially in light of the semiarid conditions of Egypt, which required the annual flooding for irrigation. Nile flow is a function of the amount of rain that falls on the Ethiopian highlands and the precipitation stored in Lake Abhe, Lake Zway-Shala, and Lake Turkana. The rainfall in these highlands accounts for 83 percent of the Nile flow at Aswan. The seasonality of rain is dependent on the Indian monsoon that falls between June and August (Barry and Chorley 1992). Therefore, any changes in the monsoon rain would have an impact on the annual amount of precipitation that would ultimately lower the level of the Nile. As stated earlier, about 2200 B.C., a severe lake level reduction was reported at Lakes Abhe, Zway-Shala, and Turkana (Gasse 2000, Johnson and Odada 1996, Ricketts and Johnson 1996, Butzer 1997). This led to a lower Nile flow and level that resulted in aridity and drought conditions in Egypt (Hassan 1986, 1997; Bryson and Bryson 1998). According to Butzer (1976), there was a significant decline in Nile flow to the order of 30 percent or more after the First Dynasty right through to the Middle Kingdom.

There were also reports of the invasion of dune sand in the valley near Memphis, suggesting the increasing aridity of the landscape (Hassan 1997). In Middle Egypt, sand dunes also invaded the flood plain. Lack of high floods from the Nile along with the dry climate led to severe pressure on the agricultural system as naturally irrigated areas for crop cultivation were reduced. Besides impacting tax collection, famine followed and has been confirmed by the ancient texts of Egypt (Hassan 1997; Bell 1971, 1975; Butzer 1976). The climatologically induced conditions led to reduced agroproduction, which, in turn, had an impact on the Egyptian economy of the First Intermediate period (Weiss 2000). Flood failures occurred between 2180 and 2135 B.C. and again between 2005 and 1992 B.C. (Bell 1975). However, by the period of the Middle Kingdom, more normal conditions returned. Signs of famine emerged again about 1750

B.C., though they were not as severe as those that occurred in 2200 B.C. (Bell 1975). Extensive desiccation of the marshlands was also reported along with mass death of adults and children along with reduced birth rates.

Northwestern India

In the case of northwestern India, high-resolution paleoclimate records for the Indian monsoon indicate signs of aridification in the late third millennium B.C. (Weiss 2001, Bentaleb 1997). Dry conditions were experienced in the Thar Desert about 1700 B.C. (Enzel et al. 1999). Ratnagar (1981) has pointed as well to this climate shift and has further suggested a small-scale oscillation to drier conditions between 1800 and 1500 B.C. Singh (1971, 1973, 1990) confirmed this increasing aridity by reviewing pollen cores from three salt lakes located in Rajasthan, Sambhar, Didwarnar, and Lunkaransar as well as the increasing salinity in these lakes between 1800 and 1500 B.C., which impacted on the Harappan civilization: "All this goes to indicate that a dry period of some intensity had set in about 1800 B.C. It is a rare coincidence that the Harappan culture is known to have started declining about 1750 B.C." (Singh 1971, 188).[6]

Such arid conditions naturally impacted agroproduction in northwestern India, especially for arid regions where minor shifts in terms of wetness would spell severe stress. This change in the natural system was also coupled with the occurrences of tectonic shifts that added further strain to the social system. Tectonic shifts alone would not immediately impact the reproduction of the social system unless they were in the immediate proximity of human communities or they reshaped the contours of the landscape by shifting river courses. The latter happened in the second millennium B.C. By diverting watercourses, the diversions transformed some rivers into dry water beds, which further exacerbated the already existing aridity, thus impacting the social system. For this period, Agrawal and Sood (1982) noted tectonic shifts that diverted the course of the Satluz and the easterly rivers away from the Ghaggar, which over time transformed into a lakelike depression during this period. The Ghaggar or Sarasvati, which feeds into the Indus River, was alive until the late Harappan period (1800 B.C.) but was dead by the time of the Painted Gray Ware period (1000 B.C.). Possehl (2000) has also confirmed this drying up of the Sarasvati and its implications for the Harappan urban complexes located on its riverbank.

The thesis of tectonic shifts impacting the reproduction of the Harappan civilization's urban complexes has also been advanced by several scholars (Raikes 1964, Raikes and Dales 1977, Dales 1979, Sahni 1956). The suggestion is that a tectonic uplift generated a dam approximately

145 km downstream from Mohenjodaro in an area near Sehwan. This caused the normal discharge of the Indus River to accumulate in a growing reservoir, which over time caused the flooding of Mohenjodaro. Mud-brick platforms were erected to keep the city safe from the flooding waters. Archaeological excavations have indicated silt accumulation up to a vertical distance of approximately 21.3 m sandwiched between successive levels of occupations of Mohenjodaro. The silt deposits are not of the type spread by normal flooding of fast-flowing rivers but seem to be of the kind similar to still-water conditions.[7] Dales (1979), building on this, has suggested that, enmeshed in this deteriorating condition, the weakened state was unable to send help to its inhabitants in the northern frontier when they were threatened by tribal incursions.

Beyond the arguments suggesting climate changes and tectonic shifts leading to structural socioeconomic and political reversals, it has been suggested that overcultivation, overgrazing, salinity, deforestation, and flooding contributed to these changes (Fairservis 1979b, Raikes and Dyson 1961, Wheeler 1968, Stein 1998). The flooding of the Indus River would have had the effect of increasing the water table for a considerable distance on both sides of the channel. With a high salt content in the water table, and the mean temperature about 90°, poor leaching led to large areas becoming unfit for cultivation over time. Along with the wearing out of the landscape through overcultivation, overgrazing, and deforestation, this would have generated severe stress on socioeconomic reproduction and hence structural reversals in the socioeconomic and political arenas. Fairservis (1979b, 88) has put this succinctly: "the evidence again demonstrates a failure to come to grips fully with what must have become an increasingly acute situation—the destruction of the local ecological patterns and the consequent failure of food resources."

Southern Levant and Eurasia

In southern Levant, aridity emerged toward the end of the third millennium B.C. (Bar-Mathews 1998, Goodfriend 1991). With such climatic change, agriculture was impacted following the lowering of the levels of the rivers and streams. Similar to the Nile floods in Egypt that the agricultural base was dependent on, the lowering of river levels led to the end of flooding of flood plains. What resulted was pressure on populated communities in terms of food supply along with the loss of cash crops. The result was the abandonment of towns and villages and it could have engendered political instability for the local elites whose responsibility was to provide resources for the populace.

Beyond the above core centers of Mesopotamia, Egypt, the Harappan civilization of northwestern India, and the southern Levant, temperature changes also impacted other ecological landscapes. In western Asia, the introduction of the Zebu cattle, which can withstand aridity, occurred during the two arid periods (2200 and 1200 b.c.) of the Bronze Age (Matthews 2002). In central Eurasia, preliminary data also confirmed marked changes in vegetation, beginning about 2200 b.c. and lasting until 1700 b.c. (Hiebert 2000, Krementski 1997). Pollen cores indicate a sharp decrease in arboreal pollen and an increase in steppe pollen. From 2200 b.c. to 2000 b.c., there was a severe drop in forest cover and an increase in steppification, leading to an expansion in steppe landscapes from 1800 b.c. to 1700 b.c. The pollen profiles for the region discussed in the previous section also confirmed the deforestation process. Arid conditions also affected arable land, which caused severe pressure on animal husbandry of the steppe population. The lush feathergrass steppe growing on the landscape near Kalmykia, for example, from 2500 b.c. to 2200 b.c. gave way to dry scrubby vegetation—wormwood steppe—and even desertification by 2200 b.c.–1700 b.c. This changed ecological landscape led to out-migration of the sedentary population from river valleys with time and exploitation of the steppes for animal feed.

Socioeconomic and Political Transformations

As discussed in chapter 1, socioeconomic and political trends during Dark Ages are reversals of what occurred during periods of expansionary growth. We note some general trends, such as a fall in population levels for some areas, especially for highly urbanized communities, decline or losses in certain material skills, decay in the cultural aspects of life, decline in living standards and thus wealth, political instability, loss of trading contacts and collapse of trade networks, and deurbanization. If we also consider Dark Ages as periods of ecological crises, the lack of available resources would lead to adaptations/innovations: in using different materials in the production of commodities, in the establishment of different social and political organizations, and in the cultural aspects of material life. These adaptive/innovative ventures seem to occur as the Dark Ages are receding, and the adaptive/innovative and learning processes developed due to scarcity and societal upheavals are adopted within the social, economic, and political fabric of life. Resource scarcity would also lead to the search for new areas for resources exploitation; hence stimulating socioeconomic and political transformation that otherwise might take a much longer or a different route in terms of social change. The latter might explain historical transformation of whole regions where the adoption of certain metals and sociocultural lifestyles occurred homogenously.

Table 3.5. Population of Major Mesopotamian Cities (in thousands), 2800 B.C.–1500 B.C.

City	2800	2500	2400	2300	2200	2100	2000	1900	1800	1700	1600	1500
Adab	10	20	10	10	30	10	10	10	10			
Akkad					30							
Akshak		10	20									
Assur								10	15	10	10	10
Babylon										60	60	
Badtibira									10			
Eshunna									10			
Girsu			40	80	50	80	40					
Isin							40	20	20			
Kesh	40	10	10									
Kish	30	20										
Lagash		60	30									
Larsa	16	10					40	40	40			
Nagar	20	15	10									
Nina						10	10	10				
Nineveh											10	10
Nippur	10	20	20	30	30	30	30	20	20			
Shuruppak	30	30	10									
Suheri	10	10	10		10	10	10					
Umma	20	40	40	40	10	20	25		40			
Ur	12	10	10	20	40	100	20	10				
Uruk	80	40	30	30		30	30	30				
Zabalam	10	10	10	10	10	10	10	10	10			
Total	288	305	250	230	210	300	265	160	175	70	80	20

Source: Derived from Modelski 2003: 28–33 and Thompson 2004.

Deurbanization and Migration

Tracking the reversals in socioeconomic trends during Dark Ages or over the very long term requires considerable effort, especially when the quantitative data are sparse. Some recent attempts such as that of Modelski (2003) and Thompson (2004) on urbanization and economic expansion have provided us with some broad contours on these processes. In terms of urbanization, by 3500 B.C. for the "heartland of cities" such as southern Mesopotamia, urban growth had progressed to such an extent that it had three cities with populations at or over 10,000 (Modelski 2003).[8] These cities (Uruk, Eridu, and Larak) formed the core of the urban system of southern Mesopotamia. Five hundred years later, about 3000 B.C., the conglomeration of cities had increased to ten with a total population of 140,000 persons. By this period of Early Dynastic I, what was also signaled was a shift of population toward the south and southeast. Between 3300 and 3000 B.C., Uruk had a population of approximately 40,000 persons and extending over an area of 200 ha (Modelski 2003, 22). Other areas of urbanization beyond Uruk at this time were Susa, located in the Susiana plain, about 25 ha in size; Chogha Mish, 18 ha; and Habuba/Tel Qannas in the Syro-Mesopotamian plain, about 40 ha (Algaze 1993a, Modelski 2003). It seems therefore that Uruk was by far the largest urbanized area during this period.

By 2500 B.C., during the period of Early Dynastic III, the rise of Sumer exhibited the largest urban conglomeration at 60,000 persons. Uruk by this time had been reduced to a population of 40,000 in comparison to 80,000 in 2800 B.C. (Modelski 2003, 28). However, the total urban population of Mesopotamia at 2500 B.C. had reached 290,000 (Thompson 2004). Outside of the heartland of cities, we find Ebla, located in northern Syria, with a population of about 40,000 and Mari in northern Mesopotamia with a similar population size. Elsewhere, we have Memphis in Egypt at 30,000 persons, and Mohenjodaro and Harappa in northwestern India at 20,000 and 15,000, respectively.

By 2200 B.C., the Akkadian period and the start of the Dark Age phase 2, the total urban population of Mesopotamia had been reduced to 210,000 (see table 3.5). This shift is also reflected in the proportion of declining urban settlement sizes (see table 3.6). During the Early Dynastic periods II and III (2800 B.C.–2300 B.C.), the percentage of urban settlements with more than 40 ha was about 78.4 percent; by the Akkadian period (2200 B.C.) it has been reduced to 63.5 percent. Further deurbanization continued so that by the Ur III and Isin-Larsa periods (2100 B.C.–1900 B.C.) the percentage had dropped further, to 55.1 percent. This slippage continued to the Old Babylonian period reducing further to 50.2 percent (1600 B.C.). Conversely, nonurban settlement sizes (less than 10 ha or less) increased.

Table 3.6. Urban and Nonurban Settlements in Mesopotamia, 2800 B.C.–1600 B.C.

Period	Percentage Nonurban (10 ha or less)	Percentage Urban (more than 40 ha)
Early Dynastic II/III (2800 B.C.–2300 B.C.)	10.0	78.4
Akkadian (2200 B.C.)	18.4	63.5
Ur III-Isin-Larsa (2100 B.C.–1900 B.C.)	25.0	55.1
Old Babylonian (1600 B.C.)	29.6	50.2
Kassite (1400 B.C.)	56.8	30.4

Source: Based on data from Adams (1981, 138).

During the early Dynastic II and III periods it was about 10 percent, and it almost doubled by the Akkadian period. With the arrival of the Ur III and Isin-Larsa periods, the percentage had risen to 25 percent and almost tripled to about 29.6 percent by the Old Babylonian period in comparison to the Early Dynastic period. The deurbanization process and migration to rural communities are also supported by the population decreases in Mesopotamian cities as outlined in figure 3.5. From 210,000 during the Akkadian period (2200 B.C.), the population in Mesopotamian cities was reduced to 190,000 by the Isin-Larsa period (1900 B.C.). This was a loss of 10 percent. The population level was reduced further to 70,000 by the Old Babylonian period (1600 B.C.). Overall, from the start of Dark Age phase 2 (Akkadian period) to its end in about 1700 B.C. (Isin-Larsa and Old Babylonian periods), we see a loss of over 66 percent of the urban population in Mesopotamia.

Deurbanization and population losses were also repeated in northwestern India. According to Possehl (2000), by the late third millennium B.C. there was evidence of abandonment of important buildings in the highly urbanized settings such as Mohenjodaro where we find the Great Bath and the Granary devoid of human use. Concurrently, the Sindh region and the Baluchi Highlands also witnessed depletion and deterioration. By the early second millennium B.C., Baluchistan was uninhabited. Cholistan, in northwestern India, experienced a drop in size in terms of settled areas from an average of 6.5 ha about 3800 B.C.–3200 B.C. to 5.1 ha by 1900 B.C.–1700 B.C., and finally to almost 50 percent less (2.6 ha) by 1000 B.C. (Chew 2005a, 2006, Possehl 2000). In the Sarasvati region, the shifting and drying up of the river system saw the abandonment of settlements in the inland delta of Fort Derawar. The latter area was the breadbasket of the Mature Harappan civilization.

Elsewhere in about 2200 B.C., similar signs of deteriorating conditions were also encountered in Anatolia, with abandonment of urban centers such as Troy II to Troy III-IV (Wilkinson 1990, Mellink 1986, 139–52). Consequently, depopulation also resulted. Sedentary population settlements on the Anatolian plateau were also abandoned. To the west of Anatolia, Palestine also suffered such crisis conditions (Butzer 1997). Unwalled villages replaced walled towns. There were signs of cave occupation and migratory movements. In some areas, settlements completely disappeared and remaining settlement sites were reduced by more than half of what existed before 2200 B.C. (Harrison 1997, 1–38). In other parts of the southern Levant, by 2200 B.C., settlement sites were abandoned (Seger 1989, Finkelstein and Gophna 1993). Population losses were also reported (Gophna and Portugali 1988). By 2000 B.C., only small villages were in place that resulted in social groupings that appeared to be nonhierarchical and pastoral in nature (Dever 1998).

Across the Mediterranean from Palestine, the Aegean experienced distress, though to a lesser extent. Between 2300 B.C. and 1900 B.C., there was a loss of sedentary population. Such losses were experienced on both mainland Greece and Crete (Jameson et al. 1994, Watrous 1994). It has been argued that such losses were a consequence of land degradation and anthropogenic soil erosion (e.g., see Runnels 1995). Others, such as Rackham and Moody (1996), suggest that the socioeconomic crisis can be accounted for via the reduction of precipitation leading to pressures on rain-fed agriculture. Depleted vegetation and aridity of the Cretan and mainland Greece landscapes further reduced soil absorption capacity, and thus any rainfall that occurred was not easily absorbed. What this leads to is an increased runoff during thunderstorms. Both sets of arguments can be summoned to account for the crisis Crete and mainland Greece were experiencing at this conjuncture in world history. The ecological degradation is either anthropogenic in origin or climatological in origin, as we have stated above. Anthropogenic-induced ecological degradation along with climatological changes have impacts on the reproduction and trajectory of the social system in question as well as the world system at large.

It should be noted that the Aegean recovered faster than the rest of the Bronze Age system, for by 1900 B.C., Minoan Crete was on an expansionary growth path in terms of palace building that lasted until 1700 B.C. Such a pace of recovery suggests that the social system in question had not reached a stage whereby ecological stress had attained ecological crisis proportions and that ecological recovery would not require a longer duration in terms of ecological time. Furthermore, at this point in world history, Crete and mainland Greece cannot be considered part of the core centers of the Bronze Age world system; so they might not have intensively exploited their environments in comparison to the other core centers. Therefore, the ecological condition of their landscapes might not have reached crisis conditions. However, this changed following periods of intensification of socioeconomic expansion that occurred for Crete between 1950 B.C.–1700 B.C. and 1700 B.C.–1450 B.C. and for Mycenaean

Greece from 1400 to 1200 B.C. whereby palace building and socioeconomic expansions were the order of the day (Chew 2001).

For central Eurasia similar stress conditions also prevailed. The changed ecological landscape led to out-migration of the sedentary population from river valleys over time and exploitation of the steppes for animal feed. Denucleation occurred with the establishment of smaller communities near oases. This spread occurred in central Asia at Korezm (south of the Aral Sea) and Margiana (Murghab Delta) in Turkmenistan, Bactria, and western China. This process, prompted by ecological degradation and environmental changes, also occurred in Syria and Jordan. Migration out of urban centers located on the coast to the interior and the establishment of smaller village-type settlements resulted (McGovern 1987, 267–73).

Loss of population through migration has been noted in several locations such as Near East, Mesopotamia, northwestern India, and central Eurasia (Weiss et al 1993, Algaze 1993a, Harrison 1997, Possehl 2000, Hiebert 2000, Fagan 2004). With climate changes between 2200 and 1900 B.C., there was desertion of the Habur Plains in northern Mesopotamia, followed with population reduction in the northern settlements such as Tell Leilan, Tell Brak, and Mohamed Diyab. Population losses for Tell Leilan were estimated to be about 14,000 to 28,000 persons. In Sumer, 80 percent of the population was living in urban centers by 2800 B.C.; however, by 2000 B.C., this number had declined to under 50 percent (Fagan 2004). For centuries, Amorite pastoral peoples had populated the open country surrounding the Euphrates. With the climate changes discussed above, they started to encroach on the urban settlements. With their movements down the Euphrates and Tigris they forced the ruler of Ur to erect a wall—Repeller of the Amorites Wall—to prevent further migration. This wall was 180 km and in spite of its length it failed in its task (Fagan 2004, Weiss 2000). The Hurrians and the Gutians to the north were also displaced. In northwestern India, migration from the urban complexes were also of the same order. Mohenjodaro and Harappa saw population disappearances as did the settlements of the Harappans in Sindh. With the drying up of the Sarasvati, the eastern region saw an increase in settlements indicating the relocation of the population in areas where the drainage system had disappeared. Similar migratory movements also occurred in west Asia and central Eurasia.

Political and Social Changes

If we examine Dark Age phase 2 (2200 B.C.–1700 B.C.), political instability is one feature that highlights the political economic events of the Bronze Age world system. For Egypt, however, Dark Age conditions did not last as long, for they started to dissipate by the Middle Kingdom period (2040 B.C.–1715 B.C.). Climate changes led to famines that in turn generated political upheavals and the dissipation of central authority in Egypt. Drought conditions and lowered Nile flooding impacted the farmers' ability to pay taxes because of lower harvest yields. This resulted in local administrators and governors, who collected taxes, having to delay their transfers to the royal house. In turn, the king's revenues plummeted and thus impaired his ability to pay for an army or to deal effectively with drought and famine. As a result, the stability of the political regime was affected. The sum effects of this in terms of political stability, as Bell (1971) has concluded, were short reigns. For example, between 2190 B.C. and 2130 B.C. there was a succession of about thirty-one to forty kings. Hassan (1997), covering the period from 2180 B.C. to 2134 B.C., reported that eighteen pharaohs reigned during this short time span. The collapse of the central monarchy of the Old Kingdom in about 2180 B.C. occurred within such dynamics.[9] The death of Pepi II in 2184 B.C. started the dissipation of central authority and Egypt was not reunified until the reign of Mentuhotep I in 2046 B.C. Political stability returned by end of the third millennium B.C. during the Middle Kingdom period.

Besides political instability occurring about 2200 B.C. in Egypt during the third millennium Dark Age, other reversals also occurred during this time such as artistic degeneration and the downsizing of monumental buildings because of diminishing resources. The size and elaborateness of the pharaonic tombs were reduced; by this time, the tombs of kings were one-chambered affairs with less ambitious layouts (Bovarski 1998, 316–19). To deal with the famine and droughts, temporary dams were built at the edges of the alluvial flats to retain much of the annual floodwaters of the Nile on the agricultural fields. Grain was stored and distributed to the famine areas to show the pharaoh's largesse. Boundaries of provinces were also closed to prevent mass migration out of famine-stricken areas. All these initiatives proved fruitless at times because riots broke out along with the ransacking of granaries. Famine was kept at abeyance during the Middle Kingdom period (2040 B.C.–1715 B.C.) with the exception of some occurrences in 1750 B.C.

Similarly, in Palestine and the southern Levant, there was a structural simplification (devolution) of sociopolitical institutions (Esse 1991; Dever 1998). There was a reduction in social complexity whereby the urban society in place with a stratified system had transformed to a less urban system determined by a clan or tribe structure and very slowly even changing to hamlets. There was the elimination of the elite structure that had control. This transformation was a reversal of structures, as even by the late Chalcolithic period, the social-political structures in Palestine had evolved to a stratified system, and the economic institutions by the Early

Bronze Age had shifted from raw materials manufacturing to agricultural surplus production with market exchange. The collapse can be seen in the oil and wine production sector. With Egypt in close proximity, the socio-political structures and economic institutions were also transformed as a consequence of trading and bilateral exchanges.

In other parts of the system such as southern Mesopotamia and north-western India, structural political, economic, and social reversals were also occurring. These transformations were extremely impactful in view of the trading relations of the region—southern Mesopotamia, the Gulf, and northwestern India—and led to the demise of the social systems in place with systemwide repercussions. As previously discussed, by the third millennium B.C., southern Mesopotamia, the Gulf region, and north-western India were linked in a trading network of commodity exchanges. Therefore, a crisis in one part of the system would also mean a translation of this stress to other parts of the system. An ecological stress in southern Mesopotamia would mean a lowering of agricultural output or produc-tion and hence a drop in imports and demand. Because of the trading linkage and networks, a division of labor had been established by this time. Therefore, reductions of demand in southern Mesopotamia would impact other regions such as Dilmun in the Gulf and the Harappan civili-zation through a diminished demand for their materials and goods. What this type of dynamics further suggests is that supply and demand might not necessarily be a consequence of the state of the economy or based on consumer tastes and needs. Rather, supply and demand dynamics are in-extricably linked to the connections between the natural system and social system. Thus, anthropogenic explanations provided for systems demise have ecological roots.

The above situation was what faced southern Mesopotamia, the Gulf region, and northwestern India. Southern Mesopotamia by 2200 B.C. was experiencing salinization problems leading to lowered agricultural productivity, and this became acute by 1700 B.C. Southern Mesopotamia never recovered from the disastrous decline in agricultural yields that accompanied the salinity issue. Deurbanization was the order of the day as we have indicated previously. Urban life and culture continued on a declining scale with the population concentrating only in major towns (Brinkman 1968). Consequently, the cultural and political centers in southern Mesopotamia continued their slide unchecked. The Harappan civilization not only had to face ecological stress, climate changes with temperature increases, and arid conditions like southern Mesopotamia, it had to undergo tectonic shifts.

The above and the economic linkages between the Harappans and other parts of the Bronze Age economic system facilitated the demise (1700 B.C.–1500 B.C.) of the Harappan civilization (Lal 1997). Its decline coincided with the demise of southern Mesopotamia and the associated trading communities in the Gulf region. After 1700 B.C., the Gulf trade disappeared (Leemans 1960). As the urbanized communities of the Harappan civilization were linked to the overarching Gulf trade and beyond, its infrastructure and surrounding hinterlands had therefore developed and specialized in the manufacture of products and natural resources for export. Thus, when its exports to the Gulf and beyond disappeared, it could no longer reproduce the accumulation process that had sustained its urban growth. This led to migration to the rural areas of the north and south. With the accumulation process slowing down, the outlying trading towns and outposts in the hinterland, devoid of prosperous support from the Harappan core, gradually merged with the countryside and the structural socioeconomic and political reversals remained unchecked.

SYSTEM RECONFIGURATION

The demise of southern Mesopotamia and northwestern India, coupled with the socioeconomic and political upheavals in the Levant and their associated hinterlands from 2200 B.C. to 1700 B.C., initiated a significant system crisis of the Bronze Age. With the socioeconomic collapse of southern Mesopotamia and northwestern India, the demise of these economies meant also the collapse of the Gulf trade. After 1700 B.C., at the social system level, despite the fact that ecological stress (at the natural system level) continued as reflected in our arboreal profiles listed in table 3.1, economic recovery resumed.

With recovery, other parts of the Bronze Age system such as the eastern Mediterranean littoral (centered about Crete and mainland Greece) along with central Europe and Anatolia increasingly began to take advantage of the vacuum generated by the collapse of the southern portion (the Gulf Trade) of the Bronze Age system. With Mesopotamian traders changing their orientation "from the East (Indus valley, Magan, and Meluhha) to the west (with Syro-Palestine, Egypt and Cyprus)" trade in the eastern Mediterranean littoral boomed (Cline 1994, 9). Egypt, Syria-Levant (such as Ugarit, Mari, Byblos, Ras Shamra), Crete, Cyprus, and mainland Greece expanded their trading volumes utilizing the peripheral areas such as central and eastern Europe and Nubia for their resource needs (Knapp 1993, Chew 2001, Kristiansen 1998b).

Long-distance trade through the travels of warriors, specialists, and merchants linked communities from Eurasia to the Aegean and Scandinavia and from the Urals to Mesopotamia (Kristiansen 2005). The Caucasus developed a metallurgical center, thus forming a Circum-Pontic province that included Anatolia, which received its metal ores from the Caucasian region. With the loss of the Gulf trade, the trading dominance of southern Mesopotamia was diminished, resulting in Mesopotamian trade shifting northward and hence making Anatolia an important eastern node of this Bronze Age trading network (Chew 2001, Larsen 1987). In sum, the eastern Mediterranean littoral became the prime axis where economic activity of the Bronze Age system concentrated.

Such social system adaptation and resolution of the 2200 B.C. crisis of the Bronze Age leading to renewed economic expansion was only temporary, as the structural rules of accumulation and social regulation were not transformed. Over the *longue durée*, these rules governing accumulation and social regulation continued to engender ecological stress (e.g., as noted in table 3.1). Coupled with climate changes and other natural disturbances, social (world) system crisis would only appear again in 1200 B.C. The system crisis of 1200 B.C. (Dark Age phase 2A) repeated what occurred in 2200 B.C., except that when it finally dissipated there was system *adaptation* and *transformation*, which we will delineate and identify in the following pages. Copper and bronze were replaced by iron underlying the material life of the world system, and hence began the Age of Iron.

A Globalized World of the Second Millennium B.C.

With the collapse of the southern portion of the Bronze Age world system, the connecting networks reconfigured and reoriented. Shifting away from the Gulf region, the trading networks ranged from Crete, the Cyclades, and the Greek mainland on one side of the Aegean Sea with Troy, Cyprus, and Anatolia located across from it. From this geographic position, further south we find the communities of Syria and Palestine and to the southwest was the kingdom of Egypt. To the southeast, we have northern Mesopotamia (see figure 3.1). This network of socioeconomic exchanges of the eastern Mediterranean region was also linked to communities of western, central, and eastern Europe and central Asia (Kristiansen and Larsson 2005). The Aegean and the Carpathians became the nodal points for these trading networks. It was a "globalized" system of trade and sociopolitical exchanges of the evolving world system.

The trade routes in the eastern Mediterranean ran counterclockwise in terms of sailing directions. The directions went from the Greek mainland to Crete and south to Egypt, up the Syro-Palestinian coast to Cyprus, and then west to the Aegean via the coast of Anatolia, Rhodes, and the Cyclades. According to Cline (1994), there was also a clockwise routing from Egypt; then along the Libyan coast to Crete and to the Greek mainland to the Cyclades, Rhodes, the southern coast of Anatolia, Cyprus, down the Syro-Palestine coast; and back to Egypt.

With the collapse of the Ur III system and the rise of the city-state of Assur, this northern locale was a center for the regional trade of the eastern

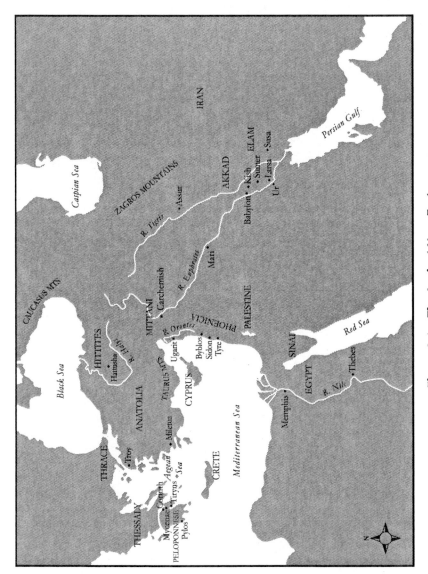

Figure 3.1. The Ancient Near East

Mediterranean by the nineteenth century B.C. and continued until 1600 B.C. under Hammurabi (Larsen 1987). From here connected by trade to Syria and the Anatolian plateau, northern Mesopotamia supplied agricultural products and textiles. In turn, copper, wood, wine, silver, gold, and tin were traded from these other regions. Assur became the nodal point for tin distribution from the Iranian plateau and Afghanistan. Copper was from eastern Anatolia and Cyprus and was distributed to Syria and the Near East. Despite the agricultural crisis, southern Mesopotamia continued to provide the textiles and wool for export northward. Within this trading zone, Syria provided the wood, wine, purple-dyed textiles, and other aromatic products (Liverani 1987). Egyptian trade flowed through the Syro-Palestinian zone and from this region; Egypt was connected to the Near Eastern trade and with the Aegean.

The demise of the Persian Gulf trade by 1700 B.C. resulted further in an increase of the trade of the eastern Mediterranean with the Anatolian plateau (Chew 2001). By the second millennium B.C., with the collapse of the Gulf trade, intermediary centers such as Crete increasingly played a part in the eastern Mediterranean within this trading network.[10] From 1750 B.C. to 1450 B.C., the boom in trade engendered a period of palace construction that followed an earlier phase between 1950 B.C. and 1700 B.C.[11] The Minoan command-palace economy was involved not only in the export of surplus agricultural produce such as grains and oil, but also in the export of textiles, metal works, pottery, woodwork, and so forth (Chew 2001, Kristiansen and Larsson 2005). Such a diversified economic structure provided it with a competitive advantage over other regions of the Bronze Age system such as mainland Greece, the Cyclades, and Europe to the north.[12] These areas provided Crete with natural resources such as silver, copper, and other much-needed metals.

Later in the second millennium, mainland Greece became also the main source for timber to meet Crete's diminishing wood supply. From the east came high-value raw materials such as tin and silver. The latter came from mainland Greece and the Cyclades in exchange for manufactured goods such as textiles, metalwork, pottery, carved stone, and agricultural produce that the Minoan civilization produced. Silver as a medium of exchange was sent to pay for imported metals and exotic products from Egypt, Syria, west Asia, and Africa.

Paralleling the trade strategies of the southern Mesopotamia of the third millennium B.C., Minoan trade was also followed with Minoan colonization of some places such as Ayia Irini, Phylakopi, Kythera, and Akrotiri in the Cyclades and eastern Greece between 1550 B.C. and 1450 B.C. (Branigan 1981, 1984; Cadogan 1984; S. W. Manning 1994). These colonies, like their counterparts that were established by Mesopotamia, Egypt, and Harappa, were gateways for trade to the eastern Mediterranean and

Mycenaean Greece. Minoan domination of the Aegean started to slip after the mid–second millennium B.C. The rise of Mycenaean Greece in this era increasingly eclipsed the role Crete played in the easternmost region of the Bronze Age world economy (Chew 2001). Minoan traders by this time began to concentrate on new western markets in the western Mediterranean such as Italy, Sicily, and Sardinia (Cline 1994). Messenia, on the western Peloponnese, benefited from the Cretan trade routes going to the western part of the Mediterranean, such as Italy, while Argolis, to the east, also rose in prominence, dominating the trade routes across the Aegean Sea to Troy and onward to the Black Sea (Dickinson 1977). These trading routes provided access to the metal-rich areas of the Danube and the Baltic that were already in place by the end of the third millennium B.C. Consequently, the lower Rhine to the north too was increasingly drawn into the orbit of the trading system.

On the above trading backbone that benefited Crete, Mycenaean Greece began to establish its economic dominance within the Aegean. Trade relations were also established with southern Italy and the Syro-Palestinian coastal areas (Chandler 1974). Similar to the Cretan economy, Mycenaean Greece exported wine, olive oil, grains, and manufactured products to eastern and northern Europe and the eastern part of the Mediterranean and, in turn, received needed natural resources such as copper, tin, and horses. Outposts were also established to facilitate commercial exchange and colonial settlement. On a comparative basis, they were much like those that were founded by Mesopotamia, Harappa, Egypt, and Crete (Chew 2001). These outposts at Miletus, Trianda, Phylakopi, Enkomi, and Cyprus grew and expanded as trade increased (Vermeule 1960, Immerwahr 1960, Knapp 1993). The colonies in Sicily and southern Italy were to connect with communities in western Europe such as those in Germany and Wessex that had trade relations with Scandinavia.

To the east of this globalized Bronze Age trading system was the kingdom of Hatti with metallic resources such as gold and silver, whereby these precious metals were exchanged for textiles, lapis lazuli, olive oil, grain, horses, tin, and so forth (Bryce 2002). Trade contacts were established with Babylon, Mittani, Assyria, Syro-Palestine, Egypt, Crete, and the Caucasus. The trade routes that the Hittites were involved with were in the control of the Assyrians, where through their established merchant colonies in Anatolia the goods were transferred.[13] This ended by the mid-eighteenth century B.C. with these outposts being abandoned.

Several cities on the eastern Mediterranean littoral such as Ugarit and Ura (on the coast of Cilicia) also played a significant role in Hatti's trade with the rest of the Near East. Ugarit was the trading emporium for goods, grain, and raw materials from Egypt, Syria, Mesopotamia, and Mycenae reaching Hatti; Syria and Mesopotamia were the sources or conveyors of manufactured products and sought-after metals. It was the principal outlet to the Mediterranean Sea for the Syro-Mesopotamian hinterland. Goods such as grains, wine, olive oil, honey, timber, resins, linens, salt, ivory, and wool textiles passed through Ugarit to and from the hinterlands. Ura, situated in the northwest, played a similar function for imports coming from that geographic direction. These international trading emporia would have products from all over the Near East: lapis lazuli from Afghanistan, gold from Egypt and Hatti, amethyst and turquoise from the Nile valley, jewelry from Minoan Crete, olive oil from Mycenaean Greece and Crete, woolen textiles from Egypt and Mesopotamia, and horses from Babylon and Egypt.

The globalizing trajectory was extended starting from the second millennium B.C. onward when these cores in the Near East, as Kristiansen and Larsson (2005, 107) put it, "turned their interest towards the barbarian peripheries in Central and western Europe" for their natural resources and livestock such as horses. In the Caucasus, the mines supplied the copper, and there was the development of a Circum-Pontic metallurgical province that included Anatolia (Chernykh 1992, Sheratt and Sheratt 1993, Kristiansen and Larsson 2005). Copper usage, however, started much earlier in Anatolia about the seventh millennium B.C., but copper with tin alloy was not fabricated until the third millennium B.C. according to Chernykh (1992). With this, tin bronze usage spread throughout the European periphery and the Near East, and between 2200 B.C. and 1700 B.C., the adoption of tin bronze was completed. Serbia, the Slovakian Ore Mountains, southeast Spain, Cornwall, Brittany, Erzgebirge, and Tuscany were the possible areas that provided sources of tin for the peripheral areas of Europe and the eastern Mediterranean (Pare 2000). With such development, the central and western European metallurgical centers were "increasingly drawn into trade relations with the palace cultures and city states of the eastern Mediterranean and Anatolia, which reached a new flourishing after 2000 B.C. when the Minoan palaces were built" (Kristiansen and Larsson 2005, 114). There arises from this the development of a European metallurgical province (Pare 2000). The trade relations were made more intense when gold and amber were included. Bullion and amber were exchanged between eastern Europe and Mycenae during the second millennium B.C. (Kristiansen 1993, 1998b; Dickinson 1977; Chew 2001; Sheratt and Sheratt 1993).

By the middle of the millennium (ca. 1600 B.C.), besides eastern Europe and the Carpathians as the source of raw materials (such as tin) on which the developed production processes in the Aegean depended, the Baltic region also became a supplier of amber (Harding 1984, Kristiansen and Larsson 2005). According to Kristiansen and Larsson (2005), the first period of most intense contacts between the Minoans and Mycenaeans and west, east, and central Europe were between 1700 B.C. and 1500 B.C., though there were earlier contacts that started about 2300 B.C. to 1900 B.C. The trade routes from western Europe linked up with other central European and southern networks to the eastern Mediterranean (Kristiansen 1998b, Sheratt 1997, Needham 2000). By 1600 B.C., this trading network, which was dominated by the Minoans, was taken over by the Mycenaeans and from then on the western network became more important in contrast to the eastern portion.

Given the mostly synchronic mapping of the trading connections of the centers of the ancient Near East outlined above, it should not be assumed that these trading networks were stable structures over time.[14] The mapping of these connections is to reveal the interlinked patterns of commercial activities that were in existence and thus underline the development of a globalized system of interconnected regions and polities.[15] Their vitality and concentration changed over time and were conditioned by the pulsations of socioeconomic, political, ecological, and climate changes. Thus, when the Dark Age returned in 1200 B.C., the collapse was systemwide.

THE FINAL PHASE OF THE CRISIS: THE END OF THE BRONZE AGE

If 2200 B.C. was the start of system crisis at both the natural and social systems levels, and with the natural system in continuous crisis, 1200 B.C. signaled the beginning of social system transformation and the final phase of the crisis leading to the end of the Bronze Age. Starting from about 1200 B.C., socioeconomic and political collapses were prevalent throughout the Near East and the eastern Mediterranean. According to Drews (1993), the crisis emerged with sporadic upheavals in the last quarter of the thirteenth century B.C. Stretching from Greece, the Cyclades, and Crete through to Anatolia, Cyprus, Egypt, Syria, and the southern Levant, the catastrophe was widespread. With the exception of the periphery, the core centers of the Bronze Age system at this time were in crisis.

Visible evidence of this crisis can be gleaned from archaeological excavations. Along with the ecological distress that is evident in the pollen profiles and the climate shifts including natural disturbances discussed in the previous pages, destruction of physical structures—outcomes of political conflicts and migratory tribal invasions—were also predominant.

Starting with mainland Greece, we find widespread destruction where palaces and large buildings with fortifications exhibited signs of fire during the Late Helladic III B phase (Hope Simpson and Dickinson 1979). Specifically, the destructions were at Thebes, Lefkandi on the Euboean coast, Athens, Corinth, Mycenae, Tiryns, Laconia, Achaea, and Messenia. In southwest Peloponnese (Messenia and Triphylia), the known number of

sites fell from 150 in the thirteenth century B.C. to 14 by the twelfth century
B.C. The Palace of Nestor at Ano Englianos was destroyed in a region of 240
settlements where a highly developed administration and the ruling elite
were turned into total desolation (Harrison and Spencer 1998, 148). In a
similar fashion, settlements were abandoned in Laconia from 30 to 7, in the
Argolid and Corinthia from 44 to 14, in Attica from 24 to 12, in Boeotia from
27 to 3, and finally in Phocis and Locris from 19 to 5. Destruction was more
sporadic on the Greek islands with some exceptions. Excavations on the
island of Paros showed similar signs of stress and for Rhodes and the other
islands of southeast Aegean. Crete also exhibited the same type of physical
destruction with the palace of Knossos at some time being destroyed.[16] In
other parts of Crete, such as at Kydonia, there is evidence of destruction
about 1200 B.C. Large urban site abandonments were also found at Amnisos, Malia, and Palaikastro during the Late Minoan III C. It seemed that
the people moved to smaller sites and hamlets (Haggis 1991).

The same situation was also visible in Anatolia. Where there were cities
in the Kingdom of Hatti, they disappeared after 1200 B.C. with the Hittites
consigned to living in small villages (Drews 1993). Evidence of conflict
between the Hittites and migratory groups can be seen in the destruction
of Hattusas at the beginning of the twelfth century B.C., the capital of the
Kingdom of Hatti, where ash and charred wood were discovered in excavated sites. Other cities such as Alaca Höyük, Alishar, and Masat Höyük
also experienced the same destructive fate. To the west of Hattusas,
Karaoglan and Miletus on the Anatolian coast were also destroyed during
the thirteenth century B.C. Further north of Miletus on the northwestern
coast of Anatolia, Troy also saw extensive damage at the end of the Bronze
Age. Troy VII A was burned about 1180 B.C. In southeastern Anatolia and
on the upper Euphrates, the excavated sites Lidar Höyük and Tille Höyük
also showed pronounced destruction by fire. In all, the disruption and
destruction was widespread throughout the kingdom of Hatti.

The island of Cyprus by no means escaped this catastrophe. Enkomi,
Kition, and Sinda were burned in a wave of destructions from 1230 through
1190 B.C. (Karageorghis 1992, Muhly 1984). Elsewhere, in southeastern
Cyprus, the settlement of Kokkinokremos was abandoned with the metalsmiths leaving their metallic valuables behind (Drews 1993). The situation
remained the same for urban sites on the western coast besides Enkomi.
Similar to Hatti, it seems the destruction was widespread on Cyprus.

In the Levant, Syria experienced the stress as well. The city of Ugarit
collapsed at the end of the late Bronze Age, about 1196 B.C. Tablets discovered revealed the threat for the city from invading groups. Ras Ibn Hani
and Tell Suki also were sacked and showed signs of fire. On the Orontes
River, Alakah, Hamath, Qatna, and Kadesh also revealed similar patterns
of destruction (Woolley 1953). In eastern Syria, Aleppo encountered the

same fate, along with Emar and Carchemish situated on the Euphrates. Carchemish was rebuilt and the local king following the fall of the Kingdom of Hatti claimed the title of the "Great King of Hatti" (Drews 1993). In the southern Levant, Deir Alla, Lachish, and all the urban communities (Ashdod, Ashkelon, Akko) on the trade routes from Syria to Egypt were all destroyed. Smaller sites such as Tell Jemmeh, Tell Sippor, and Tell Jerishe also succumbed to the catastrophe. From Hazor in the north to Khirbet Rabud in the south, inland sites were not spared the destruction.

In Egypt, though no urban settlements were burned, Nile flood failures caused tremendous stress in addition to the invasions of the Egyptian Delta by foreign forces (Butzer 1976, Bell 1975). Northern Mesopotamia escaped some of the widespread destruction with the Kingdom of Assur blocking any major incursions. Babylon, however, was sacked in 1157 B.C., with political upheavals continuing until it was destroyed by Assyria in 1087 B.C.

The explanation for the collapse of the Bronze Age is rooted in a variety of factors. On the whole, however, they have been rationalized and based on anthropogenic ones such as barbarian invasions, unceasing consumption and cultural decadence, power rivalries and state competition, vagaries of development, overcentralization of authority, military and weapon innovations, and famines and diseases (e.g., see Toynbee 1939, Childe 1942, Snodgrass 1989, Harding 1982, Drews 1993, K. Friedman 2003). Without a doubt, these factors at the social system level could have precipitated the system crisis and transformation of the Bronze Age world. Drews (1993), for example, has attributed the physical destruction and burning of the urban settlements to invading armies or tribes with military and weapons innovations. Kajsa Friedman (2003) has also recently joined Drews on this anthropogenic journey. For her, the final collapse of the Bronze Age world system was a consequence of the social, political, and economic dynamics of what she has termed the developmental thematic that "naturalistically" through incessant accumulation, core-periphery relations, and political rivalries led to the final demise of the system. Even if this were the case, such explanations only provide one dimension of system transformation. What is lacking is a consideration of the *linkage* between the social system and the natural system and how a disruption of this connection would induce crisis conditions, for the former (the social system) depends on the latter (natural system) for its continued reproduction, that is, if we are still conditioning our understanding of world history based on a historical-materialistic explanation.

The lack of such attention does not mean that there has been no attribution of natural system factors conditioning the collapse of the Bronze Age world at all. Rhys Carpenter's (1968) thesis of climate shifts affecting Mycenaean Greece and the onset of the Greek Dark Ages is a case in point, though it was severely questioned by Wright (1968) and Chadwick (1976) following its proposal. Others such as Chew (2001), Fagan (2004), and Kristiansen (1998b) have suggested an alternate route: the importance of natural system factors to system collapse and the end of the Bronze Age.

Despite the predominance of anthropogenic explanations for the eventual collapse of the Bronze Age world system, I wish once again to reintroduce the dynamics of Nature (natural system) and the link between the natural system and social system back into these anthropogenic accounts for the end of the Bronze Age. It is to underscore the point that, in the last instance, perhaps Nature had the final say.

Ecological Stress

In an earlier work, *World Ecological Degradation*, I discussed in detail the accumulation strategies of Minoan Crete and Mycenaean Greece along with the urbanization processes and the population growth that these two societies had throughout the second millennium B.C. Associated with these expansionary growth strategies, we witnessed ecological degradation trends such as deforestation, soil erosion, and species extinction (Chew 2001, Bottema 1994). Such deforestation levels are again confirmed by arboreal pollen profiles from Greece (see tables 3.1 and 3.2) and the rise of *Plantago* pollen throughout the period of examination.

For Crete, the intensive exploitation of resources for economic transactions impacted the landscape (Bottema 1994). Deforestation generated soil erosion and flash flooding; the latter impacted the manufacturing processes of Crete. Wood scarcity forced changes in production locations or resulted in the closure of facilities. Knossos suffered from these stressed ecological conditions. It has even been suggested that such land deterioration contributed to the demise of Minoan Crete (Carter and Dale 1974, 68).

These ecologically devastating trends were also repeated throughout the Bronze Age system. Mainland Greece—which provided the wood supplies to Crete when Crete's supply ran out—and other areas in Europe and central Asia showed such scars as well. Historically, since 7300 B.C., mainland Greece had an open deciduous forest (Bottema 1994). Following this time, with human activity, the forest was removed; though initially it was quite moderate, especially with hunting and gathering as a form of economic tendency (Van Andel and Runnels 1988). Associated with this economic thrust, gradually, the pollen record was changed by 6200 B.C. The intensity of deforestation in the early Bronze Age caused severe soil erosion on the hills of Berbati and Limnes in northeastern Greece (Bintliff 1992, Runnels 1995). Intensification of land use and animal husbandry led to severe alteration of the landscape. Population increases along with the adoption of the ox-drawn plow further exacerbated the intensity of land utilization. The pollen record from Osmanaga Lagoon in southwest Greece in Messina shows evidence of extreme forest removal by 2000 B.C. (Zangger 1998, 5). Between 1600 and 1400 B.C., the pine forests in Messenia were wiped out due to agriculture and overgrazing. Soil erosion was endemic and was controlled by terracing and the building of terrace walls. Consequently, agricultural production was affected. In the Argolid, production of cereals and olive oil generated deforestation of oak trees on the hillsides. It resulted in large amounts of earth and water draining from the slopes onto the plain of Argos and filling up stream beds leading to extensive flooding (Runnels 1995). As a consequence, Tiryns and its agricultural lands were affected by floodwaters (Runnels 1995). Pylos's harbor was impacted by siltation, as was the island of Melos.

Besides terrace walls to deal with soil erosion, other technological solutions were also tried, such as the building of dams to divert watercourses and dikes to facilitate drainage (Van Andel et al. 1986, Van Andel and Zangger 1990, Van Andel and Demitrack 1990). A massive dam was built between the fourteenth and thirteenth centuries B.C., about 4 km upstream from Tiryns, which was located on the southern edge of the Plain of Argos (Kraft, Aschenbrenner, and Rapp 1977; Van Andel and Zangger 1990, Van Andel and Demitrack 1990). It was 100 m wide and about 10 m high (Zangger 1993, Balcer 1974). The effort was made to divert the river, which was transporting tremendous amounts of eroded alluvial deposits from the eastern mountains away from the town of Tiryns. In Boeotia, dikes were built to facilitate the draining of Lake Copais. This was also repeated in the Argolid to contend with winter streams.

However, by the late second millennium B.C., such efforts began to fail. Erosion became uncontrollable during the Dark Age crisis of 1200 B.C. when socio-political life was at a standstill and population density had dropped precipitously. This was quite pronounced in the Plain of Argos about 1250 B.C. (Bintliff 1992). With scarcity of wood for fuel, metallurgical and pottery works were affected, which resulted in further population decline. The pottery works at Berbati and Zygouries were such cases. Population migration followed the closure of these manufacturing centers and the abandonment of Phylakopi coincided with the deforestation of Melos, where the town was located. The same occurred for Berbati, Midea, Prosymna, and Zygouries in 1200 B.C., and there were also population losses in Mycenae, Pylos, and Tiryns. Towns and settlements disappeared. In southwest Peloponnese, the number dropped from 150 to 14. Other regions experienced similar declines; Laconia, Argolid, Corinthia, Attica, Boeotia, Phocis, and Locris all registered losses (Chew 2001, Perlin 1989).

In southern Europe, there were degradative impacts on soil formation from Urnfield settlements (Kristiansen 1993). Kristiansen and Larsson (2005) have also documented widespread ecological degradation in the

Caucasus as a result of mining for metals to supply the eastern Mediterranean and the Near East. This was also repeated for the mining area of Kargaly in the Urals, which supplied metals to the whole steppe region, where deforestation was the consequence, according to Kristiansen and Larsson (2005). Tables 3.1 and 3.2 show time series of arboreal pollen profiles of central and eastern Europe, including Russia, that parallel the deforestation trajectories.

For the northern Pirin Mountains of southwestern Bulgaria (see table 3.2, Bulgaria 1 [Besbog 2]), deforestation has been continuous throughout the Bronze Age. Its occurrence during the late Bronze Age was a consequence of the reorganization of the economy of the Thracian tribes between 1000 B.C. and 800 B.C. in the production of iron and population movements into metal-producing zones and pastures of mountain regions (Stefanova 1995, 29). The former was not only for local needs, but also to supply the centers in the eastern Mediterranean. In northeastern Bulgaria (see table 3.2, Bulgaria 2 [Mire Girvan]), however, deforestation was not a consequence of metal production but one of land clearing for stockbreeding, since there are few types of cultural cereal pollen found (Lazarova 1995, 61).

Climate Changes and Natural Disturbances

A warm period prevailed over the ancient Near East between 1200 and 900 B.C. (Neumann and Parpola 1987). Arid conditions were reported for the southern Levant from 1300 to 600 B.C. (Dubowski et al. 2003). Such a warming and arid trend had an impact on the stream flow of the Tigris and Euphrates, where there was a maximum peak between 1350 and 1250 B.C., followed by a sharp drop reaching a minimum at about 1150 B.C. (Kay and Johnson 1981). Recovery of moisture only returned in about 950 B.C. Textual evidence also indicates a number of severe droughts experienced in Assyria and Babylon. About 1090 B.C., a severe drought occurred, and a period of drought years extended from 1050 to 1007 B.C. (Neumann and Parpola 1987, 176). Drought conditions also prevailed for Greece and the eastern Mediterranean from 1200 to 850 B.C. (Weiss 1982, Carpenter 1968). Bryson et al. (1974, 49) have also reported drought conditions and increases in land temperature for the Anatolian plateau. The precipitation rate was 20 to 40 percent below normal, and the temperatures were 2.5 to 4°C above normal. Circumstances were also similar for Libya, where precipitation was 50 percent below normal, and the temperature was 1.5°C above normal.

Climate changes in the form of temperature increases and rising aridity have severe implications for already ecologically stressed social systems crippled by deforestation and soil erosion. The impacts are translated to lower harvest yields, and, at times, crop failures along with loss of animal pasture. It has been estimated that a mere 1°C rise in winter temperature may reduce rainfall by as much as 30 mm. For the Ancient Near East, where 200 mm of annual rainfall is a threshold for rain-fed agriculture and any level below is dependent on irrigation, such a decrease would spell crisis for the region. Especially for areas dependent on perennial river floods, such as the southern Levant, a drop in rainfall has tremendous consequences. Lowered agricultural production would mean "the social and political instability of the period largely was a function of inadequate agricultural output. . . ." (Neumann and Parpola 1987, 173). In eastern Mediterranean, social systems, such as Crete, that relied on agricultural products as cash crops and thus were reliant on bountiful harvests to offset their imports of needed natural resources, such as metals and wood, faced extreme stress when the climate started to change during the late Bronze Age.

For Egypt, the temperature increases led to droughts, and this impacted agriculture even as far south as Nubia after 1260 B.C. (Hassan 1997; Butzer 1976, 1997). Famines extended even as far as Libya, which led to attacks on Egypt. Reduced Nile flow because of lowered volumes in the lake levels in the Ethiopian highlands from about 1260 B.C. onward further intensified the drought conditions that were being experienced (Butzer 1976, 1983). Lowered flood levels from the Nile started about the reign of Ramses III from 1182 B.C. onward. The aridity and drought conditions led to dust storms and the continued encroachment of desert sand on the urban environment. At Aksha, sand dunes spread over the flood plain, and the lack of flooding led to the buildup of salt in the flood plain (Butzer 1983). In the delta region, the reduced Nile flow led to lowered discharge along the Pelusiac Nile distributary.

Beyond the temperature changes and drought, natural disturbances in the form of volcanic activity and earthquakes have been attributed to the exacerbation of the already precarious ecological landscape. In the eastern Mediterranean, the Aegean plate straddles the Turkish, African, and Eurasian plates. Crete, for example, lies on the Aegean plate (S. W. Manning 1994). For this period, the volcanic eruption on Thera (Santorini) is one that has been widely examined as a factor in the demise of Minoan Crete (Marinatos 1939; Baillie 1994, 1995, 1998, 1999a; Pang 1991; Chadwick 1976; Warren 1985; Hammer et al. 1980; Driessen and Macdonald 2000). The exact dating of this eruption has been scrutinized closely (e.g., see Hammer et al. 1987; Kuniholm et al. 1996; Bietak 1996; Baillie 1995, 1999a; S. Manning et al. 2002). Initially, between 1400 and 1390 B.C. was identified as the time frame of the Thera eruption (Hammer et al. 1980, Marinatos 1939). This time frame has been revised by a new ice-core boring, and it is now determined to be about the calibrated age of 1630–1530 B.C. or about conventional ^{14}C dating of 1376–1342 B.C. (Hammer et al. 1987).

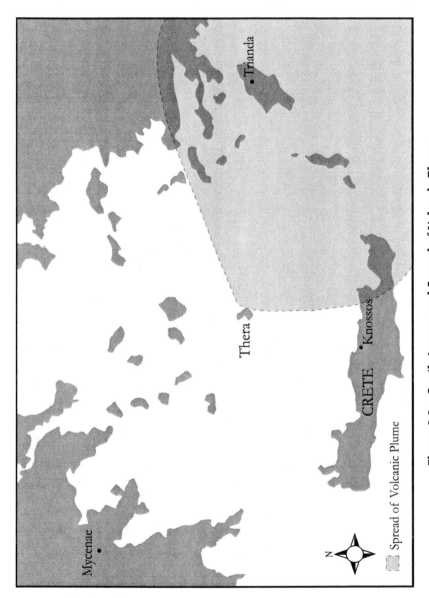

Figure 3.2. South Aegean and Spread of Volcanic Plume

By examining acidity peaks, the eruption time frame is determined to be about calibrated 1645 B.C. or 1390 B.C. (^{14}C dated) (Hammer et al. 1987). However, there has been no agreement reached on the absolute dating as both the second half of the seventeenth century B.C. and the middle of the sixteenth century B.C. have also been suggested (Driessen and Macdonald 2000, Baillie 1995). Recently, two teams of archeologists have again calibrated the eruption. S. Manning et al. (2006) have dated the eruption between 1660 and 1613 B.C. while Friedrich et al. (2006) have proposed 1627–1600 B.C. for the catastrophe.

The impact on the socioeconomic reproduction of the region, such as the impact on Crete, from such a volcanic eruption was far reaching. The spread of the plume of tephra, dust, and gases was across most of the eastern portion of the Mediterranean east of Thera, and it impacted crops, livestock, buildings, and water supplies (see figure 3.2). The eruption column reached a height of almost 29 km and penetrated well into the stratosphere. The force of this eruption is estimated to be equivalent to those of Krakatoa in A.D. 1883 and Tambora in A.D. 1815. Prior to this eruption (two to five years), there was a serious earthquake perhaps triggering the eruption. Archaeological excavations have indicated site abandonments on the island of Crete. There is also evidence of tsunamis occurring. Archaeological excavations revealed a 15 cm silt layer, which suggests a water event, and tsunami deposits overlaid by tephra on the coasts of Asia Minor. The tsunamis also destroyed ships in Cretan harbors that faced north, such as Poros, Amnisos, and Nirou Chani, and salinated the northern coastal areas, making them unfit for agriculture. Following the eruption, a massive ash fall of more than 15 cm covered the eastern portion of the island and parts of Asia Minor (see figure 3.2). One would expect that animals, plant life (olive trees and vines), and perhaps some humans would have been killed. Such devastation covered plant and animal life and as Driessen and Macdonald (2000, 85) have suggested: "Olive trees, vines and other crops may have suffered, a situation aggravated by any ash fall, which would also have been extremely dangerous for animals as it would have abraded their teeth and clogged their digestive system."

The volcanic tremors would have also shaken buildings, causing migrations out of urban complexes. What resulted would be a reduction of occupied space, absence/decrease of new constructions, erection of protective structures, abandonment of old wells and the digging of new ones, hoarding of precious metals and objects, and political fragmentation. All the Cretan settlements showed signs of the lack of new construction and settlement contraction, such as in Vathypetro, Galatas, Petras, Zakros, Kammos, and Palaikastro, where the plume of ash covered. Building construction materials utilized were of inferior quality. Hoarding was quite evident, with daggers hidden beneath pithoi and copper ingots in storage spaces of the palaces at Malia and Zakros, and in houses at Mochlos and Palaikastro. Excavations have also revealed evidence of political and economic fragmentation and decentralization with the rise of local economic and administrative systems and the failure of palatial administrations.

Furthermore, the eruption destroyed the Minoan naval fleet from the generated tsunamis and ash fallout (Chadwick 1976). This loss undermined Cretan naval supremacy, which for a long period provided Minoan Crete the power to exercise its dominant position in this region of Bronze Age world system. This demise of Minoan Crete should be considered with the political shifts occurring during this period. The increasing role of the Hittites and Kassites through their expansion and dominance of Anatolia and Mesopotamia must have impacted the economic activities of Minoan Crete. The dominancy of the Hittites and Kassites along with the ascendancy of Mycenaean Greece further curtailed the economic reproduction of Minoan Crete. The Minoans, who had relied on the import of necessary natural resources for their manufacturing processes from the trading interconnections of the Bronze Age world system following the centuries of their degradation of the Cretan landscape, experienced the loss of these sources. These sources located on the Greek mainland came increasingly under the control of the Mycenaeans. Their supply centers in western Anatolia and northern Syria were also restricted because of Hittite expansion and control. Faced with these desperate conditions, coupled with climate changes and natural catastrophes, the Minoan civilization came under severe stress in its reproductive capacities about the mid–second millennium B.C. (e.g., see Driessen and Macdonald 2000).

Besides the volcanic eruption at Thera, which impacted Crete, Evans (1921) has also remarked of the destruction of Knossos from an earthquake about 1400 B.C. According to Evans, the earthquake disrupted lamps and open fires and, fanned by the wind, the blaze destroyed the urban community and the palace. This destruction thesis by volcanic eruption has been challenged by some archaeologists (see Drews 1993).

With volcanic eruptions, climate changes would also follow, such as a "volcanic winter," with the volcanic aerosols influencing the radiation balance and thus impacting the economy and agriculture (Hammer et al. 1980, Driessen and Macdonald 2000). Besides those parts of the eastern Mediterranean that were impacted by volcanic eruption, it has also been suggested that the environment of Egypt at this time was affected by a major dust veil with reduced rainfall (Baillie 1999a).

In the other parts of the systems, such as in mainland Greece, there have also been indications of earthquakes leading to urban damage. Excavations at Tiryns on the Plain of Argos showed tectonic shift damages in the lower citadel of the city (Zangger 1998). This occurred about the Late Helladic III B period (1335/1325 to 1190 B.C.), with another round of tectonic activity during Late Helladic III C (1190–1050 B.C.). There is evidence of flash flooding that deposited alluvium. Whether the earthquakes engendered flash flooding resulting in urban damages or the flash flooding was a result of the eruption of Hekla 3 in Iceland in 1159 B.C. is difficult to determine. For clearly in the latter's case, climate changes would follow from such volcanic activity with perhaps unusually heavy rainfall that could have generated flash flooding (Zangger 1998). Either way, in terms of causal relationship, socioeconomic life would have been affected.

Other parts of mainland Greece that suffered from earthquakes were Midea and Mycenae. Iakovides (1977) attributed the destruction of Mycenae during the late Late Helladic III B period to earthquake fires, and so did Åstrom (1985) for Midea.

In Asia Minor and Syria, Schaeffer (1968) has indicated that cities were ruined by earthquakes about 1200 B.C. Ugarit, the trading center for the Hittites, was impacted. So were Alalakh, Hattusas, Alishar, Alaca Höyük, and others that were shaken by the natural disaster. Troy VI H also suffered from a catastrophic earthquake with fires ensuing from the tremors about 1275 B.C. (Blegen 1950). On the coasts of southern Levant, tectonic activity was reported during this period (Neev et al. 1987). Active tectonic activity also influenced the rate of sand supply through the Nile by a slight north-northeastward tilt of the Nile delta.

In all, climate changes and natural disturbances impacted the reproduction of these ancient economies and societies and exacerbated further the already precarious nature of the world system and the entities that form it.

Socioeconomic and Political Transformations

At the level of the social system, the stressed ecological landscapes coupled with climate changes and natural disturbances conditioned widespread socioeconomic and political transformations. It was systemwide in terms of changes, starting from 1200 B.C. onward where kingdom/ chiefdom after kingdom/chiefdom experienced changes in their social, economic, and political fabric.

Egypt

Starting with Egypt, which remained a significant power in the eastern Mediterranean littoral under Pharaoh Ramesses II (1304–1237 B.C.), rivalry with the Hittites under Muwatallish saw Syria coming under Hittite control, even though the Egyptians maintained control over Palestine. With the death of Ramesses II, Egyptian power was significantly challenged by invading forces of Libyan and Sea Peoples about 1232 B.C. that Pharaoh Merneptah decisively repelled. The origins of these Sea Peoples has been widely debated (e.g., see Drews 1993, Page 1963, Barnett 1975, Gardiner 1961, Braudel 2001, Bryce 1999) and the supposition is that they had their original abodes to the north of Egypt, perhaps in the Aegean or north of Anatolia.

The constant military and political challenges continued with Pharaoh Ramesses III fending off another invasion by the Sea Peoples from 1194 B.C. onward when they attacked the fertile lands of Syria, Palestine, and the delta, and ended by 1188 B.C. with the final victory for Ramesses III. With the death of Ramesses III, domestic and political turmoil ensued. Climate changes that forced the Sea Peoples to leave their abodes have been attributed to their migratory invasions of lands that were under Egyptian control (Weiss 1982, Hassan 1997, Braudel 2001, Bryce 1999). In a wider context and over a longer historical period, Modelski and Thompson (1999) have documented this migratory pattern of incursions that coincided with the socioeconomic pulsations of the world system.

Besides these external incursions on Egypt, there was also domestic turmoil during these turbulent times. Most interpretations suggest that the turmoil was a consequence of increased taxation and other factors related to land use, and here climate played a significant role. The decline in Nile discharge that we have discussed in the previous pages became acute during the reign of Ramesses III, and this affected agricultural production (Butzer 1976). Aridity was the order of the day, and salinization, which is hardly a problem for Egypt unlike southern Mesopotamia, became an issue in areas where lift irrigation was practiced to enhance the Nile's reduced discharge. With decreasing Nile discharge, slow moving white water with clays and sodium-rich solutes became a factor in peripheral areas of the flood plain of Egypt. These conditions led to crop failures or low harvests. As a result, grain prices rose to about eight times the normal standard, and inflation continued to its highest point in about 1130 B.C., when grain prices were twenty-four times above the standard price. During the reign of Ramesses III, the price of emmer wheat rose with respect to the prices of metals. These price increases continued until the reign of Ramesses VII and managed to stabilize about 1099 B.C. toward the end of the reign of Ramesses X.

The drop in Nile discharge also caused land prices to decline, and there was a sharp drop about 945 B.C. The price of land did not recover and stabilize until 700 B.C. In 1153 B.C., the food supply started to fail, leading to food riots (Faulkner 1975). At least six major riots occurred between 1153 and 1105 B.C. Mass dislocations followed with mass burials. In a land where the stability of the cosmic order lies in the hands of the pharaoh, crop failures and lowered harvests put severe pressure on the stability of the political order. This caused the breakdown of royal authority.

Population losses were recorded starting about 1200 B.C. for Egypt, continued for the Nile valley, and did not recover until about 700 B.C.

(Butzer 1976, 85). The population level did not return to the 1200 B.C. level until about 500 B.C. Ecologically, there were other dire situations beyond salinization and lowered Nile discharge. Reports have been discovered of species extinction of large game in the Nile valley followed with the need to import large game for symbolic hunts (Hughes 2001).

Kingdom of the Hittites

To the northeast of Egypt in western Anatolia, the Hittite kingdom experienced widespread economic and political chaos as well. From documents excavated at Ugarit, the collapse of the Hittites took place between the end of the thirteenth century B.C. and the beginning of the twelfth century B.C. Political challenges were posed by neighboring vassal rulers and the migratory Sea Peoples (Braudel 2001, Bryce 1999). Starting with the reign of Tudhaliya IV in about 1227 B.C., Hittite control of western Anatolia was precarious with the Ahhiyawans challenging Hittite authority in western Anatolia along with vassal rulers such as from Lalanda (Bryce 1999). Furthermore, there was concern of the Assyrian and Babylonian threat to the southeast over control of Syria. Alignment with the regime at Milawata helped to temper the advance of the Ahhiyawans, and thus the Hittites could then be in a better position to deal with the Assyrian threat. Conflicts ensued with the Assyrians capturing the copper mines of Isuwa from the Hittites (MacQueen 1986).

The reasons for all these conflicts and military excursions are not clearly known from the archaeological discoveries to date. K. Friedman (2003) has suggested that political violence and conflicts were outcomes of the development initiative of the world system where the accumulation of surplus and the search for natural resources were political economic activities undertaken by the kingdoms of the late Bronze Age in the eastern Mediterranean. Though important, such a rationale addresses only one aspect of world history during this *conjoncture.* Other considerations that are ecologically conduced need to be inserted, such as a continuous drought and famine condition. Gorny (1989) noted a warming trend during this period leading to crop failures, which, coupled with incursions from migrating nomads and marauding Sea Peoples, made the Hittite Empire vulnerable.

Starting from the reign of Hattusili III in 1267 B.C., the famine forced the Hittites to import grain from Egypt and Ugarit and to have trade arrangements to ensure the food supply source continued uninterrupted (Bryce 1999, 2002) (see figure 3.3). In the previous sections, we were alerted to climate changes affecting crop harvests in the Near East. Bryce (1999, 356) has indicated that the Hittites from the reign of Hattusili III onward were increasingly reliant on imported grain. The drought and famine condi-

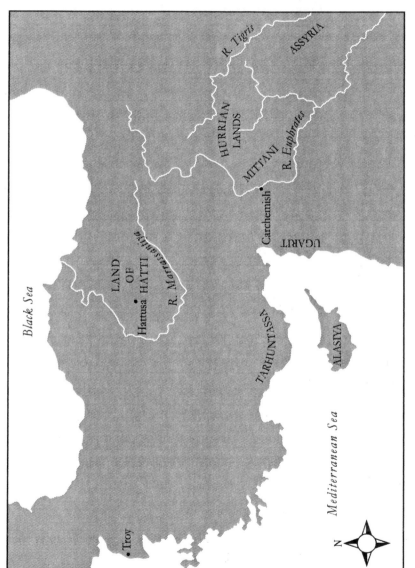

Figure 3.3. The World of the Hittites

tions experienced by the Hittites continued until the reign of Tudhaliya IV (1227 to 1209 B.C.). Tudhaliya IV wrote to the king of Ugarit, Niqmaddu III, of the need to ship, without further delay, 450 tons of grain from Mukis to the port of Ura of the kingdom of Tarhuntassa, on the southern coast of Anatolia (Bryce 2002).

Along this vein, military conflicts between kingdoms, such as those generated by the Hittites, were based on social system and natural system relations. Climate does affect crop production and prices in a materialist world. Tudhaliya IV's campaign to conquer Alasiya (Cyprus) was for its abundant copper and timber resources and its location in the northeast corner of the eastern Mediterranean (Bryce 1999). The Hittites were determined to ensure that their supply routes remained open and that the port of Ura remained under their control because the fate of socioeconomic life of the Hittites was now dependent on imported grain as well. Alasiya also supplied the Hittites' copper needs because their other supply source has been taken over by the Assyrians. Thus, the son of Tudhaliya IV was forced to undertake numerous naval campaigns "off the coast of Alasiya, almost certainly to protect the supply routes which were becoming increasingly vital to the provisioning of the Hittite world" (Bryce 1999, 358).

Besides the physical destruction to the urban areas of the Hittites that we have already discussed, the Hittite collapse was bound to climate-induced food shortages and seismic shocks (Braudel 2001, Gorny 1989). Or as Gorny (1989, 92) has stated: "the role of the environment in the collapse of the Hittite state is not well attested, but I believe future study will show that environmental factors were intimately involved in both the integration of the Hittite state and its eventual demise." Some have attributed the collapse to the invasions by the Sea Peoples with different military strategies and innovations, and regional conflicts and competition (e.g., see Drews 1993, K. Friedman 2003). Taken as a complex of factors, each of these explanations induced the final outcome. For our purpose, natural system factors played an important part. Hittite dependence on imported grain became more acute toward the final years of the kingdom and with the ecologically stressed environment forced the Hittites to subdue the kingdom of Tarhuntassa to ensure that the port of Ura was open for the Hittites' grain imports from Canaan and Egypt. Sea battles were also fought by the last king of the Hittites, Suppiluliuma, off the coast of Alasiya to protect supply lines using the naval fleet supplied by its vassal king of Ugarit (Bryce 1999). Bryce (1999) has stated that in the last decades of the Late Bronze Age, disruption of commercial networks and trading operations in the Near East was a prominent feature. Therefore, an interruption in grain supply could be a crisis if the system was import grain dependent. The Hittites' degree of dependence on imported grain at this stage can be seen in the level of consumption for urban areas such as Hattusa. MacQueen (1986) has estimated that the annual grain consumption of the citizens of the capital, Hattusa, was between 10,572 and 14,096 kl. Such production levels required at least 16,187 to 24,282 ha of land.

When the end came for the kingdom of Hittites, Bryce (1999) claims Hattusa was consumed in "a great conflagration" and its associated satellite vassals also followed suit. It seemed that very few Hittite urban sites were destroyed by fire. Site abandonment seemed to be the prevailing motif, thus underlining the process of deurbanization, which is a predominant feature of the Dark Ages as we have discussed in the previous chapters. The slide into less-than-complex lifestyles can be seen from the pottery recovered from this period. There was a falloff of the ceramic design; the color of pottery tends to be monochrome and ranges from brown to reddish-brown to red and of poor quality (MacQueen 1986). Could this drop in quality and lack of vitality be a result of the diminishing natural resources required for making this pottery? There has been no attempt to hypothesize this set of changes. In other parts of Anatolia, such as the eastern region, there was no evidence of ceramics. The argument for this total absence is that this region had retrogressed into nomadism (MacQueen 1986). Such an assertion needs to be scrutinized carefully before we can agree with it. Other reasons can be put forth; only further research and excavations can illuminate this.

Ugarit, the vassal kingdom to the Hittites, also experienced the same fate. Its political and social structures shared the same destruction as some of the Hittite cities in the twelfth century B.C. Such loss is quite dramatic when the urban complexes of the kingdom numbered about 10,000 persons, with the rural areas amounting to a further 25,000 persons (Yon 1989). Agriculturally focused in terms of its economic structure along with its external trade relations as a consequence of its coastal position on the Syrian coast, the kingdom never was a dominant military power, though it provided its military to support the Hittites. Faced with external incursions from the Sea Peoples and changing ecological environments, the end came rather swiftly.

Greece

Across the Mediterranean from Anatolia, similar socioeconomic and political changes were also occurring. Greece encountered a decline in socioeconomic life from 1200 to 700 B.C. that was characterized by decline or loss of certain material skills, decay in cultural aspects of life, a fall in living standards and thus wealth, deurbanization, population losses, and loss of trading contacts within and without Greece (e.g., see Snodgrass 1971, 1980; Desborough 1972; Deger-Jalkotzy 1998; Chew 2001; Murray 1907; Ward and Joukowsky 1992; Morris 2000; Whitley 1991; Childe 1942;

Harrison and Spencer 1998; Van De Mieroop 2004). The archaeological evidence unearthed suggests socioeconomic patterns that are distinctively different from the style and level of sociocultural life prevailing prior to the onset of the Dark Age.

Population decreases occurred between 1250 and 1100 B.C. Morris (2000) has estimated losses of about 75 percent followed with emigration from the core areas of the Mycenaean civilization with this trend continuing for central Greece as well. According to Snodgrass (1971), between the twelfth and eleventh centuries, there was a reduction of over three quarters of the population. The population level began to rise again after 800 B.C. (Snodgrass 1980).

Pottery and other objects recovered from excavated sites along with the architecture and design of dwellings reflect ecological stress and scarcity of natural resources. Architectural standards were lowered and there were very few signs of good stone-built constructions. Small stone construction was prevalent, and mud-brick construction was increasing. Mud-brick structures predominated in the building structures between the eleventh and tenth centuries. We find the emergence of a class of handmade burnished pottery, "Barbarian Ware," with few obvious links to Mycenaean styles. The appearance of this style has been attributed as an economic response to the collapse of centralized production with the demise of the palace economies and a regression to simpler technology (Small 1990). Furthermore, pottery styles of the period in Greece became austere, unlike the decadent style of the previous era.

Starting with the Submycenaean style of pottery (ca. 1125 to 1100 B.C.), the austerity of the design can be seen. As Desborough (1972) has put it, the standards deteriorated sharply not only to the making of the pottery but also to the painting and decoration. The design was of the simplest kind and there "was a virtual bankruptcy . . . and often carelessly applied" (Desborough 1972, 41). According to Desborough (1972, 293), it was "a depressed and debased style of pottery," reflecting the conditions of the period. The variety of styles in terms of vase shapes of this type of pottery were also reduced. Rutter (1989) has also suggested that luxury vases and other pottery items were quickly abandoned as necessary frills when the hard times hit. There was less variety of material goods, thus reflecting a less complex social order.

The emergence of the Protogeometric style (ca. 900 B.C.) continued to reflect the austerity of the period (Snodgrass 1971). This latter style was supposed to have originated in Athens and then was copied by all the other regions of Greece, whereas the Submycenaean was deemed to have originated in western Attica (Desborough 1972, Snodgrass 1971). Desborough (1972) has pointed out that the decorative motifs for the Protogeometric style were confined to a small area of the pottery and that decoration was used sparingly. As well, Snodgrass (1971) has also alerted us to the appearance of handmade pottery during the Dark Ages. The reversion to handmade pottery when the pottery wheel had been adopted in prior times suggests to us the decay of manufacturing production or even perhaps the loss of manufacturing skills. It could also mean that with social decay and collapse, there was a revival to the utilization of indigenous material in view of the disruption in trade routes. From the Protogeometric style, we have the transformation to the Early Geometric pattern circa 860/840 B.C. and Middle Geometric pattern circa 770 or 760 B.C., and finally the Geometric pattern by 710 or 700 B.C.

In terms of decorations and finishing, the bulk of the pot or vase was usually left plain in the natural color of the clay and the decorations covered a third of the surface area at most (Desborough 1972). The lack of intense firing also suggests dwindling energy supplies. The compass and multiple brushes were used for decorating the pottery. As recovery proceeds and the balance of Nature is restored, we find the plain, rectilinear or curvilinear patterns in pottery designs giving way to images depicting animals and humans. In the later Protogeometric-style period, we see the introduction of silhouette figures of a horse or a human on the design. If we consider the decay of cultural life and the loss of the art of writing, and view pottery design as a way the potter as artist could depict sociocultural life then, the motifs that we find in these pottery designs would summarize life in Dark Age Greece. The range of representational media in which representational art occurred during the Dark Age was also reduced (Rutter 1989). Whereas prior to the Dark Age period, during the exuberant Mycenaean times, painters produced lively colored frescoes of stylized patterns, humans, animals, and creatures from the sea (Desborough 1972). With such shifts in decorating motifs, it suggests the return of biodiversity to the environment and the loss of biodiversity at the onset of the Dark Ages. By the late Geometric-style period, we find scenes of organized groups of men in uniforms, the portrayal of warfare, and chariots depicting social life as the Dark Age was receding.

Beyond pottery styles, other objects recovered indicate a scarcity of natural resources, especially metals, or that the supply sources had dried up. The use of obsidian, stone, and bones for blades and weapons underscores such scarcity and suggests that trading routes and centers for sourcing the metals might have disappeared or have been disrupted. Other primitive materials reappear as apparent substitutes such as bone spacer beads for amber in jewelry, and stones were used to replace lead in sling bullets. Objects buried with the deceased increasingly were made out of iron such as iron pins and fibulae, and even weapons, which all in the past had been bronze, and bronze wares only returned toward the end of the Dark Age period (Snodgrass 1980). Where bronze was used, it was found on the bulb of pins thus revealing the scarcity of bronze (Desborough 1972, Snodgrass 1971). In all, as Snodgrass (1971) has commented, poverty was abounding, and the fondness for heirlooms revealed signs of deprivation. By Late Helladic III C, the production of glass and faience objects ceased in Mycenaean Greece (Deger-Jalkotzy 1998). Fine jewelry was no longer made and whatever pieces were found in the excavated tombs were heirlooms passed down and manufactured prior to the onset of the Dark Age.

Ecological scarcity required a downscaling of material and cultural lifestyles. Such changes are reflected in burial practices that exhibited a reorganization of life along modest lines. The design of clothing and shoes was of the plainest kind (Snodgrass 1971). A one-piece woolen garment that did not require much cutting or sewing to make gained popularity among the female population in Submycenaean Athens and became the predominant dress design in the Protogeometric period. Pins for dresses were scarcely used. The downscaling process is exhibited further in the formation of decentralized communities and associated population losses. The collapse of the palace-driven economies with centralized monarchies were replaced by smaller political organizations dominated by an aristocrat and his family.

Whether this lifestyle is one that was actively sought as a consequence of ecological scarcity or occurred as an outcome of the depressive conditions of the Dark Age is difficult to gauge. It is clear, however, that there was a shift from the Mycenaean way of reproducing life for they no longer provided practical models. The loss of sophistication is clearly seen and as Morris (2000, 207) has stated, "in their funerals people seem more concerned with showing what they were *not* than with what they were." What we are sure of is that as recovery proceeded—we begin to witness this by the mid-half of the tenth century b.c.—trading networks were reestablished and communities revived. Such an upswing was characterized by exuberance, materialistic consumption, and accumulation. As the social system recovered, we see the rise of the bronze industry, the increasing quantity of pottery buried in the tombs, the increasing quantity of gold deposited in the burials, and signs of social cultural recovery. This is in sharp contrast to the Dark Age when materialistic consumption declined, and most of the trading networks disappeared or were restricted only to the area of the Aegean Sea.

What the Dark Age of this period represented for the Mediterranean region was that the extreme degradation of the ecological landscape precipitated socioeconomic and organizational changes to meet the scarcity of resources so as to reproduce some semblance of cultural and economic life of prior times. Consequently, systemic reorganization occurred at various levels, from the way commodities were produced to clothing fashions and designs.

Hierarchical social structures disappeared during the Dark Age, as evidenced by burial practices, and were restored when recovery proceeded (Whitley 1991). To Whitley (1991, 20), burial practices "may be seen as an expression both of social relations and ideology. . . ." During the Dark Ages, there was a shift from multiple-tomb burials to single-tomb burials. This shift reflected the change from an emphasis on heredity signifying a stratified order with ruling classes to one that reflected no expectations of descendants and little regard for extravagance (Snodgrass 1971, Desborough 1972). The single tombs lack monumental significance and architectural quality. From the graves excavated of the Protogeometric period (ca. 900 B.C.), there are no indications of disparities in wealth and social distinction as exemplified in the Athenian graves. Distinction was based on age and sex rather than other social dimensions (Whitley 1991, 115). This was to change by the Early Geometric period (ca. 860/840 B.C.) when the status of the person buried was amplified. Social and sexual identities of the person interred became more evident. Thus, we find the return of a hierarchical pattern and a departure from the more egalitarian structure of the Protogeometric period. Such hierarchization continued in the Middle to Late Geometric periods (ca. 770–700 B.C.).[17] By this period, however, there was also a breakdown of the aristocratic order with the arrival of early state formation, though social hierarchical differentiation remained in place.

With the Dark Age, not only was there a loss of population, but deurbanization was also under way. The latter process continued, giving rise to small communities with lower population levels (Jameson et al. 1994, Watrous 1994). Seen from an ecological point of view, this downscaling provided the necessary timing for Nature to restore its balance and for socioeconomic life to start afresh when recovery returned. The collapse of the palace economies enabled the ecological landscapes, which in the past were intensively exploited by the palace-driven economics, to restore themselves. In the Argolid and Messenia, according to Deger-Jalkotzy (1998, 123–24), the land recovered and the tree population increased. Furthermore, with the loss of centralized control from the various palaces, not only did deurbanization occur but decentralization as well. Each region thus had the opportunity to search for new mechanisms and ways to administer and reproduce socioeconomic life in general. New trends emerged following the collapse of the palaces as a consequence of the unexpected liberty that resulted from the collapse, and each region/community began to make contacts with others outside Greece toward the end of the Dark Age.

From these small communities, in the case of Greece, the preconditions for the rise of the Greek polis (cluster of villages) were put into play, and what followed was a flourishing of political and economic life as soon as the social system recovered (Snodgrass 1971, 1980). Muhly (1998, 20) has put this in a succinct fashion: "the importance of the Dark Age, then, must be that it created the conditions that made possible the growth of this distinctly Greek political organization." To this extent, *the stressed ecological conditions that engendered deurbanization and the formation of small isolated communities precipitated the rise of the polis and the Greek city-states.* We need to realize, therefore, that perhaps scarcity of resources can also have productive outcomes that otherwise under bountiful conditions might not have occurred. Stanislawski (1973, 18) has suggested that instead of seeing the Greek Dark Ages as a period of darkness, it should be seen as one of enlightenment with contributions such as the first use of stone-walled agricultural terraces, the use of chicken eggs in domestic diet, the beginning of the spread of alphabetic writing, the spread of iron, the general use of the olive as food, and the first use of waterproof plaster. Morris (1997a, 547–48) has also noted a drastic change in the use of writing by 750 B.C. Writing was found everywhere in Greece even on potsherds and stone.

Systemic reorganization occurred, and the lengthy duration of the Dark Age needs to be noted. That it is of such a long duration underscores the length of time required for ecological recovery to take place and the immensity of the degradation that occurred. What followed in the recovery phase, however, was a Dark Age–conditioned social, cultural, and political lifestyle that formed the basis of western civilization as we know it today.

The Periphery

Beyond the core areas of the eastern Mediterranean littoral, the periphery of the system such as central, eastern, and northern Europe had a different rhythm vis-à-vis economic expansion. Unlike in the Near East, the Dark Age from 1200 to 700 B.C. was a period of population increases, expansion of settlements, agrarian intensification, and reorientation of trade and exchange for these peripheral regions (Kristiansen 1998b, Chew 2001). This was not the case for the societies along the Atlantic façade, that is, from England to Iberia. They were linked with the Mediterranean and hence felt the reverberations (Kristiansen 1998b, 144). With the collapse of the Near Eastern Mediterranean trade networks and the shortage of metals, metal production boomed in central and eastern Europe, and the east-west exchange connection was strengthened, thus establishing a regional system (Urnfield) of trade exchanges and production. In the Nordic area, there was settlement expansion onto more marginal soils, especially in eastern Scandinavia. Kristiansen (1998b, 102) has asserted that between 1100 and 750 B.C., along with the population increases among the Urnfield culture, there was an increase in social and political hierarchization. The pollen profiles for northern Europe, Switzerland, central Europe, Spain, and Portugal all showed open pastures and agriculture and hence defor-estation that we have indicated from pollen profiles previously.

Crisis in the regional system emerged much later, about 750 B.C., fol-lowing centuries of intensive resource extraction, land exhaustion, and climatological changes in which the climate became cooler and moister. In central and eastern Europe, we witnessed collapses of social hierarchy with communal burials replacing chiefly burials from 1250 to 750 B.C. (Kristiansen 1998b). Village societies were organized along egalitarian lines (Kristiansen 1998b, 113; Childe 1969, 200). Such unstratified social organizational patterns were to change in the early Iron Age when the centers in the Mediterranean recovered in the eighth and seventh cen-turies, and the arrival of the city-states enabled trading to be conducted between the entrepreneurs of the Urnfield hamlets and villages and these trading points in the Mediterranean. Hierarchy and fortification crept into the social organization and physical structures of these villages and hamlets of central Europe during Hallstatt B2-3 period. Such differ-ences in economic trajectories between regions suggest that at this time (in terms of world-systems development), the synchronicity of relations and processes was not as linked to the extent that crisis in the core was felt throughout the periphery. Despite the lack of synchronicity, systemic change continued to occur. As we have seen above, for central and eastern Europe, regional system changes occurred after 1200 B.C., about 750 B.C., following centuries of landscape degradation.

In other parts of the (semi?)periphery, such as in Syria, Palestine, and Jordan, there was a shift from city-state system to a more insular society with few foreign contacts and a lower standard of living (McGovern 1987). The collapse of urban coastal areas had tremendous consequences for inland communities, especially in Jordan and Palestine. Urban dwell-ers had to move to seek other means of support and thus emerged small outlying village communities. The adoption of iron as a base metal started to replace bronze wares. We find transmigration and the establishment of new settlements in the hinterland of Transjordan, where iron ore deposits were located (McGovern 1987).

SYSTEM TRANSFORMATION:
THE TRANSITION FROM BRONZE TO IRON

The trends and tendencies in urbanization/deurbanization and popula-tion levels that we have observed during the Dark Age in the separate re-gions of the Near East, Aegean, and Europe have also been confirmed by George Modelski (1999b, 2003) and Bill Thompson (2000) since 4000 B.C. Given that Dark Ages in world history are significant moments signaling system crisis and system reorganization, the final phase of the Bronze Age crisis led to ecological recovery, certain political-economic realignments and reorganizations, and the transition to a new working metal—iron. The final phase of the Bronze Age crisis was *system transformative*, for it led to fundamental social system changes that evolved to a set of new patterns (Chew 2002a, Sheratt and Sheratt 1993).

The adoption of iron was system transformative for the widely available deposits of iron ore, unlike copper that was found only in selected areas of the Near East, central Europe, the Aegean, and Iran, engendered a number of socioeconomic changes such as agricultural yields and trade expansion (McNeill and McNeill 2003, Heichelheim 1968, Braudel 2001, Polanyi 1977). The Age of Iron began, according to Waldbaum (1978, 1980), when iron ceased to be considered a precious metal and was finally accepted as the predominant material for the making of tools and weapons. The Age of Iron reached fruition by the tenth century B.C. from Greece to the Levantine coast, and about the ninth century B.C. in Mesopotamia and somewhat later in Europe.

Whereas iron was freely available, copper and tin were not; the latter metals were unevenly distributed in Europe and the Near East (e.g., see Pare 2000, Heichelheim 1968, Kristiansen 1998). Furthermore, tin bronze and arsenic bronze were in use in different areas of the Near East. Crete, for example, favored arsenical bronze and so did Egypt (Muhly 1980). Anatolia and other parts of the eastern Mediterranean utilized the copper alloy of tin bronze. With such uneven distribution of copper and tin in the ancient world and the differential use of copper alloys, access to these metals was extremely important and this became more acute during the final crisis of the Bronze Age from 1200 B.C. onward.

Since the third millennium B.C., access to the copper and tin from the core centers of the world system was through long-distance trade, and this was mapped out in the earlier parts of this chapter. Tin, a rare metal, in terms of workable deposits, was found only in certain parts of Europe and the Near East. In Europe, workable tin deposits were located in Serbia, southeast Spain, northwest Iberia, Tuscany, Cornwall, Brittany, Erzgebirge, and in the Near East, deposits were located in Turkey, Syria, Iran, and the eastern deserts of Egypt, and as far east as Afghanistan. An international tin trade came into being after the first quarter of the second millennium B.C. in Europe and central Asia, stretching from the British Isles, southern Scandinavia, Tuscany through to the Carpathian Basin, and supplying tin to the eastern Mediterranean.[18]

Copper was sourced from Palestine where there was evidence of mining. It was also found in Cyprus, in small amounts on mainland Greece in the Argolid, on Crete and some of the islands of the Aegean, and in abundance in Anatolia, and in the eastern deserts of Egypt. Iron, unlike copper, was found everywhere in the eastern Mediterranean from Egypt through to Anatolia and northward from the Aegean through to central Europe (e.g., see Snodgrass 1971, Braudel 2001, Heichelheim 1968, Kristiansen 1998b).

The dependence on long-distance trade for the supply of these metals (copper and tin) thus exposed the economies of the Ancient Near East to changing dynamics of the Bronze Age world system. Disruption in supply because of the various factors we have discussed previously would thus mean crisis conditions for the manufacture of bronze-related commodities. The basis for the transition to iron use has been discussed widely. Several arguments have been put forth: from a regional bronze shortage to the disruption of the international supply of copper and tin (Muhly 1980, Pare 2000, Wertime 1980, Van De Mieroop 2004, Kristiansen 1998b).

Besides this constriction of supply and scarcity argument that led to the adoption of iron use, S. Sherratt (2000) has offered a different interpretation of the transition to iron use. For her, instead of resource scarcity or disruption in supply, it was the overabundance of bronze in circulation during the crisis period of 1200 B.C. that led to the adoption of iron. Evidence for this are the discoveries of copper ingots and bronze found in shipwrecks, graves, and hoards and the circulation of bronze scrap, indicating of abundance (S. Sheratt 2000, 83–87). Furthermore, with the influx of European and Italian bronzes into the eastern Mediterranean in the second half of the thirteenth century, it led substantially to an increase in the amount of bronze in circulation among the diverse levels of society. The extensive trade in bronze scrap, according to S. Sheratt (2000), often undermined the economic political orders that were based on the control of the circulation of these metals in the world system (Pare 2000). Hence, the wide-scale availability and access led to disruptions in economic and political control through decentralized competition. S. Sheratt (2000, 89) claims this led also to the destabilization of the Bronze Age world system from 1200 B.C. onward:

> We end up at the end of the 13th century with a system . . . are all equal grist to a commercial, decentralized mill. . . . In short, what we are seeing is the growth of the alternative networks: the erosion of monopolistic control of entrepreneurial activity, uniting European "barbarians" and eastern Mediterranean "free traders" in a mobile commodity flow which undermined and swept away the older system. To the extent that it may sound familiar in the last decade of the 20th century, as the growing world economy, with its unpredictable currency flows, threatens the stability of the established economic, and possibly political systems of the west, we can perhaps see it as a late 2nd millennium B.C. version of globalization.

Decentralization and autonomous metal workshops were the order of the day, especially following the collapse of the Mycenaean civilization (Giardino 2000). Such development entails the collapse of political and economic control of the international trade routes by the core centers with their palace-run economies and competition from outside the core centers during a period of economic decline of the world system where the core centers are in disarray.

This development has to be considered with the discoveries of hoards. However, we should not assume as S. Sherratt (2000) has that the finding of hoards of copper objects meant that there was an abundance of copper. The hoarding process, as Kristiansen (1998b) has clearly delineated, can be explained by a number of socioeconomic reasons.[19] For us, hoarding occurring increasingly during the Bronze–Iron Age transition suggests a crisis in the system of metal scarcity thus requiring recycling rather than abundance, prosperity, and wealth of metal. Huth (2000) has suggested the difference in the type of hoards in terms of recycling. According to Huth (2000), late Bronze Age hoards contain copper ingots and damaged or broken objects, which indicates that they were hoarded for later use or for recycling; however, axe hoards of the early Iron Age do not have copper ingots or scrap and were made up of entirely recycled and recast metals.[20] This further suggests the declining value of bronze with the increasing use of iron. Was it due to a bronze shortage and/or disruption in supply?

Snodgrass in *The Dark Age of Greece* has stated that there is a shortage of bronze during the Dark Age. Wertime (1980, 1) agreed with this assessment by writing that "men were forced toward a new metal by the disruption of the trade in copper and tin in a moment of social chaos in the Eastern Mediterranean." Desborough in *The Greek Dark Ages* also shared this bronze scarcity condition and so did Sas in *The Substance of Civilization*. Kristiansen (1998b, 211) writing on the European periphery has also indicated a bronze shortage due to the disruption of long-distance trade. Waldbaum (1978) supported this scarcity and disruption thesis, but insisted that it was not copper that was scarce, instead it was tin, and the disruption in the tin trade routes exacerbated the condition. Waldbaum's position is shared by Zaccagnini (1990, 501) who has included tin scarcity as one of the factors in the transition from bronze to iron, besides the disruption in trade routes that others have also put forth. However, Muhly, who earlier in 1980 suggested a shortage of copper has since restated (1998, 1980) that there was no shortage of bronze or tin.[21] According to Muhly (1998), trade contact with Cyprus, where copper was found, was never disrupted, and there is no indication that there was a shortage of tin between twelfth and seventh centuries B.C.

However, we do know that there was tremendous recycling going on in Cyprus and in other parts of the Aegean and the eastern Mediterranean according to S. Sheratt (1998, 2000). S. Sheratt (1998, 2000), however, viewed this recycling effort as being conducted as a consequence of the institutionalized Sea Peoples using Cyprus as a base of entrepreneurial activity following the collapse of the palace economies on mainland Greece and Cyprus. Rather than viewing S. Sheratt's explanation of re-cycling as an economic activity whereby the breakdown of centralized economic control provided the opportunity for economic independence, we can also rationalize it as an effort to husband and continue produc-tion because of a bronze shortage pace as argued by Snodgrass (1971) or a disruption of trade exchanges because of a global collapse as argued by Bryce (1998), Drews (1993), Strange (1987), Van De Mieroop (2004), and others. Understood along this vein, our view of the Dark Ages as a con-sequence of ecological scarcity and crisis following centuries of excessive human exploitation of the environment is still a robust explanation.

Scarcity, disruption of supply, and collapse of palace-administered economies must have led to the adoption of iron use, as the discovery of smelting and making iron products was known in the Bronze Age as early as the third millennium B.C. in the Caucasus and Near East when copper was the dominant base metal (e.g., Braudel 2001, Snodgrass 1971, Childe 1942, Waldbaum 1978, Wertime 1980, Zaccagnini 1990). Zaccagnini (1990, 497) has put this cogently:

> The indisputable fact that in the eastern Mediterranean areas iron replaced bronze in the manufacture of weapons and tools in a comparatively short time (between the 12th and 10th century) is now tentatively explained by the hypothesis of some sort of drastic cut in the supplies of copper and/or tin—supplies previously ensured by palace administered trades—and the consequent necessity to resort to an alternative metal—iron—which was more easily accessible and required less infrastructure for its processing.

The adoption of iron brought to an end centuries of bronze use that was in the control of palace economies and elites. Childe (1942) has suggested that cheap iron with its wide availability provided the opportunities for ag-riculture, industry, and even warfare with the adoption of iron as the base metal. Zaccagnini (1990) and Snodgrass (1971) have, for example, noted the falling value of iron during the first millennium B.C., and by the mid–sixth century B.C., the price of iron had become cheaper than copper or bronze.

With trade route disruption and copper scarcity, the adoption of iron use spread further, especially among the communities in Greece that were isolated as a consequence of Dark Age conditions, for iron was available locally. It led to the development of local iron-producing industries (Snod-grass 1971). The low cost of iron because it was available locally facilitated its widespread use in agriculture and industry (Childe 1942, McNeill and McNeill 2003). Cultivation was easier with iron plowshares in heavy clay soils. This enabled the rural communities to participate further in the economy beyond subsistence and in maintaining a class of miners, smelters, and metalsmiths fabricating the iron implements to reproduce material life. Such an explanation is also supported by Heichelheim (1968) and Polanyi (1977), who have suggested that the widespread adoption of iron was the result of the opportunity for rural communities in southern Russia, Italy, North Africa, Spain, Gaul, Germany, and Eurasia to work the heavy soils with iron implements, thus increasing their production levels. Production increases can be seen by the fluctuations in grain prices according to Heichelheim (1968). The consequence of such transformation is that the urban elites in the Near East who in the past controlled the grain and other trade commodities suffered losses because of changing prices and the falling demand in the copper, tin, and bronze trade that they also controlled. In places where the palace-run economies were stronger such as Assyria, Babylonia, and Egypt, devoid of economic resources the infrastructure and bureaucracies were reduced.

As a result, the social structures were transformed by the formation of different regional centers in the periphery and in the Mediterranean. The opportunity for the farmers to farm in heavy clay soils utilizing cheap iron implements also provided the conditions for economic and system expansion following the end of the Dark Age, where in the past these areas were not as productive. It enabled economic expansion and the move into newer areas for agriculture as by this time some of the older settled areas were ecologically degraded and overworked. Complete restructuring took place over most of the Near East (Van De Mieroop 2004). Population movements took place both internally and externally. By the ninth century B.C., there were peoples in areas that were unknown in these regions before the Dark Ages. For example, in central Anatolia, Phrygians arrived in the twelfth century from the Balkans. Sea Peoples moved into Syria-Palestine. The Arameans who were located in northern Syria before 1200 B.C. moved to large areas of the Near East such as Assyria and Babylonia and were joined by the Chaldeans. By the first millennium B.C., Arabs started to move into Babylonia. Facilitated by the domestication of the camel that occurred earlier in the later second millennium B.C., the trade in incense under the control of the Arabs flourished, thereby linking the Arabian Peninsula to Mesopotamia and the eastern Mediterranean.

At the social system level, the Dark Age crisis ushered forth the dissociation of high-value commodities away from the control of the palace/state, for by the end of the Dark Age, the command palace economies in the eastern Mediterranean were dissolved. What emerged was the continued differentiation of commercial/economic structures from the political structures (Polanyi 1977). Instead of bureaucratic palace-centered trade, we see the development of mercantile city-states where merchant enterprise replaced the palace-controlled exchange. With this transformation, new forms of political powers and structures emerged. We see the emergence of a new political structure, the city-state (polis) in the Aegean, but also the continuation of empire-type political structures such as in Assyria, Babylonia, and Egypt.

The new political structure, the polis, as a social organization and political concept emerged in eighth-century Greece (Morris 1987, 1988a). As Morris (1988a, 752) has stated, it was unique among ancient states for "its citizen body was actually the state." The rise of such a state form was the result of the collapse of the aristocratic society that occurred during the Greek Dark Ages. Other factors also precipitated its formation. Deurbanization and the loss of population in the urban areas resulting in the development of isolated communities during the Dark Age engendered the structural conditions for the development of the polis. In addition, with the scarcity of resources and the abundance of poverty leading to less hierarchical social structures, the groundwork for the development of the polis was also put into place. The polis thus was one where all authority was divested to the community unlike previous political forms in Mycenaean Greece. Force, therefore, was located in the citizen body as a whole, and thus there was little need for a standing military. Individual natural rights were not sanctioned by a higher power as the highest authority was the polis, that is, the community. It set its roots in the Aegean, whereas in other parts of the Near East, divine kingship was maintained with some minor modifications such as in Assyria, Babylonia, and Egypt. The latter continued as Bronze Age states.

Recovery returned about 700 B.C. with social systems expanding and growing in complexity again. Expansion came first in the form of colonization by the Greeks in two phases with the establishment of polis-type political structures. Between 775 and 675 B.C. such expansion was for agricultural purposes, where the soils and lands of Greece, which were degraded after centuries of erosion and intensive cultivation, could no longer produce to meet the needs of the growing population. The excessive population mostly comprised poor peasants who were turned into tenant farmers *(hectemores)* who, saddled with increasing debts, migrated to the urban centers, thus swelling the cities. With the state of the degraded environment in Greece with the exception of Boetia, Attica, and Sparta (where internal colonization was still possible with some fertile agricultural land left), expansion of the system came with migration to other areas such as Italy, Sicily, southern France, and western Asia. Growth in this case came from a colonization process that was extensive in nature—a consequence of the ecological crisis of the Dark Age that had just ended.

Following the success of this agricultural colonization strategy resulting in the generation of surplus and wealth, a second round of colonization from 675 to 600 B.C. followed, mainly focusing on commercial activities. With this phase of colonization, trade routes were further fixed and strengthened. Wealth for the colonial cities came from agricultural exports, trade, and production. Besides the Greek colonies, other growth poles of the system then were Egypt, Persia, and Phoenicia, and as Braudel (2001, 225) puts it, the Mediterranean never became a "Greek Lake." With these different core centers, no polity ever gained control of the Mediterranean. However, with the arrival of Rome the Mediterranean became a Roman sea. With the growing rise of Rome and the demise of Greece, the degradation of the environment continued (Chew 2001). Forests were removed in northern Africa, and almost everywhere, Roman rule was established. Mines were dug in Spain with cities, roads, and production facilities established within the Roman Empire. Crisis emerged again starting in about the third century A.D. with similar trends and tendencies in terms of ecological and socioeconomic variables like that of the Dark Ages that occurred during the Bronze Age. This time, the collapses were not Mesopotamia, Harappa, Mycenaean Greece, Crete, or the Hittite empires, but it was the western portion of the Roman Empire and the system of the Iron Age.

NOTES

1. Our periodization of Dark Ages is based on pollen records with discrete time points utilizing trend analysis (polynomial) to distinguish the periods of deforestation and reforestation. Finer time resolution of pollen count over long periods in the future, if available, might perhaps provide more discrete periods, or even shorter periods, of reforestation and deforestation than what our analysis has provided.

2. This assumes that trade is a key avenue for the accumulation of surplus.

3. This has not been the case in the works of Huntington (1917a, 1924) and Childe (1952), for example.

4. For example, it has been estimated that a mere 1°C rise in temperature may reduce annual rainfall by 30 mm in the Near East.

5. For a discussion on how the salinization problem emerged in southern Mesopotamia as a consequence of deforestation and ecological degradation, see Chew (2001).

6. Raikes and Dyson (1961), on the other hand, have indicated that there were no appreciable climate changes during this period. There is also the critique that the increasing salinity to these lakes was a consequence of lowered rainfall. Other factors, such as the disruption in the underground drainage system due to tectonics, could have played a part in the increase in salinity (Possehl 2002).

7. This thesis has been questioned by Lambrick (1967).

8. These cities have been defined as world cities by Modelski (2003, 4–5) with population levels that meet a minimum threshold for the era. In this case, the population level is set at 10,000 based on historical estimates, allowing the identification of these cities as key urban areas of the ancient era.

9. Butzer (1997) has challenged this thesis that lower Nile floods and climate change induced the demise of the Old Kingdom. Rather, for Butzer, the collapse

of the Old Kingdom was a consequence of decentralization, dynastic weakness, a shift of wealth and power to several provincial centers during Dynasty 6, the loss of royal power due in part to the trade monopoly with Syria being undercut by the Akkadian conquest of Byblos, and civil wars, and so forth.

10. For an extensive account of the political economy of Crete and the Minoan civilization, see Chew (2001) and Kristiansen and Larsson (2005).

11. To say that Crete was in an expansionary mode during this time of the first phase of the Dark Age starting about 2200 B.C. requires clarification. This expansion during a Dark Age suggests that only the southern portion of the Bronze Age world system was deeply impacted by the downturn trends and that Crete was not in the core of the system at this time.

12. Crete's political-economic strength in the Bronze Age trading world was by no means equivalent to that of Mesopotamia, Harappa, and Egypt. Its urban settlements and palace complexes, which directed its commercial and manufacturing capacity, were much smaller in scale. Measured on the Mesopotamia-Harappa urbanization scale, the palace complexes at Crete were no larger than fair-sized villages of the early Dynastic Mesopotamia. Nevertheless, with the Gulf trade collapse from around 1700 B.C., Crete, because of its location as well, managed to exploit the trading opportunities.

13. Profits were extremely high. About 100 percent for tin and 200 percent for textiles were garnered by these Assyrian merchants (Bryce 2002, 87).

14. Thompson (2001) has periodized the pulsations of the expansion and contraction of this trading world of the Near East.

15. It is beyond the scope of this study to address the connections and exchanges between these cores and peripheries in terms of sociocultural patterns and cosmologies during the Bronze Age, and furthermore, a complete and extensive study has been made by Kristiansen and Larsson in their book, *The Rise of Bronze Age Society: Travels, Transmissions, and Transformations.*

16. There is a dispute over the chronology of this destruction. It was either during the early fourteenth century or in the early twelfth century (Drews 1993).

17. Morris (2000), however, has argued that the shift from egalitarianism to stratification might not be the case. Rather the grave burials reflecting an upper class strata, the *agathoi*, prompt some to conclude that a shift to stratified society by the eighth century did not represent the total spectrum of Athenian society, and that the lower order people were disposed of (or buried) in a different way and have not been excavated by the archaeologists.

18. The spread of tin bronze–alloying technology from the Near East and the Aegean took over five hundred years.

19. See Kristiansen (1998b) for a discussion of the various types of hoarding, the possible reasons for the practice of hoarding, and the nature of whether the hoard is a dry or wet hoard.

20. It has also been suggested that the axe hoards can be reconsidered as recycled ingots for they were cast to reflect everyday use (Huth 2000).

21. Morris (2000) has suggested that perhaps there was no bronze shortage. He says that iron items were found in the graves in a higher proportion than bronze objects because there was a shift in cultural tastes and a preference for iron pins over bronze ones.

III

THE CRISIS OF ANTIQUITY

4

Intensification of Natural and Social System Relations

DARK AGE OF ANTIQUITY

Social system restoration and expansion returned to the eastern Mediterranean about 700 B.C. after over five hundred years of ecological, socioeconomic, and political disruptions. By no means was socioeconomic rejuvenation uniform throughout the system. For peripheral Europe, especially the central and eastern parts, there were signs of ecological and socioeconomic deterioration: a consequence of the regional expansion in agriculture and mining from 1100 to 750 B.C. to meet regional demands after this region experienced trade disruption with the Mediterranean and Near Eastern economies during the Dark Age. In this regard, unevenness of economic expansion in the system does not mean the lack of connectivity of the system. Rather, it shows that at this early period of world system history, the ecological capacities differ between regions/zones. Economic expansion in the core areas after 700 B.C. does not necessarily translate to an overall system expansion, especially in peripheral areas that experienced a regional boom when the core areas were in crisis. Such was the case for central and eastern Europe, whereby centuries of regional expansion (1100–750 B.C.) led to ecological distress by the eighth century B.C., which in turn pushed these areas into socioeconomic decline at a time when the cores areas were rebounding from a Dark Age.[1]

Despite this unevenness of expansion, for the core emerging from centuries of reduced economic activities and saddled with a growing population and a landscape that had been intensively cultivated and mined for centuries, there was a need to locate new areas for settlement and production. Starting as early as the tenth century B.C., these trading and colonizing plans were under way, primarily undertaken by the Phoenicians, the Greeks, and the Etruscans. As the eastern Mediterranean was already well connected to the existing trading system, even though there were disruptions during the prior Dark Age, it was to the western Mediterranean that most of the efforts were placed. The rich resources of Iberia, Italy, North Africa, and so on were potential areas for such expansion and colonization. Included in this expansionary thrust is the further intensification of trading relations between the Mediterranean and Europe utilizing the river systems such as the Rhône-Soane.

The above initiatives were similar to the later "voyages of discovery" undertaken by the western European powers in the fifteenth and sixteenth centuries A.D., for they established trading posts, settlements, and towns to facilitate trade and resource extraction. Such designs naturally led to capital accumulation and increased urbanization. As always, population growth ensued. What followed were centuries of socioeconomic expansion and political developments and conflicts that stretched from the western Mediterranean to the Near East. From Philip of Macedon to Caesar, we find the further intensification of empire building and slavery along with the slow evolution of the city-state and citizen rights. Such were the socioeconomic and political tendencies that shaped the world (social) system. The incessant socioeconomic and political forces that underlay this system expansion meant that the natural system continued to be under great assault. The resiliency of Nature to such anthropogenic acts of violence finally gave way about A.D. 300/400 with the onset of another Dark Age. By this period as well, the weather had also started to change. As I have indicated previously, Dark Ages are conjunctures whereby ecological ruptures occur periodically when the natural system is under tremendous stress; therefore the Dark Age of Antiquity that follows parallels the prior Bronze Dark Age with its ecological distress, its deurbanization and population losses, its climate changes, its diseases, its large-scale migrations, and its political collapses. It is to this systemic collapse that we now turn.

WESTWARD AND EASTWARD EXPANSIONS

Westward economic exploration ensued with much fervor after 800 B.C. by the Greeks with the establishment of city-states and colonies, though the Phoenicians and Minoans initiated these exploratory ventures much earlier, about 1300–1100 B.C. Whereas the Phoenicians were focused on setting up trading colonies, leaving governance to the local elites, the Greeks pursued their economic objectives via the establishment of the polis or city-states and migrant settlements, thus transforming the politi-

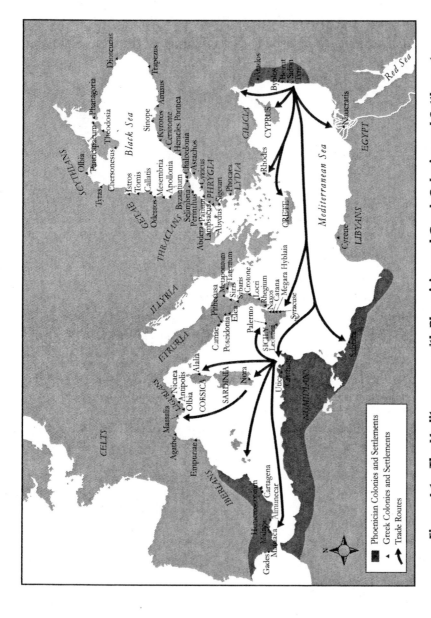

Figure 4.1. The Mediterranean with Phoenician and Greek Colonies and Settlements

cal arena where these entitles were founded. Geographically, the Greeks focused closer to home—they concentrated their activities in Italy and Central Europe—and the Phoenicians directed their efforts on Iberia and North Africa (see figure 4.1).

At this stage of global development, there were essentially three routes to sail to the western Mediterranean (see figure 4.1). The first was to keep close to the northern edge of the eastern Mediterranean, thereby hugging the coasts of Greece and the Greek islands as far as Corfu. From Corfu, the trip would be across the Strait of Otranto to the Straits of Messinia. This route naturally was the choice of the Greeks. The second route was to sail through the Mediterranean by way of Cyprus, Crete, Malta, Sicily, Sardinia, and the Balearics. This was the rapid route and one that was taken by the Phoenicians. The final route is the southern trip, hugging the African coastline and sailing to the Pillars of Hercules and the Straits of Gibraltar. From these routes, the migrants and the merchants sailed to establish colonies, settlements, and trade exchanges. These socioeconomic thrusts into the western Mediterranean led to a further intensification of the natural system and social system connections. From lesser-scale intensity in terms of resource extraction fulfilling a trading arrangement between the eastern and western parts of the Mediterranean that occurred in the past, the transformation that followed from these colonization schemas led to wide-scale changes in consumption patterns and urban development. Where in the past (1300–1100 b.c.), the local elites of the western Mediterranean were the main consumers of the luxuries of the eastern Mediterranean manufactories, the initiatives of the Phoenicians and the Greeks led to the development of urban communities with their specialized division of labor and a heightened consumption pattern.

Initially, the Phoenicians and the Greeks were quite competitive in establishing their trade relationships and colonies. Phoenicia with its city-states lies on a long, thin strip of what is modern-day Syria and Lebanon. From Tyre in the south to Arados in the north, its width is only about 11.3 km littered by small ports with a mountainous backbone. The Phoenician motive to explore the western Mediterranean was prompted by its political situation. Having to pay tribute to the Assyrians, it needed the necessary silver as payment for the Assyrian Empire's needs (Frankenstein 1979). Phoenicia's developed industry specializing in luxury goods provided it with the advantage to be able to move goods across the Mediterranean to places of high demand. Its seafaring ability enabled it to then take advantage of the metals from Iberia and the Atlantic, exchanging them for its manufactured items such as metal vessels, glassware, ivory carvings, alabaster, and textiles. Its skilled artisans, weavers, ironworkers, goldsmiths, silversmiths, and shipbuilders were often sought after by other states (Braudel 2001). The textiles of Phoenicia were colorful cloths sought after by the elites. Glassware such as globules, amulets, pendants, beads, and vases were traded all over the Mediterranean.

The Phoenicians initially acted as go-betweens for the local merchants in the West and the trading emporia in the eastern Mediterranean (Frankenstein 1979). The impetus behind this was to seek access to the metallurgical riches such as the gold and silver of western and southern Iberia and the Atlantic (Kristiansen 1998b). Over time, and after 700 B.C., this intermediary role was to change, whereby trading colonies and settlements were established to exploit the silver mines of southern Iberia. According to Harrison and Spencer (1998), a string of colonies were in place by the seventh century B.C. The division of labor seemed to be the local elites controlling the mining of the silver while the Phoenicians through their factory sites in the colonies undertook manufacturing with their skilled artisans. Such scale of economic activity naturally transformed the local Spanish landscape. An urbanization process ensued, with communities averaging about 40 ha in size. After 573 B.C., however, the Phoenicians started to withdraw from the western Mediterranean following the absorption of the city-states of Phoenicia into the Babylonian Empire. Such a change left only Carthage where Phoenician interest could still be pursued.

Founded on the North African coast, Carthage had open access to the African hinterland. Along with this were the establishment of villages and towns on the coast of Algeria: Collo, Djidjelli, Algiers, Cherchell, and Guraya. Carthage became the gateway to the cheap metal sources of the western Mediterranean. Tin was from the Cassiterides and northwestern Spain, copper and silver were imported from Andalusia and Sardinia, and gold from the African interior. Carthage was the transshipment point between the western Mediterranean and the East. On this basis, Carthage grew in size. Multistoried buildings dominated its urban area, with a public square and agora in place. In it were countless numbers of artisans, metalsmiths, laborers, slaves, and sailors. In all, it is said that the population numbered over 100,000 persons. Its role, however, was susceptible to the ebb and flow of the political economy of the Mediterranean. With the increasing presence of the Greeks after 573 B.C., Carthaginian dominance started to eclipse. There were periods of uncertainty with Alexander's attempt to build an empire (334–323 B.C.), which forced Carthage into a more diminished role. This threat ended with the death of Alexander and with Alexander's general, Ptolemy, seizing the eastern part of Alexander's empire. Such change put an end to the subversion of Carthage's position in the western Mediterranean with Ptolemy's rule. The end of Carthage's dominance came in about 146 B.C. when its was defeated by the Romans.

Unlike Phoenician expansion in the West, which was motivated by Phoenicia's relationship with the Assyrian Empire, Greek expansion was prompted by internal processes. Following the end of the Dark Age, with population growth and degraded landscapes (as discussed in chapter 3), along with improvements in agricultural methods and iron making, the Greeks began colonization in order for the political economy to expand (Snodgrass 1971, Kristiansen 1998b, Chew 2001). Along with these trends and tendencies, following the Dark Age, new elites emerged who were free landowners and citizens within a governmental structure of a polis replacing the old palace aristocracy (Morris 1989).

Such political and social development occurred within a larger frame-work of a number of city-states in competition with each other to secure political and economic dominance. This transformation led to a number of citizens with their newfound statuses without corresponding economic opportunities. Colonial migration thus provided the avenue to meet such interests with the formation of new settlements in the western Mediterranean from mother cities on mainland Greece. By the early eighth century B.C., we find the first colonization in southern Italy and after 600 B.C., we find settlements in the western Mediterranean and the Black Sea coast, especially following the decline of the Phoenicians after 573 B.C.

From 700 B.C. onward, southern Italy became part of the Greek world. Colonies after colonies were established and a trade explosion ensued (Collis 1984). According to Braudel (2001), there were two periods of colonization with their distinct characteristics. The first, from 775 to 675 B.C., was made primarily for agricultural production to supply mainland Greece with food. The second, from 675 to 600 B.C., was primarily commercial to enhance the trading relations and to export manufactured products, such as pottery and textiles, in return for natural resources and grain.

Besides pursuing colonization in the West, to the east, the Greeks penetrated the Bosporus and founded three colonies by the middle of the eighth century B.C. (Appolonya, Sinopa, and Herkyla). The founding of Apsar followed by the end of the eighth century B.C. (Bondyrev 2003). Colonization also dotted the Black Sea coast between the eighth and seventh centuries with the city-state of Miletus founding Fasis and Amis, and Athens establishing Guenes and Dioskurya. Ecologically, such colonization efforts were degradative for the Greek mainland as well as for the colonized landscapes. For example, the colonization of Pontus required approximately ten thousand to twelve thousand ships of different sizes. Bondyrev (2003) estimated that a total 153,600,000 ha of forests were cut to meet the shipbuilding needs between the eighth and fourth centuries B.C.

In the western Mediterranean, the Greeks shared control of the island of Sicily with Carthage. Massalia (modern Marseille) was founded about 600 B.C. by the Phocaeans. This colonization firmed up the trading route along the Rhône River. It ensured that the natural resources of western Europe were secured and established a further trading route besides the trip across the Alps. The founding of Massalia also linked the silver and copper mines of Spain to the Greek trading zone. The new colonized areas of the western Mediterranean provided a bountiful surplus of grain. Grain yield was a hundred to one according to Braudel (2001). Not only was grain production an asset, there was also the minting of Greek coins using the silver from Spain. This was done in Sicily. With the linkage to the mother cities on mainland Greece, the colonies traded extensively with the homeland, extracting the local and hinterland resources to meet the trading demand. Braudel (2001) has suggested that such a period was a "take-off" for the ancient world economy and the emergence of a type of merchant "capitalism."

The vast expansion of trade and production continued uninterrupted in the Mediterranean. The arrival of Alexander of Macedon in the fourth century B.C. generated further Greek influence in the eastern Mediterranean and beyond. With the exception of changing political hegemonies due to the fall of the Persian Empire and the arrival of Rome by 146 B.C., this period of socioeconomic expansion that started after the eighth century B.C. led to an intense relation between the social system and natural system. The annexation of the Persian Empire meant opening a new world for Greek colonization. Greek city-type colonies were established in the Ancient Near East. The Hellenistic cities in the East were patterned after the Greek polis with its agora (marketplace), theater, schools, fountains, and office buildings. The grid system became the norm of building organization. Pirene was approximately 21 ha and Pergamon was established to approximately 21 ha in size. In these urban enclaves, Greek merchants, bankers, artisans, and officials reside. In the countryside, the Greek farmers cultivated crops for export back to mainland Greece. Specialized farms were established as far away as Russian Turkestan and India (Childe 1942). In turn, the ceramic industries of Athens and the Greek islands found new export markets in these colonial cities. Such expansion and economic transformation continued unabated, further intensifying the natural and social system relations.

Caravans and flotillas brought to the Mediterranean perfumes, spices, drugs, ivory, and precious stones from central Africa, Arabia, and India. Gold, forest products, and fur were shipped from Siberia and central Russia, with amber coming from the Baltic and metals from Spain and the British Isles. Such scale of economic activity in the eastern Mediterranean was followed by the rise of Rome, where Roman subjugation of Etruria, the Samnites, and the Gauls led finally to an undisputed Rome in the western Mediterranean. Such an extended period of intensified socioeconomic expansion did not exhibit any signs of crisis at the natural system level, but this was to change following a long period of Roman expansion throughout the Mediterranean and Europe.

THE WORLD ACCORDING TO ROME

It is clear that by 146 B.C., Roman rule was undisputed in the Mediterranean following the end of the third Punic war with the final defeat of Carthage. Roman control sparked a cycle of urban expansion throughout the Mediterranean leading to a "Romanization" of the landscape influenced by Hellenistic sources. The Roman Republic was dominated by the Roman Senate. Political power thus resided among the patrician clans that populated the Roman Senate. The citizenry of Rome elected Roman consuls to the executive offices of the senate, but in reality, the patrician class monopolized these positions. As a result, over time and due to public pressure, a parallel structure emerged with the formation of the tribunate of the plebs whereby the mass citizenry of Rome elected officials to protect the poor from the oppression of the rich. Yearly elections by a tribal assembly led to the election of the Roman Tribune. Such political structures and development corresponded to the democratic-type polis system of Ancient Greece. On this basis, Roman Republican rule followed and extended throughout the Mediterranean.

Unlike other conquerors, Roman rule of conquered territories initially was somewhat lenient, and populations seen as ethnically and linguistically close to Romans were eventually offered Roman citizenship (Braudel 2001, Rostovtzeff 1930). Following conquests, colonization followed with the formation of settlements that were peopled by either Romans or Latins. In Italy, the conquered Italian cities provided troops for the Roman legions in lieu of having to provide monetary taxes to the Roman treasury. These structural trends benefited the evolution of the Roman Empire and marked a notable advance in empire formation (Braudel 2001, Anderson 1974).

Continuous Roman conquest of the western Mediterranean and its northern hinterlands through extended military campaigns connected these lands to the classical world of the Ancient Near East (see figure 4.2). As Richardson (1986, 178–79) has noted, "what the Romans were doing in Spain was essentially the same as what they were doing in the Greek east, that is using all means available to ensure that the peoples of the Mediterranean did what the Romans wanted them to do." Spain, Gaul, and Britain, which did not have much of a history of urban lifestyles, were transformed. The river systems of Spain and Gaul assisted the invasions for they carried the legions and later provided the transportation of food and manufactured products from the heartland of the empire to the frontiers (Drummond and Nelson 1994, Millar 1981, Garnsey and Saller 1987). What followed was the transformation of the rural landscape with agricultural estates and resource extractive industries. Along the river systems, towns were established that represented the terminus for surplus extraction. Towns such as Cordoba, Lyon, Amiens, Trier, and others were

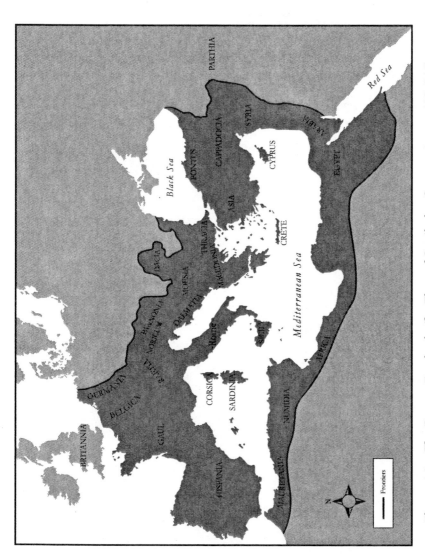

Figure 4.2. The Roman Empire in the Time of Septimius Severus (r. A.D. 193–211)

built. Hence, we find continuous urbanization where the landscapes, which in the past were natural areas, were transformed.

Roman penetration of the East, however, was more cautious. Faced with established urban communities and civilizations, client states were encouraged and fostered instead of being replaced with a conquered administration. Only minimum social-political interference was exercised, and taxation was the medium of economic extraction from the East.

The natural system and social system relations during the Roman period were characterized by a number of economic strategies. The early Roman Empire was organized around autonomous towns and tribal territories connected by means of roads and forts (Jones 1974). Underscoring this projection of control were the accumulation needs of the patrician class. In Italy, the establishment of slave *latifundium* peopled by slaves derived from the various Roman wars of conquest such as the Macedonian, Punic, and Gallic wars spurred agricultural expansion. By the first century B.C., each *latifundium*-style estate amounted to approximately 81,000 ha in size. Such increases led to great extensions in pastoral ranching, cereal, olive, and grape cultivation. A slave-driven economy emerged with the proportion of slaves to free persons in Italy reaching almost 67 percent by 43 B.C. (Brunt 1971, 34–35).

Beyond Italy, Roman expansion also brought in revenues from the conquered land in the form of goods, slaves, agricultural products, and silver and gold bullion. Based on this evidence, we know that the social stratification heightened and the social-natural system relations intensified. This rhythm continued through the centuries with the provinces providing revenues from tribute levied on land and population, rent on mines, and other taxes on commercial activities. For example, the silver mines at New Carthage brought in about 9 million denarii a year. Besides this transfer of resources to Rome, coin and bullion also were shipped to Rome as indemnities and booties from war conquests. Carthage paid 28 million denarii after the first Punic War and a further 60 million denarii after the Second Punic War, and Macedonia and Greece paid booties and indemnities amounting to 70 million denarii between 201 and 167 B.C. (Jones 1974).

Roman attempt at pacification of the conquered population and territories utilizing the Roman legions led to the development of free commerce in the provincial towns and markets and the establishment of trading networks. Consequently, appropriate manufacturing and extractive industries followed with production in leather, wool, pottery, and other metals. Not only were the provincial towns stimulated, but the communities external to the empire were also transformed. Such socioeconomic change led to the rise of provincial elite members that over time resulted in further urban growth. Provincial centers such as Aquileia on the Adriatic and Narbo and Tolsa in Gaul rose to be regional centers and had trade connections beyond the provinces with other foreign communities. In the eastern portion of the empire, with its established towns and trading networks, Roman rule meant the circulation of products from other parts of the empire into the region and beyond.

WESTERN FRONTIER OF THE EMPIRE

By 27 B.C., the Roman Republic was effectively over, and during the reign of Augustus (27 B.C. to A.D. 14), the foundations of an imperial government were put in place. With this imperial government, a fixed and fortified frontier was established in the West following the conquest of Britain in A.D. 43 and Dacia in A.D. 105–106 (Drummond and Nelson 1994, Millar 1981). Implementation of this policy rested on the military strength of the Roman legions that were dispatched to safeguard the territorial lines. Legions and auxiliaries were spread out in permanent fortified positions along the actual frontier instead of being based as a group poised to attack in case of an incursion (Millar 1981). Such defensive arrangements orchestrated by the Roman legions along with the demobilized veterans of the Roman legion—who chose to settle in the *coloniae* of the empire—determined the socioeconomic and political trajectories of the western frontier of the empire (e.g., see Drummond and Nelson 1994). The relations with the natural system began to intensify, and the landscape that had already been transformed was changed further according to the needs of the Roman legions and, from time to time, the imperial dictates of successive Roman emperors.

To supply and feed a standing army requires a continuous flow of resources. Transportation of these resources via overland routes often was extremely difficult and expensive, and the only available choices were packed animals and carts. The river systems were the other alternate mode for shipment, and they were often used for bulk items. It is clear that with the level of resources required, it was not the intention of Imperial Rome to supply the legions in the West forever with food and resources from the heartland of the empire. Instead, it was deemed that the immediate surroundings in the West were to provide for the legions' needs after the legions had the opportunity to establish themselves following the implementation of Roman imperial rule. Thus, provisions were provided at first by Rome, following which, the forts, camps, and military settlements of the Roman legions in the West became self-supporting by living off the surrounding native resources.

Such a structural requirement led to the transformation of the economic and social structures of the frontiers in the West to meet the needs of a military institution (Nash 1987, Caselgrove 1987, Wells 1999b). Coupled with the provision of material and food needs for the Roman military, imperial dictates also required the natives to pay taxes to Rome. This collection was made either in monetary terms or in kind and was duly enforced by the Roman legions. Whatever the case, the levying of taxes entailed that the local population needed to generate a surplus to pay their taxes. As a result, what followed was an intensification of whatever economic activity these populations were involved in. Therefore, the natural system relations became further heightened and the landscape further degraded to ensure the surplus was generated.

Beyond tax collection, the Roman military installations would also automatically generate demand in the local commerce and markets. Roman military agents along with the legions injected cash to purchase necessary items from the local economy. In this fashion, the presence of the Roman military became the driving force spurring demand in the local markets. What types of products were required to reproduce this standing military complex to ensure that it met its declared mission of frontier enforcement and pacification? A range of commodities was sought to reproduce the Roman legion. With infantry and cavalry troops, there was a huge demand for leather, meat, horses, wheat, and barley. The latter served as food for the troops, the horses, and other pack animals such as donkeys and oxen. Roman enforcement of the territories of the empire and pacification of the local populace required the establishment of forts, stone walls, and other military installations to enforce order. Such physical structures required large supplies of tiles, bricks, lead pipes and pellets, iron nails, heavy timber, and cut stone. In one instance, one million nails weighing about 10t were found at the fortress of Inchtuthil in Scotland (Garnsey and Saller 1987). Leather, woolen cloth, and textiles were required for fastening armor, saddles, and tunics for the infantry and the cavalry. Initially, this material demand was satisfied through local manufacturing by the Roman legions themselves using local resources, but over time, the local populations also learned how to supply the legions' needs. Following this, we witnessed the economic transformation of Gaul, Britain, Spain, and Germany as a result of Roman military rule.

The Roman Legion and Resource Needs

The Roman imperial army was composed of various specialized units, of which the most highly regarded infantry troops were the legions. Each legion was organized and trained to fight as an independent force supplemented by cavalry troops and Roman auxiliaries. These auxiliaries were recruited from the provinces and mostly performed functions such as signal operations and staffing small forts on the frontier. Later on, the difference between the auxiliaries and the Roman legions became blurred when recruitment for the legions was extended to frontier regions.

A Roman legion at full strength consisted of approximately 5,280 infantry troops with a 120-cavalry unit attached. Along with headquarters staff, medical personnel, and other specialized occupational troops (surveyors, weapons-makers, engineers, miners, carpenters, stonecutters, etc.), the total number in a legion would be about 6,000 men (MacMullen 1984, Webster 1985, Parker 1958, Garnsey and Saller 1987). This wide array of skills meant that the legion could perform a wide variety of tasks. From building roads and bridges, mining and smelting ores, setting up brick and tile factories, making shoes, and building cities and forts, these various functions were carried out by the Roman army (Parker 1958). There was not a frequent turnover of personnel unless there were losses due to military conflicts because the enlistment period lasted for 25 years. Frequently, following the end of the enlistment period, these veteran troops with their varied skills, mastered over a quarter century of service, most often settled in the frontier provinces, thus further enhancing the local economy and commerce. However, this situation changed toward the end of the empire, when increasingly, the recruitment sources came from the local areas.

By the time of the rule of Emperor Augustus, there were about twenty-eight legions in place totaling almost 170,000 men (Parker 1958). At the beginning of the second century A.D., a total of seventeen legions were based in the western frontier: three in Britain, four on the Rhine, and ten on the Danube (Drummond and Nelson 1994). Along with the auxiliaries, the total number of troops in the western portion of the empire totaled about 200,000 men. In terms of resources, to supply and maintain the legions based as far as Spain and Britain meant an intensification of the natural system relations. To minimize the impact on the Roman imperial treasury with this high number of troops deployed, levies in kind in lieu of taxes began as soon as the legions established their installations and forts. Land use was intensified by the arrival of the troops to the frontier and by the nonagricultural population of administrators, artisans, merchants, and their families that accompanied the troops. All these people engendered an additional need for foodstuffs and natural resources.

Because the traditional agricultural focus of local native populations (the Celts and Germans) in the western frontiers was pastoralism, the need to increase the harvest of grain, such as wheat and barley, became a priority for the Roman army. This was alleviated through the provision of free land to agricultural developers and agricultural workers who were either Romans or Romanized persons. The result of all this was the eventual increase in agricultural products and the subsequent growth in new markets following the arrival of these new civilian populations to the frontier.

As with the other parts of Italy following Roman conquest, the establishment of the Roman estate, the villa, as a mode of organizing agricultural production was also established on the frontiers. A typical Roman villa was more like a village than a farming organization (Davies 1969). The villa comprised several buildings. It had both slaves and free laborers involved in a set of functions from processing animal and agricultural products to light manufacturing. The size of the villa expanded as the owner would purchase abandoned farms, thus increasing the field of operations. In places that were close to the heartland of the empire, there would be slave gangs; this type of labor was not as plentiful for those villas closer to the territorial lines of the empire because the opportunity to escape from Roman rule existed. As a result, slaves were often traded closer to the interior and free persons were often utilized to man the villas nearer to the territorial boundaries. Where they exist, we find trained slaves with expertise in accounting, winemaking, pottery, carpentry, and other professions. Such trained slaves along with skilled management led to highly productive capacities of these villas and was the preferred means by which the Romans exploited the landscape of the frontiers. In the absence of slaves, tenant farmers and salaried workers and artisans were often employed to meet the labor needs of agricultural cultivation and harvesting.

Over time, the successful villas became like a small Roman urban enclave with a library, bath facilities, and entertainment structures including planned gardens and architectural works. In addition, these villas also became storage places for the rural farming community and became the source of information for which crop to plant. It was also a site for the repair of farming equipment and a source of agricultural knowledge and technology. The villa on the territorial frontiers became also a place for salaried employment.

Villa ownerships were in the hands of transplanted Romans or local elites. Vast amounts of new land were brought under cultivation to meet military needs, and coupled with the villas were also smaller native farms and villages supporting the production process. The demand needs generated by the Roman legion ensured that agriculture was a lucrative economic activity. It led to the widespread purchase of small farms and their consolidation to large villa complexes, thus further intensifying the social stratification. All over the western part of the empire, such as Gaul, Britain, Pannonia, and the Rhineland, villas were established.

In terms of the scale of demand to meet the Roman legions' needs, for example, the Roman military in Britain required approximately 18,677 kl of grain a year as rations for men and horses (Davies 1969). This level of grain production required an extensive amount of cultivable land. Approximately 80,938 ha of land would have to be brought under cultivation, and an additional 80,938 ha would also have to fallow. To till nearly 81,000 ha would require about 10,000 draft animals, thus requiring an additional 12,141 to 20,235 ha for grazing and winter feed for these draft animals. When translated to land mass, cereal provision for the Roman military in Britain would have required about 2,072 km^2 and a population of 60,000 to undertake the task (Drummond and Nelson 1994, 53). The natural system was transformed quite extensively and so were social relations.

Such agricultural transformations were repeated in other parts of the western frontier. In Pannonia, agricultural development moved south and west from the middle of the Danube through to the Julian Alps. We also witnessed similar changes in Illyria on the Adriatic coast. Cultivation along villa lines spread from the upper Save and Drave rivers to as far as Sirmium on the Save and the Danube. By the third century A.D., smaller villas were abandoned and larger estates became the norm.

Along the Danube, villas arose near fortresses such as Aquincum (Budapest), Brigetio, Carnuntum, Vindobona (Vienna), and Singidunum (Belgrade). Such villa construction led to population increases, which is evident from the remains of the villas that have been excavated. As the center of economic enterprise, the Danubian villa paralleled those in other parts of the western frontier in terms of supplying local military and civilian needs. The number of villas increased over the course of the third century A.D. Such development led to a further increase in the local population and deepened further the natural system relations in this area.

With retirements from the Roman legions, the veterans proceeded to settle and remain on their properties (Garnsey 1970, R. E. Smith 1972). Over the course of the next century, despite the changes undertaken by successive emperors, from Severus to Caracalla, to increase the soldiers' payments, such augmentations were unsuccessful because they were accompanied by currency devaluations. This condition was later exacerbated by currency devaluations without any further pay augmentation. As a result, the legions experienced a steady decline in real income that led to reverberations throughout the markets and the economy of the frontier. Decline came almost a century later (fourth century A.D.), for example, for the Danube region, where the focus of wealth shifted from the frontier to agricultural estates in the interior.

In Dacia, where extensive mineral resources were present, especially gold, the province was added to the empire by A.D. 107. The villas established were more like working farms with a wooden stockade built to surround these structures. Their functions were to provide the supplies needed by the legions and the miners that were relocated to mine the gold. Roads were built by the legions to transport the miners out of Dacia for transshipment to Rome and the other urban areas. Such pacification of the area led to an economic boom and the opening of trade of the lower

Danube from the cities of Belgrade to Stukten. This also extended to the towns on the Black Sea coast. Such expansion ended by A.D. 270, when the Roman Emperor Aurelian withdrew the legions from this part of the empire.

In Roman Spain, Hispania, the mineral deposits of the land were also thoroughly exploited (Orejas and Sánchez-Palencia 2002). Around Cartagena, in an area of some 259 km², 40,000 men were involved in extracting silver, producing about 2,500 drachmae per day (Richardson 1986). Translated to yearly production, the mines of Cartagena produced over 4,900 kg of silver each year. Spanish mines in Galicia, Lusitania, and Asturias produced about 10 t of gold each year (Howgego 1992, Chew 2001). Silver production can be estimated to be about 40 to 45 t for one year in the first century A.D. More than 40,000 slaves were used to work the silver mines in Carthago Nova (Chew 2001).

Besides grain, the Roman legion also required other supplies such as leather, horses, timber, and other animal by-products. Timber was needed for the building of forts, barricades, and stockades, while the leather and horses were necessary components for outfitting the legion and the cavalry. With perhaps 200,000 troops in the western frontier and with each soldier requiring his own suit of armor, a large amount of leather and leather products were needed. The suit of armor consisted of a covering for the upper body made up of iron plates held together by a complex internal system of leather straps. Guards for the shoulder were constructed in a similar manner and held together by leather straps. In addition, senior personnel also wore leather straps hanging from their waists to protect their thighs and legs. Besides this armor for the body, leather was also required for belts, scabbards, and chinstraps for the headgear, which was often also made of leather covering an iron helmet. The shields carried by infantry were made of layers of laminated wood with glue made from horns and hooves of animals. A pair of sandals made from heavy leather secured together by a complex set of leather thongs finished off the outfit of an infantry soldier.

In addition to armor that required a substantial amount of leather, the Roman legions required shelter on their military campaigns. The tents constructed for shelter required even more leather. Tents comprised a number of leather panels, and calf hide was used extensively for these (Connolly 1981). Each standard-size tent required about 42 panels, whereas a centurion's tent took up to 168 panels of leather. Two panels would require a calf hide that included the back, neck, and belly of the animal. If this was used as a base to calculate the amount of calves required to outfit the western frontier army of approximately 200,000 men, it is estimated that one and a half million calfskin panels cut from the hides of 750,000 calves were required. By A.D. 1, the Roman army required fewer tents as by this time permanent shelters were erected. Nevertheless, the army utilized a great deal of livestock. In Britain, 132,000 head were needed; in the Rhineland, 176,000; and in the Danube, 440,000 livestock were employed for such purposes (Connolly 1981).

Transportation also engendered the use of leather. Most goods, such as grain, beer, preserved meats, and vegetables, were shipped in leather sacks and bags. In terms of volume of hides required, it is estimated that the frontier army in the western provinces required yearly shipments of 77,526 kl of grain requiring 1.1 million sacks derived from 275,000 head of cattle (Drummond and Nelson 1994). Given this scale of utilization of leather for tents and sacks, it is estimated that Britain had to provide over 180,000 hides; the Rhineland, 241,000; and the Danube areas, over 500,000. All this underscores the intensive utilization of natural resources to reproduce an imperial army.

The Roman legion had cavalry troops that formed part of its contingent. In addition, by the first century A.D., the Roman army also included 80,000 mounted auxiliaries with about 50,000 assigned to the western frontier besides legionary cavalry, which were smaller in number. The legionary cavalry in Britain had about 360 horses, and there were 480 cavalry troops on the Rhine, with the Danube having the largest assignments of 2,000 cavalry mounts. Such a wide utilization of cavalry stimulated horse breeding in the frontier regions, and importing of horses from the regions external to the frontiers. Imperial stud farms were established in Spain, which was part of the western frontier, and in Thrace and Cappadocia.

The requirement for live animals, such as cattle and horses, and their products to reproduce the Roman legion necessitated undertaking ranching besides agricultural production of cereals. This was pursued in the western frontier, and in a way, it was not an alien practice for the local population in these areas, for they were pastoralists prior to the arrival of the Romans. This pursuit of ranching also stimulated the territories in the periphery beyond the Roman Empire with the barbarian tribes' crossing over to exchange their horses and hides for Roman goods and currency. The excavated fortress at Carnuntum on the Danube showed evidence of it functioning as a livestock market (Drummond and Nelson 1994). What this led to was the growth of the forts not only as military strongholds, but also as trading centers beside the urban settlements that were in place along the trade routes of Roman Europe. The villas were also a source for these animals and their products. This can be seen in the large villa estates—for example, in Pannonia and Moesia—with these establishments exporting large quantities of grain and cattle (Mocsy 1974). Such demand for animals and their by-products led to some villas shifting away from agricultural production to ranching, and what followed was the transformation of agricultural land to pastoralism.

Beyond the western frontier of the Empire, Garnsey and Saller (1987) have estimated that the whole Roman military required over 150,000 t of wheat per year in terms of consumption needs. This scale of consumptive requirements when added to the needs of the city of Rome, which was about an additional 200,000 to 400,000 t, meant that the Roman provinces of the empire had to transform the landscape to meet imperial needs. The burden for this was distributed among the provinces. Wheat provision for Rome came from the western part of the empire such as North Africa, Sicily, Sardinia, and in the East, Egypt. For the Roman military, the main burden fell on the northern and northwestern provinces as two-thirds of the legions were based in the western part of the empire. Besides wheat, money taxes were also collected whereby the provinces in the Iberian Peninsula, Gaul, and western Asia Minor were the main contributors. Almost half of the taxes (about 400 million sesterces) were used to cover pay and discharge settlements for the soldiers.

In all we can surmise from these trends that the Roman Empire greatly intensified the natural system relations with the burden of maintaining the empire in the hands of the provinces. Rome was engaged in tapping the resources of every corner of its imperium.

THE EASTERN PROVINCES OF THE EMPIRE

Resource use was not limited just to the provisions required to maintain the Roman legions and their military auxiliaries. The empire had exorbitant needs whereby taxes collected in currency or in-kind were levied to meet the reproduction of Rome itself. Thus, besides the western frontier of the empire, North Africa, Egypt, Greece, and other parts of Asia Minor also contributed to the taxation process. Because of their proximity to Rome, North Africa and Egypt were major areas whereby the local landscapes were transformed for agricultural production to supply the needs of Rome.

The transformation of North Africa was not started by the Romans, though they heightened it by extending the urban enclaves that were established earlier by the Phoenicians. Tunisia was one such geographic locale that contained Roman and Latin colonies. Conjointly with this process of urban development, the Roman military facilitated further the transformation of this landscape with its building of military roads in North Africa. A total of five hundred cities in North Africa became centers of agricultural production (Millar 1981). Inhabiting these cities and urban enclaves were Roman and local aristocracies and elites.

In Egypt, faced with a civilization of comparable antiquity that was infused with Hellenistic influence, Roman rule embodied minor modifications of the already established administrative system with the sole aim of maximum revenue extraction. The Romans perceived the difficulty to remodel Egyptian life and so continued the administrative systems of the Ptolomies (Rostovtzeff 1957). Egyptian grain and corn were sought after along with the implementation of a poll tax on the general population. Under Roman rule, Egypt was divided into three main districts comprising the delta, middle Egypt, and upper Egypt. This mode of governance was extended to the Greek provinces and areas in Asia Minor under Roman control. The favoring of urban enclaves populated with hereditary ruling and colonial elites was the order of the day. Such a governing principle ensured that the loyalty to Rome was preserved and also ensured the efficient collection of taxes on behalf of Rome (Randsborg 1991, Millar 1981). It is clear that when Rome was faced with established kingdoms, it did not overtly try to overwhelm the social and institutional structures. Instead, it chose to rule through co-optation and compromises as long as the taxes were paid and Roman resource needs were met. Besides which, the western part of the empire required a fair amount of military resources and political energies to be devoted to ensure that the empire's territorial boundaries stayed intact.

Beyond taxation and land transformation, the eastern provinces offered Rome the bridge to kingdoms and lands beyond the empire to the East such as India and China. Trade circulated freely throughout the empire via cities that were united by the roads that the Romans constructed and the sea-lanes kept free of pirates by the Roman fleets. Pottery manufactured in Italy has been found in Asia Minor, Palestine, Cyprus, Egypt, North Africa, Spain, and southern Russia (Childe 1942). Regular caravans brought spices and precious stones from southern Arabia and Mesopotamia.

Such a globalized connection at this stage of world development led to major natural landscape transformations. Trade and urbanization were two key processes that underlined the continued growth of the Roman Empire. We need to turn to these processes to understand further the social system and natural system linkages.

TRADE AND CITIES

In my earlier work, *World Ecological Degradation*, the processes of trade and urbanization were traced for the Roman period to show the extent and intensity these processes had developed since the Bronze Age. What is important to note is that with Roman rule, these processes spurred on changes in the lands that became the Roman Empire and those areas that were external to the empire. In so doing, such a structural process transformed further the world beyond Rome.

Roman merchants in the western provinces not only sought the products needed by Rome and its provinces, such as precious gems and other
natural resources, but they also traded with local German tribes for local
products, such as beeswax, horses, furs, and even the hair of German
women, to make into wigs for the women elites of Rome (Drummond and
Nelson 1994, Childe 1942). An aspect of this trade that impacted wildlife
was the import of live animals from the provinces to Rome. For the imperial games and *venations,* several species from the northern frontier were
used such as the antelope, elk, bison, wild boars, bears, and stags (Brogan
1936, Jennison 1937, Chew 2001). Notwithstanding this, live animals were
also used in the provincial games and shows of the urban centers in the
territories.

These tribes in the western part of the empire brought to the trading
stations commodities for exchange beyond horses, leather, and stock
animals. Apparently, this was a case whereby the developed urbanized
community shaped the peripheral areas of western Europe. On the Romans' part, silver and gold coins were used for the exchange (Brogan
1936, Tacitus 1925). As trading volume increased, the merchants located
in the provinces began to become more dominant in the trade, thus eclips-
ing somewhat those Italian merchants based in Italy (Rostovtzeff 1957).
This trade intensity had grown to the extent that by the first century
A.D., the Germanic tribes were conversant with Roman coinage (Tacitus
1925). Such an engendered need spurred on the extraction of silver and
gold in parts of the empire such as Hispania and North Africa. Besides
these areas, the provinces in Great Britain were a good source for mineral
resources such as gold, silver, lead, and tin. By the second century A.D.,
provincial and frontier regions were opened up for exploitation. Lead was
an important item that the Romans sought as it had many uses in the lives
of the Roman elites (Elkington 1976, Chew 2001). Some of these mineral
mines in Britain, Dalmatia, and Gaul were operated by the Roman legions
along with some private entrepreneurs.

Such opening up of natural resource areas also precipitated the rise
of local manufacturing that later supplanted products from Italy. New
mining techniques were introduced and a high return was obtained from
these extractive operations. However, by the third century A.D., diminishing yields were starting to show (Drummond and Nelson 1994).

Over time as well, an appetite for Roman manufactured wares was
also developed. Where Roman merchants had provided silver and gold
coins as payment for horses, leather, and other local items for military
consumption, this money was then returned to the Roman economy as
payments for the manufactured goods. As the century progressed and
until the second century A.D., products manufactured in Italy predominated the trade exchange. A substantial amount of Roman exports such

as silverware, pottery, textiles, and glassware have been uncovered in all parts of the western portion of the Roman Empire (Childe 1942). By the third century, however, relocation of industries occurred as local manufacturing was relocated to the Roman colonies and settlements, and thus local manufactured wares began to replace those imported from Rome (Chew 2001, West 1935). These goods were manufactured in Gaul and the Rhineland and with some production in the Black Sea area (Wells 1999). Pottery known as Samian ware that was originally produced in Italy by the first century shifted to Graufenesque in southern France, and by the second century had expanded to Lezoux, which was approximately 161 km north on the Allier River. Furthermore, operations were started at Rheinzabern on the Rhine. Glass manufacturing also followed the same route. In the course of its growth, it started in Gaul, Belgium, and parts of the Rhine. To this extent, towns such as Lyons, Arelate (Arles), and Treves became main centers for manufacturing and distribution for Gaul, Germany, and Britain. A significant glass industry was established at Cologne. Most of these industries were established by the second century A.D. Textiles were produced in the western part of the empire in Gaul and in Syria for the eastern empire. All in all, these provincial centers began to displace the Italian centers in overall production for the empire's needs (Rostovtzeff 1957). Mass production seems to have been the order of the day due to the lowered purchasing power of the lower classes and the peasants.

The proximity to the markets of the products manufactured in the provinces also provided an advantage over those produced in the heartland of the empire. Transportation costs were lower, and the local manufacturers were more conducive to producing items that were suited to local tribal needs. With the help of the Roman state, these manufactories were supported for they were in line with long-term imperial policies for the stabilization and self-sufficiency of the frontier. By the end of the third century A.D., the bulk of the manufacturing potential had moved to the frontiers of the empire. Accessibility to cheap natural resources was a major factor that forced the relocation, along with dwindling energy supplies in Italy.

In all, however, the balance of trade favored Rome. Numerous advantages were also gained with the local elites being tied into the Roman economy via their purchases of Roman goods, and their tastes were also shaped by the Roman culture. Such influences were not restricted to consumption and lifestyle; the short Roman sword influenced the style of the German sword, but later on, the German sword became the standard type for the empire. Roman plowshares and agricultural tools have also been uncovered in Germania, indicating the technological influence the Romans had on local free tribes. The adoption of new agricultural techniques meant the modification of the local landscapes, hence the further intensification of the natural and social systems connections.

The Roman Empire, though self-sufficing, was not a closed system. It interacted with the ongoing trading systems and participated in the ongoing trading routes that were in existence prior to the rise of Rome. In the eastern portion of the empire, regular caravans brought spices, aromatics, and jewels from southern Arabia and Mesopotamia. There was intensified sea trade between Rome, Egypt, and India. In the Far East, Roman trade reached as far as China and Southeast Asia. The trade routes spanned eastward across Asia Minor to China and southeastward via the Persian Gulf to India and Southeast Asia. The types of products exchanged with India, China, and Southeast Asia emphasized a division of labor between more technologically developed areas and those that were less so. This was the case for Southeast Asia.

The trading routes extended across land and sea. Geographically, from Rome exports moved on the trade routes to China, India, and Southeast Asia, branching off in three circuits (see figure 4.3). The northernmost circuit ran via the Black Sea through Byzantium and central Asia. The central route went via Syria through Antioch and the Euphrates to the Persian Gulf and beyond. The southern circuit was through Alexandria, northern Africa, and Petra via the Red Sea and the Nile and beyond.

The easternmost point of the trade routes radiating from the West was Loyang, China. This route, the Silk Road, in the first century A.D. stretched from China—traversing several political entities such as the Kushans and the Parthians—to the West and ended at Antioch via Seleucia and Ctesiphon. Along this nearly 7,970-km road products from China, such as silk, ginger, cinnamon leaves, cassia bark, and other spices and semi-manufactured goods such as steel and ink, were transported (Miller 1969). From the West flowed gold and silver bullion and coinage, fine cloth, and other fine manufactured items.

The central and southern routes primarily connected the West with India, the Arabian Peninsula, Egypt, and Africa. The southern routes connected Rome to Egypt, Africa, India, Sri Lanka, and Southeast Asia. The port of Alexandria was the connective point and acted as collection center (entrepôt) for products from the East. Other ports on the Red Sea coast were also very active in this overall trade. From the late first century B.C. to the second century A.D., the ports of Clysma, Myos, Hormos, Philoteras, Leukos Limen, Nechsia, and Berenice on the Red Sea were on the trade routes (Sidebotham 1991). From Babylon and Persia came embroidered stuffs, bitumen, dates, asafetida, asphalt, fine linen, and precious stones (Jones 1974). China, India, Sri Lanka, and Southeast Asia exported not only luxuries but also steel, iron, fine muslin, silk pearls, teakwood, ebony, ivory, tortoise shell, cinnamon, cloves, nard, cassia, exotic animals,

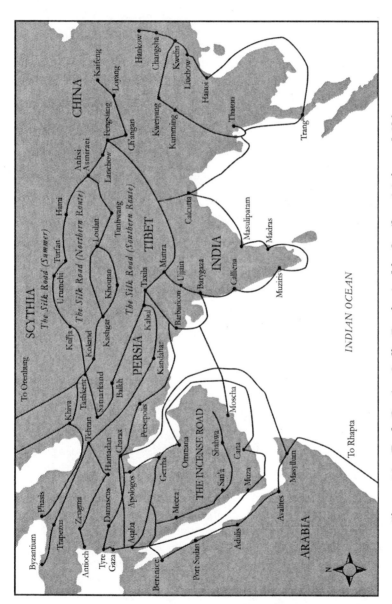

Figure 4.3. Trade Routes: India, Persia, Arabia, Southeast Asia, and China

precious stones, cotton, millet, frankincense, myrrh, and even slaves. All of this passed through these ports on the way to the Mediterranean (Miller 1969, Deo 1991, Stern 1991, Carswell 1991, Jones 1974, Rostovtzeff 1957). Iron was mined from early Han times in the provinces of Shensi, Hupei, Kansu, and Szechwan. Animals were also imported to the West to meet the needs of the elites of the Roman Empire. They ranged from parrots and cockatoos to tigers. Several ports on the west coast of India emerged to become part of this trading circuit. They included Barbaricon, Barygaza, Muziris, Nelcynda, and Becare. Mantai in Sri Lanka was also a major conduit to the Persian Gulf and beyond. Rome sent gold and silver bullion, plate and coinage, glass, barley, wheat, sesame oil, wine, fine silk and cotton cloth, bronze statuettes, cameos, mirrors, and pottery in exchange. India was primarily a source of natural resources and manufactured products, whereas Southeast Asia and Ceylon provided wood, spices, and products from the sea.

The southern trade route, which covered Africa, was the source for grain, wood, oils, exotic animals, and slaves. From the first century A.D. onward, Rome imported at least 528,000 kl of grain per year from North Africa and Egypt (Casson 1954). By the fourth century A.D., Africa became the principal source of grain and oil for Rome (Fulford 1992).

Such trading patterns of the empire led to trade deficits with the East by the first century A.D. To cover the deficits, the Romans compensated with gold coins. Annual loss to India alone amounted to 55 million sesterces. It is estimated that annual trade deficits with India, China, and the Arabian Peninsula totaled 100 million sesterces combined (Miller 1969, Hopkins 1988). This amount is equivalent to about twenty-two thousand Roman pounds of gold. By the fourth century A.D., it has been estimated that two-thirds of the stocks of gold and half the silver of the empire had mostly been transferred eastward (Childe 1942).

Towns and Cities

The Roman world was "a world of cities" (Finley 1977, 305; Rostovtzeff 1957; Hopkins 1977). This means that urbanization was a key element in the overall formation and consolidation of the empire. Such a process meant the intensification of the natural system and social system relations. Despite the importance of the rural agrarian economy, the population in the countryside also lived in urban environments of villages and towns instead of on isolated farms. Such an urbanizing trend continued along a trajectory similar to the world of classical Greece that preceded the rise of the Roman Empire. From republic to empire, urbanization continued uninterrupted, spurred on in the later period of "High Empire" (first two centuries A.D.) by the increase in the volume of trade (Chew 2001, 81).

What is remarkable to note is that, according to Hopkins (1977), this level of Roman urbanization was not surpassed until a millennium later.

The firming up of the territorial lines of the empire directed further the urbanization process. Provincial centers came to be collection points of trade, and what also emerged were towns surrounding Roman forts and emplacements. These urbanized areas also served trade beyond the boundaries of the empire. Urbanization along these lines was fostered further by the increase in the number of Roman officials and administrators who were involved in governance. Artisans, merchants, and other workers also swelled these communities.

The system transformation following the Bronze Age crisis that led to the emergence of the Greek polis was followed through by the Romans in the western part of the empire. An assemblage of city-states or *civitates* each surrounded by a dependent countryside was the basic political organizational unit that defined the empire, though in the eastern portion of the empire, there were other political arrangements that were leftovers from the period prior to the Roman conquest (Fischer 1961, Jones 1974, Hopkins 1977). Each city-state had its own council drawn from the *curiales* (middle class) of the town. The political apportionment via the city-state concept provided the basis for local tax collection and legal jurisdiction. In turn, this benefited Rome, for local elites were charged with enforcing Roman laws with the assistance of the Roman appointed administrators. As a source of tax revenues, each town and city contributed their individual shares. For example, in sixth century A.D., Edessa contributed about 16 kg of gold per year, and Egypt's Heracleopolis's annual contribution was nearly 363 kg of gold derived from the corn levies (Jones 1974). It seemed that agriculture, which was Heracleopolis's main emphasis, was more productive in terms of generating taxes than trade and industry, which was Edessa's focus. The latter was located on the trade route whereby silk and other goods from the Far East passed through from the Persian frontier at Nisibis to Antioch and the West.

Spatial designs of these towns and cities were along Roman lines where the larger cities and towns had their own theaters, stadiums, temples, gymnasia, and circuses (Frere 1967, Salway 1965, Frank 1927, Rostovtzeff 1957). They were like little Romes providing their residents with various amenities. What this meant was that taxation became the source for funding such initiatives. Assessments became unrealistic by the third century A.D., and this led to declines in the urbanized areas. However, before the third century A.D., the cities and towns of the frontier region in the West were vital economic centers with their links to trade and to Roman fortresses.

One of the most significant aspects of such an urbanization trajectory was the building of roads to facilitate communication in terms of moving the army as well as manufactured and other trading goods. The Roman military constantly expanded an extraordinary system of all-weather roads and constructed massive bridges across rivers and streams. Wagon roads were cut into impassable terrain. Seventeen roads pierced the Alps. According to some estimates, there were about 90,123 km of paved highways in the Roman Empire by the second century A.D., and this network of highways was supplemented by more than 321,870 km of secondary roads (Hopkins 1988). In addition to roads, the navy built river ports along the Danube and the Rhine and dredged the bank of some rivers to make them more navigable. Canals were also constructed to facilitate the flow of goods and soldiers. All these massive constructions meant that the face of the natural landscape was transformed drastically.

Where roads were constructed, towns emerged and the population moved to them. For example, the supply roads built along the Lower Rhine saw the villas emerging along with towns. Tongres, Bavay, Cassel, Tournai, and Thérouanne were such urban communities that grew and became collection points for the military and manufacturing centers producing tools and equipment (Mertens 1983). Some of the great cities of the Rhine-Danube region, such as Cologne, Coblenz, Mainz, Vienna, Belgrade, and Budapest, were founded from this type of origin.

The number of towns of the empire was high, indicating an urbanized environment. According to Hopkins (1977), there were nine hundred in the eastern provinces, over three hundred along the North African littoral excluding Egypt, and a similar number in Italy and Iberia. Sizewise they were of different scales. For example, Leptis Magna covered an area of 120 ha, Timgad was 50 ha, Thugga was 20 ha, Caerwent was 18 ha, London was 121 ha, New Carthage was 485 ha, Alexandria was 920 ha, and, finally, Rome (third century A.D.) was 1,238 ha.

The large urban enclaves that were built or developed following the Roman conquest were extensive and became competitive to Rome itself. Cities such as Alexandria, Antioch in Syria, Ephesus in Asia Minor, Carthage in Africa, and Lyons in Gaul were such urban environments. Behind these major cities are Pompeii, Puteoli, Ostia, Verona, and Aquileia in Italy; Tauromenium, Syracuse, and Panormus in Sicily; Massilia, Narbo, Arelate, Nemausus, Arausio, Augusta, Treverorum, Colonia Agrippinensis, Bonna, Moguntiacum, and Argentorate in Gaul and Germany; Londinium and Eboracum in England; Tarraco, Corduba, Hispalis, Italica, Emerita, and Asturica in Spain; Hadrumetum, Cirta, Hippo Regius, and Caesarea in Africa; Numidia and Mauretania; Cyrene in Cyrenaica; Tergeste and Pola in Histria; Salona in Dalmatia; Emona and Poetovio in Pannonia; Thessalonica in Macedonia; Athens, Corinth, and Rhodes in Greece; Smyrna, Pergamon, Sardis, and Miletus in Asia; Ancyra and Antiochia Pisidiae in Galatia; Pessinus and Aezani in Phrygia; Tarsus in

Cilicia; Nicaea and Nicomediain Bithynia; Cyzicus and Byzantium on the Sea of Marmora; Sinope on the Black Sea; Tyre, Sidon, and Aradus in Phoenicia; Heliopolis, Palmyra, Damascus, Philadelphia (Amman) and Gerasa in Syria; Seleuceia in Mesopotamia; Petra and Bostra in Arabia; and Jerusalem in Palestine (Rostovtzeff 1957).

The urbanization trajectory continued uninterrupted until the third century A.D., which suggests a period of social system expansion and complexity. As with past rhythms of the social system, disruptive changes began to occur at the social system levels about the third century A.D., which we will discuss in chapter 5.

NOTE

1. Regional pollen profiles of land use and deforestation and the distribution of human settlements suggest widespread ecological degradation from the twelfth century onward in Europe (Kristiansen 1998b, Chew 2001, Berglund 2003).

5

A Period of Darkness

Periodization of historical epochs has often been subjective and dependent on what the scholar wants to depict and examine. For most historians and archaeologists, the periodization has been based on a number of variables, such as societal complexity, political organization, and cultural development to economic forms of organization and production. Most often, the focus has been on the core political entity and defining the period as, for example, the Roman period or the Hellenistic period. Such broad temporal descriptive depiction does not offer us much understanding of the ecological, social, economic, and political environments. To get a sense of the direction of what is occurring on a regional or a world system basis, we need to be more analytical in our periodization by demarcating periods of stress that are punctuated with climate changes and ecological degradation within an established political-cultural complex such as the Roman Age.

In this sense, periods of Dark Ages over world history can be considered as chronological markers indicating moments of system stress at both the social and natural system levels. At the social system level, Randsborg (1991) attempts to periodize macrolevel social change for Europe and the Mediterranean during the first millennium A.D. by pinpointing the start of the third century A.D. as a "time of crisis and reorganization of the Roman Empire," and the fifth century A.D. as "the time of great migrations" and the collapse of the western Roman Empire. Such an effort gives us a sense of direction in terms of the social conditions of the times and suggests to us that starting from the third century A.D., Europe and the Mediterranean were experiencing structural changes, especially for the

Roman Empire, which at this point covered a large portion of the European/Mediterranean land mass. At the macrolevel, it seems that it was a prolonged crisis that spanned a number of centuries that finally ended by the tenth century A.D., albeit with some periods of efflorescence.

There have been widespread accounts of socioeconomic and political transformations and stress during this period; however, there has been no attempt to periodize, at the natural system level, the ecological stress that the system is encountering. There have been limited efforts to periodize climate changes occurring during this time (e.g., see Curry 1928; Lamb 1968, 1982a; Brown 2001; Randsborg 1991). This provides another opportunity to examine some of the structural changes that were occurring and compare this crisis of antiquity with the Bronze Age system crisis that we analyzed in chapter 3. What follows is an attempt to juxtapose climate changes and the ecological conditions at the natural system level with the ongoing socioeconomic and political transformations occurring during this period of darkness.

CLIMATIC CHANGES AND POLITICAL UPHEAVALS

As we have stated in chapter 3, climate changes such as reduced precipitation or temperature increases could affect socioeconomic activities particularly in the agricultural sphere, and especially so, in marginal areas. Besides this, the physical changes that are caused by humans, such as erosion because of intensive cultivation, and climate changes connected with the reduction of forest cover or agriculture would further have a significant impact on the landscape and the reproduction of the social system.

Just like the third millennium B.C., as depicted in chapter 3, there were climate shifts in Europe and the Mediterranean in the first millennium A.D. For the first two centuries after Christ, there were signs of higher humidity followed from the third century onward with relative dryness (Briffa 1999, Randsborg 1991, Lamb 1981, Allen et al. 1996). This was to change after A.D. 400 with relative precipitation going up until A.D. 500 and then followed with increasing drought from A.D. 500 until the end of the millennium.

During this period in Africa, there was relative aridity from about 800 B.C. to A.D. 400 and between A.D. 600 to 1250 with regular rainfall in the fourth and fifth centuries (Veschuren 2004). The water levels of the Nile were lowered from A.D. 600 to 850 (Robertshaw 2004). For Asia, specifically China, climate changes also occurred between A.D. 300/400 to 900. Abnormal drought conditions were observed between A.D. 400 and 700 (Needham 1959). There was a warm period between A.D. 1 and 240 followed by a cooling period between A.D. 240 and 600/900 (Bao et al. 2002, Ge et al. 2003). Others such as Tan and Liu (2003) and Brown (2001) have indicated of a warm period from A.D. 600 to 800. The aridity extended from the fourth to the sixth centuries A.D. (Brown 2001).

It is clear that there were climate changes occurring in Europe, the Mediterranean, and Africa, though the changes seemed to appear at different times. A warming trend started about the third century A.D. and was repeated in other parts of the world in a later period, for example, in Africa and China. Adding to such climate changes, Curry (1928) has even suggested that there was a regular succession of climatic cycles lasting approximately 640 years in duration, with about 300 years of increasing aridity. As a consequence of such climatic turbulence, a series of alternating periods of migration and consolidation in Europe and Asia can be traced from the fifth century onward (Teggart 1969). Gibbon (1966) in his major study on the decline of the Roman Empire had referred to the cold temperatures leading to frozen rivers such as the Rhine and the Danube that allowed barbarian (Germanic) armies to cross, enabling them thus to invade the western Roman Empire. These invasions generated disturbances and stress to the social system. The invasions were at times a drain on the Roman treasury, which had to fund war campaigns or to transfer tax collection rights to the Germanic tribes and/or buy them off with gold and silver, thus further crippling the Roman economy.

The start of the third century A.D. was a period of crisis throughout the Roman world, especially in the western part of the empire. Incursions increased in frequency, especially in the western portion of the empire after A.D. 259. On the eastern frontiers, the Goths were attacking the lower Danube, while the Persian kingdom under the Sassanids was creating unstable conditions in the East. In the West, the Franks were pressuring the frontier on the lower Rhine, and the Alamanni tribes during the A.D. 270s were raiding the frontier. By A.D. 330, the imperial capital of the empire was moved eastward to Byzantium and rechristened as "Constantinopolis" (see figure 5.1).

By A.D. 400, the Roman army in the West could no longer defend the frontier adequately, and the battle with the Visigoths clearly showed this. Such a defeat meant that Goths had invaded the northern empire, finally leading to the attack on Rome in A.D. 410. Eventually, through a set of compromises, the Goths settled in southwestern Gaul. Other Germanic tribes followed with the Swabians moving into northwestern Spain and the Vandals taking over western North Africa by A.D. 435. At the same time, the Roman army was also preoccupied with handling the Huns, who had left their pastoral lands due to arid conditions. This was the first wave of tribal incursions.

By A.D. 476, the various kingships of the Germanic tribes took over some of the Roman emperor's rights in the western portion of the empire. By A.D. 500, the Franks controlled northern Gaul, the Burgundians were

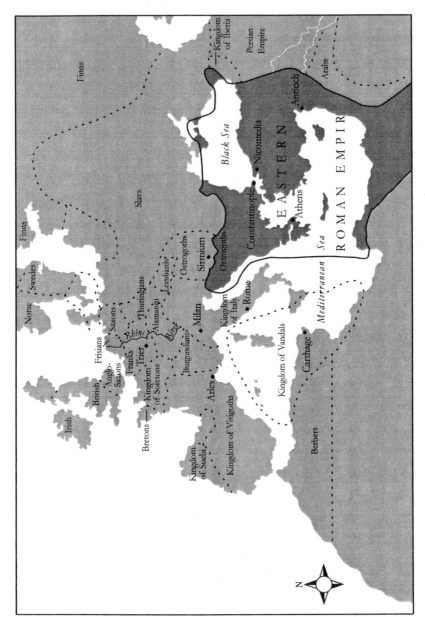

Figure 5.1. The Eastern Roman Empire

in eastern Gaul, and Spain was under the Visigoths. The Ostrogoths governed Italy and Dalmatia.

The above political situation did not last long as Justinian, the eastern Roman emperor, began to reclaim Africa, southern Spain, Italy, and Dalmatia during the A.D. 530s through several conflicts that did not end for some time. The wars occurred within a period of aridity especially about A.D. 535 to 538, probably caused by a volcanic eruption generating a dust veil leading to cold weather and dryness (Baillie 1994). Briffa (1999, 6) has also confirmed this as indicated by a pronounced decrease in oak growth.

The extent of impact was global in nature. Crops failed in Italy and southern Iraq; there was a drought in China, Japan, and Korea that led to famine. Mesoamerica and South America were also experiencing the changed weather pattern. Drought was prevalent over Eurasia, leading to migrations such as that of the Avars, who in turn put pressure on the eastern portion of the Roman Empire as well (e.g., see Keys 1999, Teggart 1969). The Avars migration formed the second wave of migratory flight that lasted from the A.D. 560s to 650s. In A.D. 566, Italy was reinvaded by warriors from Pannonia. At the same time, the Persians, who were being affected by the changed weather conditions, were waging war against the eastern Roman emperor (Keys 1999). The political upheavals were also evident in Britain whereby Anglo-Saxon supremacy was finally established. By A.D. 600, both sides of the Rhine and the Upper Danube were under the Franks. In short, by this time, the western portion of the Roman Empire no longer existed as a contiguous entity.

Besides forcing migrations, climate changes have the potential to create an environment for the transmission of diseases. Changing weather patterns can cause the outbreak of a disease such as the bubonic plague. Such occasions arose during the sixth century (McNeill 1976, Keys 1999, McCormick 2001). With climate changes such as excessive rainfall or a prolonged drought followed by rainfall, vegetation growth likely will increase. With either of the climate scenarios, the outcome is usually that more food becomes available for herbivorous animals (gerbils), insects, and rodents. This in turn leads to prodigious breeding leading to multiplication. Rodents are carriers of the plague bacterium. With the increase in the numbers of these animals as a consequence of a wider availability of food due to climate changes, a population explosion occurs. What this leads to is a need to widen the range for food foraging due to the population increase. Such wider foraging for food increases the potential of the rodents, carrying the plague bacterium to encounter other plague-free rodents leading to the latter being infected. The latter via the flea would then transmit the disease to humans.

For the sixth-century pandemic that hit Europe, it has been accepted that it was spread by the rats that were transported on ships sailing from either east African or Indian ports (McNeill 1976, Keys 1999). The evidence has suggested that one vector of the disease rolled northward up the Red Sea to Egypt, and in its wake wiped out some of the urban communities such as Rhapta and the ports of Opone, Essina, and Toniki. It struck Europe and the Roman Empire about A.D. 539. Besides the plague, smallpox caused a diminution of the population of the Roman Empire. The occurrence of diseases over time and the extent of their geographic impact can be found in table 5.1.

In terms of population losses, these plague pandemics had severe mortality rates. According to Ruddiman (2003), the major plague pandemic that occurred in the sixth century A.D. saw the loss of 25 percent of the population in Europe and North Africa. These deaths had severe consequences for the Roman Empire (Millar 1981). Not only was the tax base reduced, but recruitment levels for the legions were also impacted. Consequently, the imperial government increased the rate of taxation to ensure that its financial obligations could be met. However, such circumstances led to financial difficulties for the Roman treasury and, in some instances, led to the destabilization of the military. It is estimated that for the period A.D. 541 to 602, the population of the empire shrunk by 33 percent and its overall gross national product (GNP) was reduced by 15 percent (Keys 1999). Toward the beginning of the seventh century A.D., over 30 million gold solidi of the economy were lost due to the plague. Besides this, urban markets were destroyed because of the spread of the plague, and thus the commercial activities of the Roman Empire were curtailed.

The population losses due to diseases also impacted on the available labor for agricultural production, especially when the availability of slaves was becoming scarcer and scarcer from the absence of Roman territorial expansions that in the past had provided a supply of slaves (Jones 1966, Hughes 1975, Drummond and Nelson 1994).

It should also be realized that climate changes had great consequences for agricultural production. Because agricultural production accounted for some 60 percent of the Roman Empire's GNP, losses in production levels

Table 5.1.   Disease Pandemics in the First Millennium A.D.

Year	Region	Disease	Intensity
164–189	Roman Empire	Smallpox	Regional Epidemic
250–539	Roman Empire	Bubonic Plague	Regional Epidemic
540–542	Med/Europe	Bubonic Plague	Pandemic
540–590	Med/Europe/Africa	Bubonic Plague	Pandemic
664	Europe	Bubonic Plague	Regional Epidemic
680	Med/Europe	Bubonic Plague	Regional Epidemic
746–748	Eastern Med	Bubonic Plague	Local Epidemic

Source: Based on data from Ruddiman (2003, 281).

had severe consequences (MacMullen 1997). To this extent, Huntington's (1917a, 1924) arguments on climate changes impacting the agricultural production of the Roman Empire and consequently the state of the Roman Empire can be introduced here. The lack of rain led to poor crop harvests as well as scanty pasture for pastoralists. What followed were abandoned fields. According to Huntington (1917a, 196), "Thus by A.D. 395 'the abandoned fields of Campania alone amounted to something over 528,000 jugera.'" Not only do these changes in climate affect the Roman Empire, according to Huntington (1924), but the arid conditions also impacted the barbarian tribes in terms of suitable pastures for their animals. As a result, migrations were the order of the day. The tendency thus was to invade the seemingly more prosperous Roman Empire. Or as Drummond and Nelson (1994, 12) put it: "The time would come in the early fifth century when the Germans . . . would cross the frontier to take by force those things they had come to appreciate over the centuries." The Germanic tribes were not the only ones affected by these weather conditions; the tribes in Central Asia suffered as well. In all, for the first millennium A.D., climate changes seem to have had consequences for the reproduction of the social system via the various stresses that emerged affecting human activities.

ECOLOGICAL DISRUPTIONS

In *World Ecological Degradation,* I stated in detail the level of ecological degradation that the Roman Empire generated. In that study, the aim was to provide the scope and extent of the ecological damage caused by the Roman Empire so as to primarily alert the reader to the fact that extensive ecological degradation is "as old as the hills," and not a feature only of the late twentieth century. What was not discussed fully were the various ecological degradative trends and processes occurring during the first millennium A.D. that were anthropogenic in origin and that resulted in generating reproductive issues for the Roman Empire, especially its western portion during the Dark Ages.

Several studies have indicated the failure of the Roman Empire to adapt harmoniously with its environment (e.g., see Hughes 1975, 2001; Chew 2001).

The trend of the Romans' actions affecting the environment over the centuries was destructive. They exploited renewable resources faster than was sustainable, and consumed nonrenewable resources as rapidly as they could. They failed to adapt their economy to the environment in sustainable ways and placed an insupportable demand on the natural resources available to them. Thus they failed to maintain the balance with nature that is necessary to the long-term prosperity of a human community. They depleted the lands they ruled, and in so doing undermined their own ability to survive. Environmental changes as a result of human activities must be judged to be one of the causes of the decline and fall of the Roman Empire. (Hughes 2001, 77)

One such primary act is deforestation (Randsborg 1991, Behre et al. 1996). This attitude to the forest is summarized best when the Romans, for example, referred to Germany as a great forest, and it is to Germany that Rome looks to for its forest needs in the later period of the Roman Empire after it had exhausted the forests of its immediate surroundings in Italy. This heavy demand for wood can be realized in the number of structures that have been excavated in the western part of the Roman Empire. As Drummond and Nelson (1994, 116) put it, "a plank was seldom used where a beam would serve the same purpose."[1]

Besides the army, the Roman navy also used an extensive amount of wood especially from the North African coast. The scale of wood consumption can be seen, for example, during Emperor Hadrian's rule. For frontier building, a total of two-and-a-half million trees were felled. Such a scale of deforestation was also matched by the need to remove the forest to protect the legions on the march. A defensive rampart enclosure of about 610 by 915 m would be deforested for three legions when it halted its march and camped (Dornborg 1992). This use of wood is just the tip of the iceberg. Urbanization needs and forest removal for agricultural lands were the other two main anthropogenic acts of deforestation undertaken by the Romans, and this was explicated in *World Ecological Degradation*.

Table 3.2 (see appendices 1 and 2 for specific pollen profiles for each area) provides details of deforestation in various parts of Europe and the Mediterranean through pollen analysis. In Belgium, Germany, France, Hungary, Poland, Byelorussia, Greece, Italy, Spain, Syria, and Turkey—all parts of the Roman Empire—we find deforestation from about the fourth century A.D. onward (in some instances, such as Germany, from the third century onward) until the tenth century in most cases, and in others, even longer (Lazarova 1995, van Zeist et al. 1980, Allen et al. 1996, Randsborg 1991). Brown (2001), writing about the Dark Ages occurring between A.D. 300 and 900, has noted such deforestation levels in northwestern Europe as a whole. In most cases also, as we have indicated in chapter 3, deforestation has been occurring since the third millennium B.C., and in particular, ethnographic studies of human settlement in southern Germany have clearly shown the deforestation patterns (Jacomet 1990, Rosch 1990, Behre et al. 1996). Deforestation seems to have gone beyond the Roman Empire and extended to the northern peripheries such as Sweden, Norway, Latvia, and Finland. To the eastern peripheries, we find deforestation in the Ukraine and Russia. This lengthy period of arboreal pollen drops coincided with the Dark Age periodization defined by social historians. The anthropogenic removal of the forests is confirmed by the rise in ruderal species pollen count such as *Plantago lanceolata* that grows following deforestation (see table 3.1 and appendix 2).

Appendix 3 outlines the percentages of arboreal pollen to nonarboreal pollen and details the deforestation in terms of the lower percentage of trees to grasses, weeds, and such, for Germany (Lake Steisslingen, Ahlenmoor); Switzerland (Lobsigensee); France (Le Marais St. Boetien); Bulgaria (Besbog 2, Mir Girvan); Hungary (Lake Balaton SW); Poland (Bledowo Lake, Puscizna Rekowianska, Kluki); Byelorussia (Dolgoe, Osvea); Ukraine (Kardashinski Swamp, Starniki, Stoyanov 2, Ilvano-Frankovskoye, Dovjok Swamp); Sweden (Ageröds Mosse, Kansjon); Norway (Grasvatn); Latvia (Rudushskoe Lake); Greenland (Lake 31); Finland (Kirkkosaari, Mukkavaara, Hirvilampi); Greece (Khimaditis 1 B); Italy (Selle Di Carnino); Spain (Saldropo, Sanabria Marsh, Lago de Ajo, Laguna de la Roya); Syria (Ghab); and Turkey (Köycegiz Gölü, Beyshir Gölü).

It should also be noted that deforestation is not necessarily the dominant feature during the Dark Ages, for there are occasions when reforestation did recur during Dark Age periods due to decreased socioeconomic activities as we have indicated in chapters 2 and 3 during the Bronze Age. We can also see such reforestation in the rise of arboreal pollen count as indicated in appendix 1. According to Kempter et al. (1997), this occurred during the Dark Ages for areas such as southern Bavaria, the central Massif, and the Eifel. Appendix 3 outlines specific areas of the world system where reforestation occurred following deforestation during this period when there were increases in arboreal pollen percentages in proportion to nonarboreal pollen. It occurred in the following areas: Belgium (Moerzeke); Germany (Lake Steisslingen, Ahlenmoor); France (Le Marais St. Boetien); Ireland (Arts Lough); Bulgaria (Besbog 2); Hungary (Lake Balaton SW); Poland (Bledowo Lake, Puscizna Rekowianska); Byelorussia (Dolgoe); Ukraine (Kardashinski Swamp, Ilvano-Frankovskoye, Dovjok Swamp); Sweden (Ageröds Mosse, Kansjon); Norway (Grasvatn); Latvia (Rudushskoe Lake); Greenland (Lake 31); Finland (Kirkkosaari, Hirvilampi); Greece (Edessa, Khimaditis 1 B); Italy (Selle di Carnino, Saldropo, Lago de Ajo); Spain (Laguna de la Roya); Syria (Ghab); and Turkey (Köycegiz Gölü, Beysehir Gölü). This further suggests that the vulnerability of the landscape during certain periods, and in different geographic locations, could continue to sustain socioeconomic reproduction, though perhaps at a lowered level than before the onset of the Dark Ages. What this also implies is that recovery in terms of reforestation seems to occur after a certain period when Dark Age conditions reduced the level of socioeconomic activity and hence the overall impact on the landscape. We see this from the rising percentages of arboreal pollen to nonarboreal pollen over the period of the Dark Age of Antiquity. We assume that ecological recovery resumes after Nature has the time to rest, that is, after less intensive draw-down of the natural resources by the social system processes.

One of the major outcomes of anthropogenically induced deforestation is soil erosion and degradation. This phenomenon has been argued as one of the stresses that caused reproduction difficulties for the Roman Empire (Hughes 1975, 2001; Hughes and Thirgood 1982; Chew 2001; Jones 1959b, 1974). Not all social historians share this view (e.g., see Rostovtzeff 1957). However, the titanium count found in soils of the central Massif, the Black Forest, southern Bavaria, the Hohe Venn, and the Eifel has indicated massive soil erosion in these areas during the Dark Age period (fourth to fifth centuries A.D.) where there was Roman occupation (Kempter et al. 1997). Even during the Roman Republican period, prior to this, there was soil erosion and exhaustion. Later on, the soils of Sicily, Sardinia, Spain, Gaul, Greece, and Africa, according to Abbott and Johnson (1968), were exhausted due to erosion or intensive cultivation without replenishment. Vladimir Simkhovitch (1916) has suggested that deforestation is one of the main causes of the calamity of soil exhaustion. This has also been supported in other studies (e.g., see Abbott and Johnson 1968, Hughes 2001) in which deforestation played a large part in destroying agricultural lands. *World Ecological Degradation* discusses how this happened.

In all, there are striking parallels in terms of ecological stress and climate changes during this period of the first millennium A.D. with what happened in world history during the late Bronze Age. What were the socioeconomic life and conditions like during this Dark Age of Antiquity? We turn to this next.

SOCIOECONOMIC LIFE AND CONDITIONS DURING THE DARK AGES

At the social system level, Dark Ages are viewed by most scholars as periods of regression or reversal. This assessment is based on the expectation of continuous socioeconomic growth and expansion as social systems evolve. Instead of conceptualizing along such lines, we can look at these periods as structural moments of social and natural systems rebalancing, and perhaps even as structural adaptation/transformation following the evolutionary trajectory of the social system in question as we have theoretically delineated in chapter 1. Clearly, in my view this was the case for the social system in Europe and the Mediterranean starting from the late third century A.D. onward.

The social world at the end of the third millennium in Europe and the Mediterranean was one that was quite urbanized in the core areas of most of the provinces of the empire. As we have stated previously, throughout the empire "mini Romes" were being reproduced with their majestic public buildings, coliseums, amphitheaters, temples, and aqueducts (Duncan-Jones 1990). Local aristocracies were in place, imbued with Roman values governing the provinces on behalf of Roman interests and their own. As Duncan-Jones (1990, 159) has so vividly stated, "the rites of urban life meant ceremonies, shows, handouts and new public buildings." The city-state political setup with municipalities was followed as much as possible in the western portion of the empire and in the east as well, though the latter had an established political complex by the time of Roman arrival. Instead, the Romans either supplanted or superimposed the Roman political arrangement or gave local municipalities a relative level of autonomy. Such social and political order formed the local senates in the municipalities and city-states, and these local elites paid for the costs of the public buildings and local administration through taxes.

By the third millennium A.D., taxes were raised to finance the needs of the empire, such as funding civil and foreign wars, and when agricultural production was reduced, it fell on the municipalities to meet the increased burden. This caused local aristocracies to suffer losses in their fortunes and statuses to meet the tax burden. We find evidence of increasing attempts to seek exemptions from public office by the local elites through either petitions or evasions. Some even fled from their cities to escape from their obligations. Furthermore, in such drastic environments, peasants deserted their lands, and local leading families were reduced in number. We interpret this to be the beginning of a less stratified society; though the ultrarich of Rome, the aristocracy, continued.

Such a depressive economic environment was coupled with high prices. As a result, inflation followed fueled by governmental expenses. With the existing silver and gold mines in the provinces producing at maximum capacity, and intensified to near exhaustion in terms of yield with minimal attempt to seek new sources, the easiest route was to debase the coinage (Abbott and Johnson 1968). At A.D. 54, during the reign of Nero, the silver content in Roman coinage was about 91.8 percent. By the time of Septimius Severus's reign (A.D. 193 to 211), it had reached 58.3 percent in terms of silver content (Bolin 1958). There were attempts by subsequent emperors such as Diocletian (A.D. 284 to 305) to reform the debasing of Roman coinage in an attempt at price control. It proved fruitless in the long run.

Such an economic environment with political uncertainties due to short reigns of Roman emperors was further exacerbated by tribal incursions that occurred in the western part of the Roman Empire. For the former, over the course of three hundred years, there were a total of sixty Roman emperors and some reigned for as little as one to two years. The most turbulent period of political instability was during the third century A.D., which had a total of twenty-eight emperors.

Besides political turmoil, social conditions were stark for the urban poor. Slum conditions existed in the urban areas. The working poor were on the edge of starvation and often took advantage of the free or subsidized handouts in grain that were provided. The peasants in the countryside were no better off than their urban counterparts were. Increasing taxation to meet state budget needs meant an inordinate amount of taxes to be paid by these tenant or free farmers. The land tax reached over one-third of gross harvest by the time of the rule of Emperor Justinian in the sixth century in the West and even more in the East. In Egypt, for example, it was half the harvest (Jones 1959, 1974). They lived a laborious life, existing for the most part at the subsistence level. Unable to accumulate surplus, most often, they relied on the large landowners for aid. Those that owned their land were in constant danger of losing their holdings when crop failures due to climate changes made it impossible for them to meet their expenses or pay their taxes. This led to the transformation of these peasants to tenant farmers. Marginal lands were taken out of production, and those in distress sought employment in the cities or became brigands. By the sixth century A.D., the life conditions of these farmers dropped to desperate levels, and they sank to the status of serfs (Rostovtzeff 1957; Jones 1959, 1974). Instead of being free farmers, their status was reverted to that of a serf-type relationship with the landlords, who in most cases were absentee ones, therefore tying them further to the land (Childe 1942). Being further committed to the farm, the free peasants, who in the past were a constant source of recruits for the Roman legion or auxiliaries, were no longer in a position to meet the recruitment needs. This forced the legion to settle for tribal (barbarian) communities for its recruitment sources.

After A.D. 400, German officers began to assume positions of power in the military following a major influx of Germans into the western provinces of the empire. During Theodosius I's reign (A.D. 379 to 395), the Roman legion suffered from a shortage of recruits. The employment of tribal recruits, who were mostly from the Goths, Huns, Alans, Franks, and Alamanni, satisfied these shortfalls.

By the fourth century A.D. we also witnessed the emergence of a new stratum of Christian clergy. As a social group, it sought material benefits from the government through endowments and political support. This group representing the church was adept at court politics and was a social force within the Roman political economy. Later on, following the decline of the Roman Empire in the West in the latter part of the fifth century, the monastery replaced the urban community or city as the center of socioeconomic life. This decline followed the splitting of the empire into two empires following the death of Theodosius I in A.D. 395.

The eastern portion of the Roman Empire fared much better. As Jones (1959) has stated, the decline of the western part of the Roman Empire was not followed by the eastern portion; the latter continued for another thousand years. The eastern portion suffered from fewer incursions from barbarians and had a larger and established resource base to rely on. Its middle class staffed the administrative branch of governance, and the tax returns provided a higher portion to the treasury than what was received in the West. However, from the third century to the sixth/seventh centuries, there were signs of socioeconomic decline (Rostovtseff 1930).

Deurbanization and Population Decreases

Deurbanization became a trend that was very evident (Wells 1999). In Roman Europe, urban centers declined in size, and there was an end to building programs, which caused rural settlements to return to patterns of pre–Iron Age. Settlements in rural Italy were marked by a further decline from the third century onward (Randsborg 1991). Theaters, public baths, aqueducts, and all city life decayed (Katz 1961). Villas that were the centers of socioeconomic life were not being built in Italy or the provinces. Old buildings were being reused. For example, utilizing the building of public works in Italy as a proxy, we find that during the Republican period there were 317 buildings, such as temples, aqueducts, basilicas, baths, and theaters, being constructed. This number increased to 347 by the first century A.D. However, by the second century A.D., the decrease had started to show. The total number of buildings constructed was 192. By the third century, the total had dwindled to 58 only to decrease further to 41 buildings by the fifth century A.D.

In the western provinces of the empire, deurbanization and decay were most prominent during the fifth and sixth centuries (Drummond and Nelson 1994). For the Netherlands, urbanization was at a high level until the last half of the third century A.D., and following this it went into a dramatic decline. In lower Saxony, the number of settlements went down starting about A.D. 200 and never reached the heights achieved at A.D. 100 (Randsborg 1991). In the Cologne area, the height of urbanization occurred in the last half of the second century, and from the third century onward, decline followed and was the most drastic between A.D. 400 and 500. In Gaul, the second and third centuries were periods of villa building with decline starting about the beginning of the fourth century. This was also repeated in the Alsace-Lorraine region and west of Mainz. However, in Britain, villa settlement increased in the fourth century but declined at the start of the fifth century A.D., which is the time when the imperial military system started to decline. In southeastern Europe, villa complexes vanished as well by A.D. 400. In northwestern Europe, a large number of towns ceased to exist after A.D. 400, and in the Balkans, there were signs of recession and decay.

In North Africa, deurbanization also occurred starting from the third century to the period of the Islamic conquest. The construction of public works reached a height of 272 buildings by the second century A.D. followed with decreases to 234 buildings by the third century and to 82 buildings by the fifth century. The same pattern was also repeated for utility structures such as baths, amphitheaters, and basilicas. From its height of thirty-six buildings in the third century, the number dwindled to eight by the fifth century. In Boeotia, Greece, the same trend was also encountered with an upward surge until the early Roman period of A.D. 250 and trending downward from A.D. 250 until 900. The same trend was also followed in Argolis. In the Near East, this was also the case, with some minor differences. Instead of a decrease in the fourth century, there was a peak in urbanization during this period and one in the sixth century, but by the seventh century decline followed. The number of church buildings in Palestine also followed the same trend. If we move further east, in the Susa region of southwestern Persia, we find as well rapid expansion until A.D. 250, with a dramatic decline after this.

Along with deurbanization, we also witnessed population reduction during this period of decline (Wolfram 1990). As we know, diseases such as plague and small pox were widespread and this caused a large number of deaths in urban centers. Agricultural harvest failures because of climate changes caused famine and starvation among the poor and the lower classes. Political unrest through ever-occurring civil wars and tribal invasions also saw a high number of deaths and suffering. Losses were evident everywhere.

Population decreases can be seen, for example, in the case of the city of Rome. Between the first century B.C. and A.D. 367, Rome had a population of a million persons. By A.D. 452, following the crisis of the third century, its population was reduced to about 400,000 persons (Wolfram 1990). In less than a century, Rome's population was reduced by more than half. By the end of the tenth century A.D., the population of Rome was reduced to about 30,000 persons (see figure 5.2). Constantinople also suffered the same fate though its decrease happened much later (Treadgold 1997). About A.D. 540, it had a population of 345,000 only to be reduced by the plague of A.D. 542. By A.D. 780, along with the economic crisis, its overall population was less than 100,000.

Russell (1971) in an overview of the population trends for Europe from A.D. 500 onward has commented that prior to the beginning of A.D. 500, the two halves of the Roman Empire seemed to have experienced a sharp demographic difference. The West suffered severe losses, and climate changes due to warming seemed to have benefited the North and less so the South. About A.D. 500 for over fifty years, there was a slow rise in population level that followed attempts by the Emperor Justinian to reha-

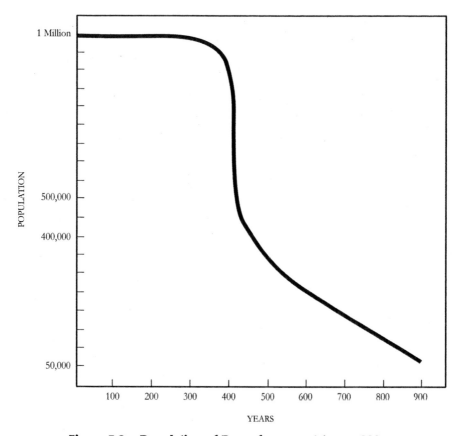

Figure 5.2. Population of Rome from A.D. 1 to A.D. 900

bilitate the empire. However, this advance had rolled back by the mid A.D. 500s, when the series of epidemics of the plague covered parts of urban Europe (see previous section). This loss further affected the empire and it was not until A.D. 650 to 700 that some growth in population returned. The Byzantine and Carolingian empires benefited from this demographic increase.

Overall, the decrease in population in Europe and the Mediterranean was noticeable (Millar 1981). The reduction did not follow a uniform trend from A.D. 300 onward until 900. During certain periods, there were spurts of renewed growth in some regions as a consequence of more moderate temperature changes returning as well as the decline in mortality from diseases.

Elsewhere beyond Europe, in Egypt, for example, the demographic trend follows the same tendency (Cohen 1995). There was an increase from A.D. 250 to 500. After this, the population level dropped until the early

Table 5.2. World Population Estimates, 400 B.C.–A.D. 1000 (in thousands)

	−400	−200	100	200	400	500	600	700	800	900	1000
China	25	45	70	60	25	32	49	44	56	48	56
India, Pakistan	30	55	46	45	32	33	37	50	43	38	40
Japan	1	1	2	2	4	5	5	4	4	4	4
Rest of Asia	3	4	5	5	7	8	11	12	14	16	19
Europe	23	26	35	42	36	29	22	22	25	28	30
Former USSR	13	14	12	13	12	11	10	10	11	12	13
North Africa	10	14	14	16	13	11	7	6	9	8	9
Rest of Africa	7	9	12	14	18	20	17	15	16	20	30
North America	1	1	1	1	2	2	2	2	2	2	2
C/S America	5	6	8	8	9	11	12	13	13	13	14
Oceania	1	1	1	1	1	1	1	1	1	1	1
Total	162	231	255	256	206	206	206	207	224	226	254

Source: Based on data from Biraben (1980).

A.D. 600s when slight growth returned. However, the decrease started again from A.D. 641 and continued until A.D. 719. Following this, growth returned but did not reach the population level of A.D. 641 until 1000.

If we examine table 5.2, most of the areas of the world that are economically connected via trade and political relations suffered population losses between A.D. 300 and 1000. Europe and North Africa, of which the Roman Empire encompassed a significant amount of the land mass, suffered losses from the A.D. 200s until 1100, and most of the severe losses started about A.D. 500. Clearly, this pattern repeats the population declines we witnessed in the late Bronze Age crisis as well. Figure 5.3 shows the trend line of world population increases and decreases from 1600 B.C. to A.D. 2000. If we follow this trend closely, there were two periods of reduction: a period during the late Bronze age, and the other during the crisis of antiquity starting in the third century A.D.

Invasions and Political Changes

The broad trends exhibiting the socioeconomic changes (outlined above) occurring from the third century onward need to be elaborated at the level of the provinces in the western portion of the Roman Empire if we are to understand the structural changes that were occurring. By the beginning of the sixth century A.D., the Germanic and other migratory tribes were firmly established in the lands of the western Roman Empire when Romulus Augustulus lost his throne in A.D. 476. The Burgundians were in southeastern Gaul, the Visigoths in southwestern Gaul and Spain, the Vandals in Africa, the Franks in northern Gaul, and the Ostrogoths in Italy (Downey 1969). We increasingly find evidence that the blending of two cultural groups with Germanic kingdoms was being established in

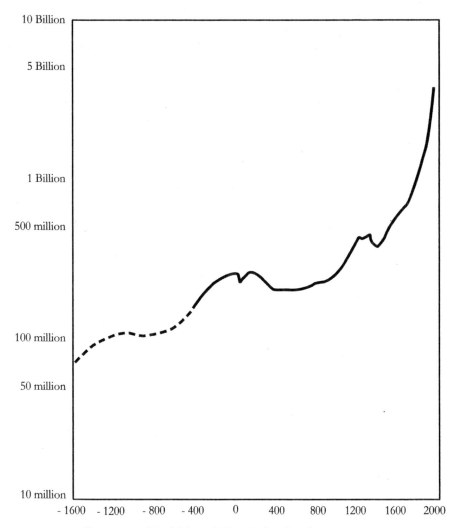

Figure 5.3.   World Population Estimates since 1600 B.C.
Source: **Biraben 1980.**

the West (Goffart 1980, Randers-Pehrson 1983, Wells 1999). The invaders retained the structure of the Roman civil administration and adopted Roman law (Goffart 1980, Downey 1969). However, trade and commerce continued to slide, and the urban environments decayed. Abandonment of cities was quite common while others survived only as civil and ecclesiastical centers (Katz 1961). Agriculture, however, started to recover, as the tribal invaders started to settle on pastoral lands, and the large estates that were owned by Romans saw ownerships transferred to the invaders (Goffart 1980, Katz 1961, Wolfram 1990). In some cases, rich Roman families changed their names to fit in with the new power structure. The eastern portion of the Roman Empire escaped from such invasions and continued from the fifth to the fifteenth centuries. Emperor Justinian attempted to recover the western portion of the empire from the Adriatic to the West starting about A.D. 533 with the battle for Africa under the Vandals. However, Gaul under the Franks, Spain under the Visigoths, and Britain remained firmly under the invaders' control.

With the Germanic kingdoms firmly established by the sixth century A.D., the eastern Roman Empire, which was not under as much or as severe duress from invasive tribes as the Western part of the empire was, started to face threats first from Persia and later from the powerful Muslim caliphates with their centers in Baghdad, Cairo, and Cordova. In the A.D. 630s, Muslim armies conquered the southern Mediterranean basin, the Levant, and Mesopotamia. By the latter half of the seventh century, they had conquered Egypt and North Africa. These conquests further eroded Roman influence. Spain fell to the Muslim armies in the eighth century and by this time with some difficulty; the eastern Roman Empire, or Byzantine Empire, managed to retain control of the Anatolian plateau, the Greek coastlands, and some parts of southern Italy (Treadgold 1997).

By A.D. 718, the eastern Roman Empire was largely diminished, and by A.D. 763, the Abbasids were in control of Baghdad. With debasements and inflation, the money economy had largely collapsed. Building construction stopped in the Roman/Byzantine Empire (Treadgold 1997). A process of simplification began to take place to meet the fiscal and economic crisis (Haldon 1990, Treadgold 1997). Furthermore, in the late sixth century, there was a rapid simplification of culture that obliterated the boundary between the aristocratic and popular culture (P. Brown 1971). In the West, the secular elite totally disappeared. The Byzantine fiscal administration underwent a simplification process (Haldon 1990, Tainter 2000).

The ninth century witnessed a general collapse of interregional contacts and social systems (Randsborg 1991). The Abbasids in Mesopotamia suffered an almost total collapse, and Islamic trade with China was curtailed. In the west, the Carolingian era suffered political setbacks with the division of the realm into several parts. Structural transformations continued to take place in the Carolingian kingdoms, and this world continued to be shaped by appearances of more monasteries, royal centers, and towns.

Cultural and Intellectual Patterns

Despite the macrolevel trends of decay and distress during this Dark Age period, cultural and intellectual patterns continued. In other words, it was not completely barren of intellectual activity (Katz 1961, Barnes 1965).

Between the sixth and eighth centuries, the cultural regression was more marked, especially in Gaul and in Germany (Barnes 1965). In the East, it was between A.D. 610 and 780 (Treadgold 1997). It was a period of decline prior to intellectual revival of the twelfth century and the initial stages of the rise of Moslem science and scholarship. Devoid of outstanding writers and painters, there were at least competent writers and artists, though the masses lost all semblance of literacy. Schools continued based mostly on Greek and Latin curricula and were taught by the clergy. The main western educational institutions were catechetical, monastic, and Episcopal schools.

Science was on the decline, and accordingly, superstition and pseudo-science were on the rise as classical thought and scholarship were gradually obliterated (Katz 1961). Natural science knowledge was dependent on compilations of less competent classical scientists or upon compilations of compilations (Barnes 1965). Medical knowledge emanated from fragmentary translations of the treatises of Hippocrates and the practice of medicine was chiefly in the hands of monks. Astronomy was fused with astrology, magic, and mysticism. The important scientific aspects of astronomy were placed in the service of church rites and festivals. Physics was scarcely studied at all, and chemistry was relegated to a description of stones and minerals with their magical qualities (Barnes 1965). Biology was used to emphasize scriptural lessons and shaped to support the teachings of the church. The shift away from paganism to Christianity was beginning to show. Intellectuals were pursuing the ideals of Neo-Platonism. Some of the main scholars of the Dark Ages were Bede, Alcuin, Servatus Lupus of Ferrières, Gerbert of Aurillac, and Faubert of Chartres (Barnes 1965).

In art, the works produced during the period lacked originality, realism, and balance. It was more imitative and conventional (Katz 1961). As the Christian Church began to emerge as a major force, it needed places of worship worthy of the religion, thus generating a need for statues, paintings, and elaborate mosaics. Instead of copying Roman temples, the architects for the church copied the Roman basilica that was used for law courts and other public businesses. Besides this, with the sociocultural decline, we also find the flourishing of local cultural designs. For example, in Gaul nonclassical styles appear on pottery and other decorations (Millar 1981). Representations of local cultural objects emerged and inscriptions using local languages came into being. In Phrygia, inscriptions in local language have been found. Christian literature written in Syriac was evident in Edessa, and in Egypt, the first Christian works in Coptic were produced. In all, there seemed to be the abandonment of the traditional classical art form. However, what was produced was of a lower technical standard.

In western Europe with the absence of strong government following
the demise of the western Roman Empire, the church stepped into the
void. It started to undertake civic functions, and as the municipal gov-
ernments decayed, the political power of religious leaders, such as the
bishops, grew. The Germanic invaders by this time had been converted
to Christianity. The church started to alleviate the distress of the poor and
thus began to have an increasing voice in civic affairs. One important dimension of this religious influence is the rise of the monastic movement
in which the monasteries later became influential centers of learning and
economy. From its original home in the East, in Egypt, this movement
became quite a force in the West as its teachings and philosophy began
to take hold. According to Bergmann (1985), the early monks, frustrated
with urbanized life and the declining economy, rejected the social order
and opted for the wilderness. In Egypt, it was the desert oasis. It was a
life of complete autarky and self-sufficiency—living in unity with Nature. Unmodified Nature was sought and exploitation of Nature was
disdained. Monastic life became dominant in the West via St. Benedict
of Nursia, whereby Benedictine monasteries were established in numerous places all over the Roman Empire. Each Benedictine monastery was
self-sufficient with its own lands capable of sustaining life without any
reliance on the surrounding society (Tierney and Painter 1992, Munro and
Sontag 1928, Cantor 1993).

Where a monastery was placed, fields were normally reclaimed, and
the wilderness was turned into an agricultural estate. Consequently, peasants came to live close to the monasteries and trade grew around it with
the establishment of a town. The monasteries also became places of peace
and an escape from temptation and worldly pursuits. They were also a
place for an ordered life of labor. All classes of people were included in
monastic life from the rich and the poor to the educated and the illiterate
(Cantor 1993). The monks maintained and improved old techniques of agriculture and used these ideas to teach the tribal invaders who had settled
in the West. The monasteries also founded libraries and copied classical
and other texts. Thus they were responsible for preserving the literature
during the Dark Ages. To this extent, in the West, the monastery replaced
the functions of the city, which during the Dark Ages had undergone
decay and lost its prominence as a focal point of commerce and civic administration. The monasteries fit the tendency of localism because of their
emphasis on efficiency and self-perpetuating nature and thus fulfilled
educational, economic, political, and religious functions. From the sixth
to the twelfth centuries, the monks were key factors in the education and
organization of Dark Age society of western Europe.

By the tenth century A.D., it seemed that a reurbanization process and
recovery was under way. Archaeological finds and sites in western Eu-

rope indicate that stability and social continuity were in place from this period onward. In Britain, the image is one of economic development and resource renewal as indicated by large farmsteads built of timber. Population levels began to recover in most regions to levels prior to the Dark Age period that started in the third century. Such was the state of structural transformations of the Roman Empire and the Mediterranean during this period of darkness.

Elsewhere, Dark Age conditions also prevailed. To the east, in China, deteriorating conditions appeared from the end of the Han Dynasty (A.D. 220) until the emergence of the Tang Dynasty (A.D. 618). Political disorder dominated the political landscape following the end of the Han Dynasty. Fragmentation occurred leading to three kingdoms—Wei, Shu Han, and Wu—with continuous wars lasting for about four centuries. Coupled with changing climate conditions followed by drought and famine, socioeconomic activities were curtailed. Trade with Japan and Korea was reduced and trade linkages were disrupted. With such disruptions, we find that the pottery in Japan and Korea taking a different style from what it was prior to the Dark Ages (Sarabia 2004). Before the arrival of socioeconomic and ecological distress, the pottery in these areas either was imported from China or copied the Chinese styles. Stressed ecological resources even led to unglazed pottery being manufactured (Honey 1948).

How did the periphery fare during this Dark Age period? The crisis was far-ranging as well in terms of its impact. The peripheral areas, especially northern Europe, also underwent structural changes because of its trading and sociocultural linkages with the other parts of Europe and the Mediterranean. We discuss this next.

THE NORTHERN PERIPHERY

Peripheral transformations followed Roman economic growth from first century A.D. onward (Randsborg 1991, Berglund 1969). In northern Germany and Scandinavia, we find evidence of this growth in the grave inventories containing consumer items such as Roman weapons and jewelry such as neck, arm, and finger rings. By the late Roman Iron Age (A.D. 200), we find a massive concentration of wealth in the graves ranging from Roman glass to gold jewelry (Hedeager 1992, Randsborg 1991). Hedeager (1992), having made a comprehensive survey of grave inventories for Denmark from early pre-Roman period Iron Age (500 B.C.–A.D. 1) through to early Germanic Iron Age (A.D. 400–600), has identified a pattern of grave deposits that seems to shift according to the period in question. Burial rituals in the early Roman Iron Age shifted significantly from the early pre-Roman period. By the early Roman Iron Age, the collective deposits ceased to be the case and were replaced by great quantities of foreign Roman luxury goods deposited in single male or female graves. Such changes in the early Roman Iron Age do suggest the increase of wealth notwithstanding the evidence of social stratification.

Archaeologists, such as Hedeager (1987, 1992), have concluded that this shift represents the appearance of a new structure or ideology. However, changes occurred again in the early Germanic Iron Age whereby ritual investments ceased and votive deposits proliferated comprising mostly locally produced items. By the late Germanic Iron Age (A.D. 600–800), votive deposits according to Hedeager (1992, 81) disappeared, and "neither graves nor votive hoards show anything more than the slightest material trace of a social elite, perhaps because the social, political and economic situation was relatively stable." The anthropological reasoning—based on the thesis of the appearance of prestige goods signaling the emergence of an elite class and/or new ideology—for such shifts in the type and quantity of grave deposits has to resort to the viewing of such changes as the stabilization of elite rule or the development and legitimization of the ruling ideology (e.g., see Hedeager 1992).

What if we do not rationalize such changes wholly along the above line of reasoning? If we follow our Dark Age thesis, in which Dark Ages occur as a consequence of ecological exhaustion and stress and exhibit losses in wealth, trade disruptions, and simplification of lifestyles and less hierarchization and more egalitarianism of the social structure, we can offer another explanation for the shifts in types and quantity of grave deposits from the early Roman Iron Age to the late Germanic Iron Age. As discussed above, the early Roman Iron Age to the late Roman Iron Age (A.D. 1–400) was a period with increases in grave deposits comprising imported Roman luxuries and indications of the formation of an elite class structure with its ideological structures. This time phasing reflects the period of economic expansion of the world economy, and hence the northern periphery of the Roman Empire expanded accordingly. By the early Germanic Iron Age as indicated above, the quantity of grave deposits went down, and the type of goods deposited changed dramatically, leading to Hedeager (1992, 81) concluding that "neither graves nor votive hoards show anything more than the slightest material trace of a social elite." If we periodize the early Germanic Iron Age as being between A.D. 400 and 800 as Hedeager (1992, 13) has done, and for us a Dark Age period, such a dramatic change in quantity and type of grave deposits are reflections of Dark Age conditions as we have listed above. In fact, by the late Roman Iron Age in Denmark, burial practices have begun to exhibit the "onset of egalitarianism" (Hedeager 1992, 148). Such absences of foreign prestige goods continued in the early Germanic Iron Age (A.D. 400–800) when their disappearances were noted.

The explanation for the disappearance could be as follows. One explanation that fits within our model of Dark Ages would be the disruption in supply of the foreign prestige goods. The other explanation would be that these foreign goods had played out their role in terms of legitimating the social hierarchical order, and hence there is no longer the need for them.

Beyond the appearance and disappearance of prestige goods in grave finds paralleling with periods of economic expansion and Dark Ages, land resources and climate changes also underlined the changing dynamics of socioeconomic reproduction over the course of the Iron Age (Berglund 1969, 2003). Widgren (1983) has reported on socioeconomic decline between A.D. 400 and 900 for Sweden. It is clear, according to Hedeager (1992, 206), that the "resources of the land were so hard-pressed that the ecological balance became more vulnerable to climatic variation and soil exhaustion (for instance) than it had previously been. . . . Changes in the ecological circumstances and in agricultural production are therefore central to an understanding of Iron-Age society."

It has long been argued that the climate during the Iron Age was much colder and wetter for northern Europe in contrast to the Bronze Age when it was warmer and drier. Recent opinion on this tends to be more differentiating. Rather than assuming a continuing sequence of colder and wetter conditions, a cyclical pattern has been suggested as being more representative of the conditions. In other words, there was a turnaround in conditions after A.D. 1 whereby the temperatures and rainfall were warmer and drier in comparison to the beginning of the Iron Age. Later on, however, this sequence was to change again. Temperature changes and rainfall patterns do not necessarily mean that agricultural production is impacted if the temperature becomes cooler and the rainfall increases. Depending on the land use, such changes might not be as impactful. Livestock farming, for example, does not suffer undue stress if the temperature falls provided leaf production continues. However, if deforestation occurs, followed by the loss of leaf production, with open pastures providing the sources for grazing, livestock farming can continue. However, pressure emerges if the weather pattern changes to one that is warmer and drier. If this warmer, drier change occurs, after much deforestation has occurred, then grasses and cereal farming will be impacted, and in turn, fodder for the livestock will be threatened. In this fashion, climate changes can impact socioeconomic life much like what happened during the Bronze Age crisis.

Agricultural expansion in Denmark continued after the Bronze Age (Randsborg 1991). During the early Iron Age, this expansion led to further deforestation (Berglund 1969, 2003). With cooler and wetter weather conditions, the deforestation did not impact arable farming as forest loss was replaced by open pastures; therefore, leaf fodder was replaced by grass. However, such conditions became tenuous when the weather again changed to warmer and drier conditions. To meet this contingency, cereal cultivation replaced grass pastures, and the changed weather conditions facilitated the cereal harvests. What this led to was a further need for manure, which meant increases in cattle stock. Consequently, we have the boom in the population of both humans and animals. Such expansion led to further deforestation and a greater increase in available pasturelands.

However, such intensive utilization of the land resources meant land exhaustion, and this was reached between A.D. 200 and 500. After A.D. 500, there were increasing signs of soil exhaustion leading to famine and depopulation of the landscape. Whether it was light soil or heavy soil, the outcomes remained the same—soil impoverishment was the result of the intensive agriculture. Migration did have an impact on overall land use; in the later Iron Age, population losses as a consequence of perhaps diseases, such as the Justinian plague that impacted Europe and Asia in the sixth century A.D., must have cut deeply into the population, especially those in the urban confines. As a result, we see the return of the forests in some parts of Denmark along with continued cultivation of cereals, such as rye and oats, in eastern Denmark, especially in impoverished soils of open pastures. Such trends suggest that reforestation can occur because of depopulation, and thus deforestation is not a continuing phenomenon during critical periods such as Dark Ages. This realization does not discount our thesis of Dark Ages and its consequent ecological and socioeconomic conditions and characteristics, for the general tendencies that we have delineated for these Dark Age periods continue.

Not only were these stressed ecological conditions leading to social transformations such as depopulation and migration, but these conditions could have also contributed to the consolidation of political power when the village society was reorganized into new farmsteads and the emergence of landless workers. In the later Roman Iron Age, we find in northern Europe the development of a kingship system with a network of vassal lords. Hedeager (1992), after reviewing the evidence, has suggested that such a development of the social formation was more likely a consequence of the reorganization through redistribution and assessment of the land. In short, the changing social rules led to the reconfigured articulation of the social structure; however, she has not dismissed completely the ecological and demographic factors as possible contributory ones to such a development (Hedeager 1992, 247–48). By the early Germanic Iron Age period, this social structural formation was further consolidated, and it did not change much until the Middle Ages. By this time, central power existed in a fixed number of kingdoms.

REPRISE

Unlike the late Bronze Age crisis, which witnessed a transition from the utilization of bronze to iron following the end of the crisis, there was not an adoption of a new metal for the base material of commodities after the crisis of antiquity (ca. A.D. 300–900) was over. Nevertheless, the trends and tendencies of structural transformations that occurred during the late Bronze Age crisis, such as ecological degradation, climate changes, deurbanization, population losses, political upheavals, social simplifications, economic and trade decay, and social migrations, were repeated during the crisis of antiquity. In this sense, there are parallels that we should take note of in our attempt to understand dynamics of the interactions among the social system and natural system and the evolution of the world system.

In the case of the crisis of antiquity, these trends and tendencies delineated above impacted the social, economic, and institutional structures of Europe and the Mediterranean and conditioned these structures and institutions in the post–Dark Age period. For the more economically focused scholars such as Robert Latouche (1961), the economic aspects of the Dark Ages of Antiquity led to the birth of the western economy. In other words, the economic conditions shaped the post–Dark Age economy that later formed the basis of the economy of western Europe. If this is the case, Dark Ages are significant for they conduced structural/systemic changes that otherwise would have taken longer to emerge in an evolutionary sense or might not have occurred at all.

It is very clear that one of the major changes following the Dark Age crisis of antiquity was a shift in western Europe from centralized political control in the form of an empire under Rome—albeit during the Roman period there was a level of local autonomy delegated to the city-state/municipality political format—to a set of kingdoms. With this, there were also the simplification and localization of economic functions. However, the simplification process was not restricted to the West; in the East, there were such simplifications as we have noted in the previous pages, even though the eastern Roman Empire had survived much longer following the collapse of the western portion of the Roman Empire. How did such a political transformation emerge?[2] Clearly, climate, ecological degradation, soil exhaustion, agricultural failures, excessive taxation, wars, and diseases all contributed to the social system stress that started from the third century A.D. onward. Was this decentralization of political control a structural change from the past? For a while, it looked to be the case. However, it seemed that this process came to a stop with the arrival of Charlemagne (r. A.D. 768–814). Centralization and decentralization of political power are swings that have occurred in world history. Even when there was decentralization in post-Roman western Europe, the other parts of the Near East did not decentralize. For a start, the eastern Roman Empire continued as a centralized entity when the western Roman Empire had collapsed into a number of Germanic kingdoms, and centralized systems continued as well in Persia and Arabia, which later challenged the eastern Roman Empire. What is important to note, however, is that the period of decentralization following the collapse of the western Roman Empire and the emergence of Frankish kingdoms established the structural political framework for the emergence of political relations in the medieval age that followed—one of decentralized political authority depictive of what is commonly known as "feudal relations."[3] Whether or not we agree with A. G. Frank's (1991) and Frank's and Gills's (1998) dismissal of utilizing feudalism as a conceptual lens to understand the specificity of the medieval period, it is clear that during the medieval period there was a decentralized set of political relations in western Europe as compared to a centralized empire-type system that was evident in other parts of the world system.

Agricultural failures due to climate changes and ecological degradation, such as soil exhaustion, coupled with increased taxation by Rome to pay for exuberant consumption and war campaigns to thwart tribal incursions had severe consequences for the social and economic structures. Due to a dwindling supply of slaves following the end of Roman territorial conquest and crop failures coupled with increased taxation, the villa, which was the agricultural production unit, saw the influx of free farmers (*colonus*) turning their farms over to the rich landowners. It led to the exercising of the Roman law of *precarium* that tied the free farmer to the soil/villa. In other words, because of a set of conditions, such as economic decline, poor harvests, and increased taxation, that were conduced by climate changes and environmental degradation, free farmers turned over their property to the rich landowners for protection (*patrocinium*) or moved to the villas after losing their land. Such situations established the serf-type relationship that distinguished the rural social relations during the period of the Dark Ages. The result is that the villa stood out as "a vital factor in the social and economic evolution of the Early Middle Ages" (Latouche 1961, 26).

The villa or estate later evolved to what we commonly know as the manor in the Middle Ages (Katz 1961, Herlihy 1974, Anderson 1974). From A.D. 750 onward, the manor became the main socioeconomic structure that formed the backbone of agricultural production in Europe and defined the social relations between the classes in the rural areas. In many ways, the manor as a social, economic, and political unit with its set of socioeconomic obligations mirrored the villa or large estates of the late Roman and Carolingian periods.[4] Combined with this socioeconomic institution was the predominance of the Catholic monastery. We find the rise of these self-contained monasteries following Frankish rule in western Europe. The expansion of these monastic retreats was supported generously by the Frankish kingdoms that consigned lands to the newly founded monasteries and bishoprics (McNeill 1963). Such an outcome thus determined the rural landscape's socioeconomic and political relations that were established as a result of Dark Age conditions.

Clearly, crisis conditions resulting from ecological degradation and climate changes engendered socioeconomic, political, and cultural transformations that might not have occurred if these crisis conditions were not present. The unbalancing of the social system and natural system interactions has an important moment in system transformations and socioevolutionary changes. By the conditions of deurbanization, population reductions, diseases, and trading downturns, which are some of the characteristics of Dark Age conditions, the shift was made to simplified and self-sustaining communities established in more rural environments such as the monastery and the villa/manor at the end of the Dark Ages.[5] These structural entities coupled with the church then determined the political economy of the landscape as the Middle Ages unfolded in western Europe. The Dark Age crisis itself with its reduced socioeconomic activities enabled the rejuvenation of the ecology and the landscape and thus provided the conditions for the next expansion of the social system. In certain ways, the Dark Age of Antiquity was a rebalancing of Nature-Culture relations following centuries of anthropogenic stress of the landscape. It was a period of system restoration and recovery.

NOTES

1. The dimensional size of a beam is much larger in volume than a plank. Usually, a single tree trunk would make up a beam.

2. There have been many explanations for the collapse of the Roman Empire ranging from social/cultural to economic/political/environmental reasons. See, for example, Gibbon (1966), Kagan (1992), Jones (1959a, 1966), Teggart (1969), Anderson (1974), Rostovtzeff (1957), Millar (1981), Huntington (1917a, 1919), Tainter (1988), and Hughes (2001).

3. The issue of feudalism as a mode of production has been questioned by A. G. Frank (1991).

4. For a discussion of the nature of socioeconomic and political relations of the manor, see, for example, Anderson (1974) and Herlihy (1974).

5. Self-sustaining communities, such as the monasteries, were like islands surrounded by the seas of socioeconomic changes. Their self-sustaining nature is very similar to the attempt to develop bioregional communities in the late twentieth centuries. For the latter, they are also supposed to be organized around self-sustaining organizing principles of living within the contours and limits of the landscape (e.g., see Thayer 2003).

IV

SYSTEM
TRANSFORMATION

6

From the Past to the Future: Whither System Transformation?

The global environmental crisis looms on our horizon. As a result, whether it is global warming, deforestation, or species extinction, there is an overwhelming concern of the dangers we face in the twenty-first century. Such fears are further wedded to the view that the impending crisis of the environment is a new phenomenon that humanity faces, and that this new thematic is the result of the excesses of capitalism, and the associated economic and social changes that have occurred over the twentieth century.[1] This latter assumption, however, is historically myopic, for it does not take into account the many phases of environmental crisis that have occurred throughout the course of world history for the last five thousand years (Chew 2001). Historically, socioeconomic and political crises are connected with such an environmental crisis period. Therefore, it is also a period of crisis when human evolutionary transformation has been stymied. A phase when human economic progress is at a standstill. A time widely known and commonly understood as the Dark Ages of human history.

From the previous chapters, over world history, there have been at least three occurrences (2200–1700 B.C., 1200–700 B.C., A.D. 300/400–900) of these devolutionary phases or Dark Ages. Given the reduced socioeconomic activities, Dark Ages provide opportunities for ecological restoration as well. From historical records, in spite of their devolutionary tendencies, Dark Ages should also be seen as moments of opportunity for societal learning and power shifts, for crisis conditions often provide other possibilities. Therefore, what results from these devolutionary periods are system reorganizations and transformations as we have seen in this book.

Given the above, such a trajectory of historical recurrences provides us with the opportunity of realizing the past in order to understand the present and possible future(s). However, the historical myopia of the social sciences has traditionally prevented a consideration of the past with its patterns and structures in order to understand the present. This concluding chapter is an attempt to overcome this. What follows is an attempt to be mindful of past patterns for an understanding of our present conditions—one that is fraught with global ecological, socioeconomic, and political crises.

FROM THE PAST TO THE PRESENT

Global pasts as periodized via Dark Ages reveal trends and tendencies of the evolution of the world system. From the Fertile Crescent five thousand years ago, the occurrences of Dark Ages have revealed not only the intensive relationships of human communities with the natural environment, but also the outcomes of these encounters. As the world system evolved over time, the occurrence of Dark Ages extending over wider and wider geographic space revealed the interconnectivity of socioeconomic and political relationships. Places where Dark Ages have not been experienced or appeared later in time suggest to us that these locales had not been incorporated into the evolving world system at that particular point in time when a Dark Age was occurring. Given these parameters, we can demarcate this ever-widening spread of Dark Age conditions in the course of world history when such a period appears. Table 6.1 and figures 6.1 to 6.3 outline the impact of Dark Ages across the zones of the evolving world system over world history. It is very clear from table 6.1 and figures 6.1 to 6.3 that with the occurrence of each Dark Age in world history, the geographic spread has widened increasingly from one Dark Age to the next. It also underlines the continued socioeconomic expansion, evolution, of the world system. The first Dark Age, from 2200–1700 B.C., demarcates the impact from the Fertile Crescent to the eastern Mediterranean and all the way to northwestern India and traversing right through to the borders of western China (see figure 6.1). Besides those areas that were impacted during the first Dark Age, the second Dark Age (1200–700 B.C.) encompassed central, eastern, and northern Europe and Arabia (see figure 6.2). The last known Dark Age that occurred in antiquity reveals the extensive nature of the spread of Dark Age conditions in Europe and Asia (see figure 6.3; Chew 2005b, Sarabia 2004). With the state of globalization of the socioeconomic and political processes of the world system to date, such historical trends and tendencies of past Dark Ages suggest that should the next Dark Age appear, the geographic impact no doubt will encompass all the continents of the world.

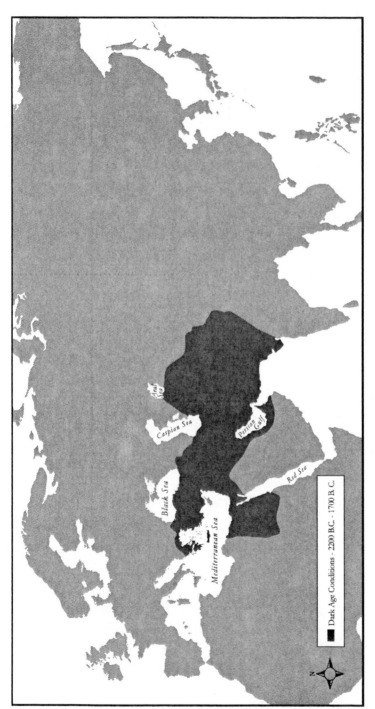

Figure 6.1. Dark Age Crisis 2200 B.C.–1700 B.C.

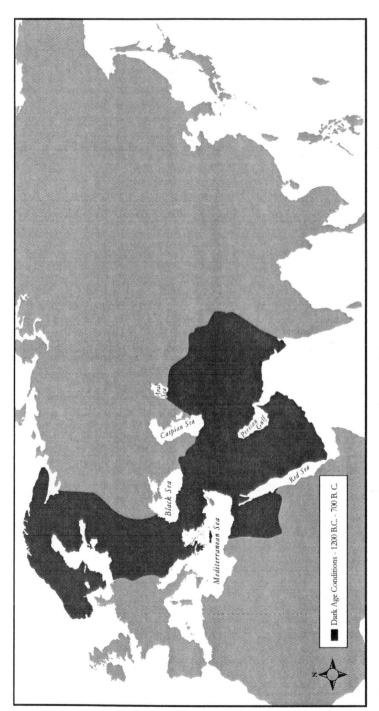

Figure 6.2. Dark Age Crisis 1200 B.C.–700 B.C.

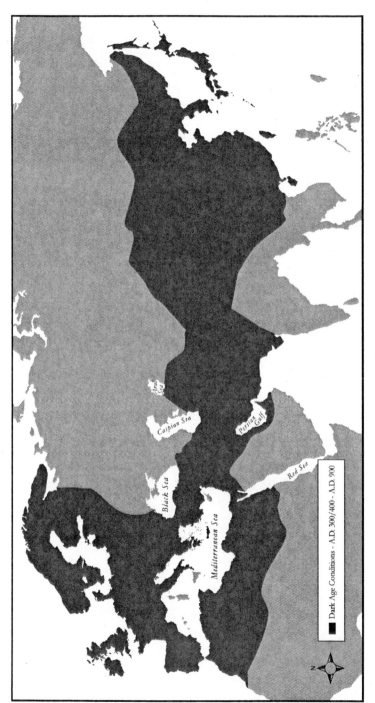

Figure 6.3. Dark Age Crisis A.D. 300/400–A.D. 900

Table 6.1. The Geography of Dark Ages over World History,
**   2200 B.C.–A.D. 900**

Period	Geographic Coverage
Bronze Age	
2200 B.C.–1700 B.C.	Northwestern India, Persian Gulf, Mesopotamia, Turkmenistan, Egypt (recovered by 2040 B.C.), Anatolia, Greece, Crete (recovered by 1900 B.C.), southern Levant (Palestine, Sinai, Jordan)
1200 B.C.–700 B.C.	Egypt, Crete, Greece, Anatolia, Persian Gulf, Mesopotamia, Turkmenistan, Israel, Palestine, Jordan, Sinai, Arabia, Central, Eastern, and Northern Europe (from 750 B.C. onwards)
Iron Age	
A.D. 300/400–A.D. 900	Spain, Gaul, Britain, Germany, Italy, Greece, Southern Levant (Palestine, Sinai, Jordan), Anatolia, Mesopotamia, North Africa, Central, Eastern and Northern Europe, China, Japan, and Korea

Nobel Prize winner Paul Crutzen (2000) has declared that we are in an epoch unlike any of those that have preceded it. Instead of considering ourselves as living in the Holocene period—the period since the last glaciation—we should consider that we are now in an epoch of what he has defined as the Anthropocene. The Anthropocene is a period that is defined by one creature: a creature that has dominated all other species and has become so dominant that its actions have altered the planet on a geological scale. That creature is the human being. The start of this epoch is supposed to be about the 1780s, when the steam engine was invented. For us, however, this demarcation of when the epoch started is not crucial nor that important. Rather, what is important is the acknowledgment that an epoch has begun whereby stressed ecological conditions engendered by humans has been initiated again.

Within the ambit of our generalized theory of Dark Ages, this indicates the possibility of the start of another Dark Age phase. Others who have not utilized long-range analysis nor shared our perspective on this are also in agreement that we are facing a global environmental crisis. Warnings of the environmental crisis trends have been announced at various global meetings organized by the United Nations from Rio de Janeiro to Johannesburg since the 1980s. Studies have been published sounding global environmental alerts starting from the Brundtland Commission on the Environment to the World Commission on Forests and Sustainable Development (1999) and through to the Intergovernmental Panel on Climate Change. In addition, selected scholarly publications, such as Paul and Anne Ehrlich's *One with Nineveh,* James Speth's *Red Sky at Morning,* Edward Wilson's *The Future of Life,* and Meadows et al.'s *Limits to Growth: The 30-Year Update* have also addressed this issue.

The prognosis is dire regardless of which study or intergovernmental report one considers. Global warming, species extinction, soil erosion, pollution, fresh water and resource scarcities, and deforestation are the major signs and tendencies that the current globalized world faces. These trends and tendencies are hardly new in the course of world history, as the previous pages on the characteristics of Dark Ages have outlined. They are repetitions of the past, albeit in the past they might not be as intense, as widespread, and as globally encompassing.

We know from our previous discussion that Dark Age tendencies operate in phases that are not necessarily periodic in nature. Hence, we cannot pinpoint a possible beginning or end of the crisis, as the latter timing depends on the state of degradation of the environment (assuming the reproduction of material life is dependent on natural resources), and the opportunities for recovery depend on either natural renewal or the incorporation of new territories. Furthermore, the data presented in the previous chapters are too limited to allow us to project dates for crisis emergence or its end. What we can do, however, is to look for similar ecological and socioeconomic trends and tendencies comparing past Dark Ages to our present conditions. If we hypothesize along this line, we can begin to see such parallels of present conditions with the past (Chew 2002a).

Before we do this, let us reiterate what we have traversed in our long journey in the previous chapters of identifying trends and tendencies of previous Dark Ages so that an assessment and comparison can be made with current and projected conditions that are ecological, climatic, socioeconomic, and political in nature.

History has shown that prior to and during Dark Ages, there are signs and indications of climate changes. These occurrences appear with temperature increases or decreases and with either increases or decreases in rainfall. As we have indicated in the previous chapters, any changes in temperature or rainfall have tremendous consequences on human economic activity, as well as for the occurrences of diseases that are either directly or indirectly a consequence of these changes. Ecologically, the landscape shows signs of wear and deterioration. Deforestation, soil erosion, and species extinction are evident when combined with a denuded landscape.

Intertwined with these trends, we have also witnessed socioeconomic reversals in terms of the growth and progress of human communities, kingdoms, and civilizations. Population patterns start to show signs of leveling off or dropping. We also have deurbanization and migration of populations, in most cases, from the peripheries to the core areas. Political instability becomes the order of the political landscape with wars and conflicts emerging over natural resources.

Simplification of lifestyles and innovations to meet contingent stressed ecological, socioeconomic, and political conditions emerge to deal with the transformed environment that has been conditioned by scarcity and climate changes. The result is a set of structural changes followed with system transformation.

PRESENT AND POSSIBLE
FUTURE ECOLOGICAL AND CLIMATIC CONDITIONS

Numerous studies have documented present and possible future ecological and climatic conditions that face the planet. Starting from 1982 in the United Nations Charter for Nature, the planet's ecological resources were seen as limited. Five years later, one of the major global warnings came in 1987 from the World Commission on Environment and Development. In its report, *Our Common Future,* the characteristics and extent of the condition of the species and ecosystems were outlined. Even in 1987, there was already scientific consensus on the rate of species extinction never before witnessed in the history of the planet. Habitat alteration was being conducted on such a global scale that it posed a grievous threat to biodiversity. Besides an impending biodiversity crisis, the report warned of the scale and pace of deforestation and noted extinction patterns that were unprecedented on a global scale in world history. Associated with this is the likelihood of climatic changes, and along with the accumulation of greenhouse gases, global warming is anticipated in the early parts of the twenty-first century. This global warning of the Brundtland Commission also alerted us to the impending crisis of global energy resources.

Aware of the fact that the primary energy resources we use are nonrenewable, the commission alerted us to the finite nature and the impending scarcity that we face. The scale of global threat is further increased in the area of global warming and environmental risks with the nonrenewable energy sources that we use. Of these threats, the Brundtland Commission identified four that have severe repercussions for the environment: (i) carbon dioxide emissions from the burning of fossil fuels leading to climate change, (ii) urban-industrial air pollution caused by atmospheric pollutants, (iii) acidification of the environments from pollutants, and (iv) the risk of nuclear reactor accidents and the problems of waste disposal and the dismantling of reactors after their service life is over (World Commission on Environment and Development 1987, 172). In all, the greatest threat, as the commission viewed it then and it continues to this day, is global warming causing climate changes on a world scale.

Population growth was one of the key trends that the Brundtland Commission declared should not continue in light of the available natural resources. Consumption patterns are uneven, with those in the core consuming much more than those in the periphery, thus further deepening the ecological crisis. Decreasing mortality rates in the periphery in the 1980s further added to the rate of population growth. At 4.8 billion in 1985, the commission projected that the world's population will reach 6.1 billion by 2000 and will top 8.2 billion by 2025. Such rates of growth will imperil global food security situations, and food security will be at risk with climate changes.

Urbanization was also identified by the Brundtland Commission as an issue in light of ecological scarcity besides the other social problems that it generated. According to the commission in 1987, the number of people living in urban areas tripled in the thirty-five years since 1950 to 1.25 billion. Knowing the amount of resources urban communities have utilized throughout the course of world history, as we have discussed in *World Ecological Degradation*, this size of growth over such a short period with continuing diminished ecological resources meant impending crisis if this trend was not arrested. The commission came to the same conclusion in its report.

Completed almost twenty years ago, the Brundtland Commission's warnings about crisis conditions and ecological stress have been repeated almost word for word over the years in governmental and scholarly studies. Without going into each specific report or scholarly study, let us briefly review a few of the key ones to show the echoing of the trends and tendencies that the Brundtland Commission had already identified twenty years ago. The United Nations Conference on Environment and Development held in Rio de Janeiro in 1992 announced similar trends and tendencies in its Earth Summit '92 report to the world. Harvard biologist E. O. Wilson's *The Future of Life* approaches the ecological degradation and crisis from the view of the natural sciences. Indicting humanity, Wilson (2002) joins the many noting how we have decimated the natural environment and drawn down the nonrenewable resources of the planet. In doing so, according to Wilson, we have accelerated the destruction of ecosystems and caused the extinction of species, some that have been here for at least a million years. Beyond this, just as we have mentioned in the previous chapter, Wilson also raised the issue of global warming as a consequence of anthropogenic activities.

Along a similar vein, but more comprehensive in nature, are Paul and Anne Ehrlich's *One with Nineveh*. The Ehrlichs' book mirrors the Brundtland Commission's report and Earth Summit '92 except that the Ehrlichs, writing almost twenty years later, identified environmental trends and tendencies that have changed somewhat to a situation that is even more critical. With the exception of population trends, what was discussed by the Brundtland Commission and at Earth Summit '92 were repeated, albeit with different emphases reflecting the interests of the Ehrlichs. According to the Ehrlichs, despite the fact that the world population will keep growing to 10.6 billion by 2050, based on a high projection, the United Nations has projected a slow decline. This projection is interesting if we consider vis-à-vis our theory of Dark Ages whereby there is a population loss or decline during a Dark Age period.

James Speth's *Red Sky at Morning* repeats the trends of all the previous studies that we have discussed briefly in the previous pages. As such, it confirms the scenario of a natural environment that is devastated ecologically through deforestation, pollution, landscape transformations, and species extinction. The condition is made worse with climate changes and an approaching natural resource scarcity, especially in the area of nonrenewable energy. Projections of natural resource scarcity on a global scale have also been made by the Club of Rome (Mesarovic and Pestel 1974) and Meadows et al. (1972, 1992, 2004). It is a common theme among most reports and studies that have been published for the last thirty years. The most recent update by Meadows et al. (2004) outlines very severe impending scarcities with declining availability of natural resources, water, and agricultural farmlands. Of these resources, the declining availability of water is a serious threat to the reproduction of socioeconomic life. To Meadows et al. (2004, 71), the major rivers of the world such as the "Colorado, Yellow, Nile, Ganges, Indus, Chao Phraya, Syr Darya, and Amu Darya Rivers are so diverted by withdrawals for irrigation and cities that their channels run dry for some or all of the year."

Deforestation is epidemic throughout the planet (World Commission on Forest and Sustainable Development 1999). Before the advent of agriculture, there were about 6 to 7 billion ha of forests (Meadows et al. 2004). Now there are only about 3.9 billion ha left. It is clear that only one-fifth (1.3 billion) of the planet's original forest cover remains. Half of this is in Russia, Canada, and Alaska with the rest in the Amazon. The United States (not including Alaska) has lost 95 percent of its original forest cover, Europe essentially does not have any left, and China only has about three-fourths of its forests.

Species extinction is also the trend of the late twentieth and twenty-first centuries. It is estimated that 24 percent of the 4,700 mammal species, 30 percent of the 25,000 fish species, and 12 percent of the 10,000 bird species are in danger of extinction (Meadows et al. 2004). For plants, 34,000 of the 270,000 plant species are at risk. Overall, the average species population has declined by more than one-third since 1970.

Just like the scarcity and availability of nonrenewable resources at the end of the Bronze Age, we are also approaching scarcity and availability of fossil fuels, such as oil, for this Iron Age. There is substantial consensus that the world production of petroleum will reach its maximum by the first half of this century, after which it will start to dwindle in terms of output. After three decades of exploitation starting from the 1970s, according to Meadows et al. (2004), 700 billion fewer barrels of oil, 87 billion fewer

Table 6.2. Annual Production and Resource Life Expectancy of Oil, Gas, and Coal

Resource	1970 Production	2000 Production	Resource Life Expectancy
Oil	17 billion barrels	28 billion barrels	50–80 years
Gas	1.1 trillion m³	2.5 trillion m³	160–310 years
Coal	2.2 billion tons	5.0 billion tons	very large

Source: Based on data from Meadows et al. (2004, 90).

tons of coal, and 1,800 fewer trillion cubic feet of natural gas are available. Meadows et al. (2004), estimating resource life expectancy, projects for oil a life span of 50 to 80 years (see table 6.2) and for coal a very large life expectancy. The latter, however, could not be much of a substitute because of its climate-warming tendency.

The Intergovernmental Panel on Climate Change and the United Nations Environment Programme (2002) issued alerts projecting warming of the global climate and the likely aridification of some portions of the globe. According to the panel, the global surface temperature has increased by 0.6°C over the twentieth century, which is the largest increase of any century during the past 1,000 years. Snow and ice cover have decreased about 10 percent since the late 1960s with rainfall increasing in some areas especially in the mid to high latitudes of the Northern Hemisphere and decreasing over much of the Northern Hemisphere's subtropical land areas.

Given the above trends and tendencies of the global environment, what does it tell us about the present and the future conditions in terms of another Dark Age? We discuss this next.

Dark Age Conditions?

The recurring nature of these Dark Ages over world history does suggest certain tendencies that we might wish to consider in light of the ecological crisis that we face today. The indicators of current ecological stress, socioeconomic trends, and climatological changes do suggest certain comparability with the previous Dark Ages that we have examined in the previous chapters. If this is the case, we might be approaching another Dark Age, if we are not in it already.

We know from the past, the changes that occurred in the ecological, socioeconomic, political landscapes and climate during the past Dark Ages. To reiterate, during those Dark Ages, deforestation reached extreme levels as a consequence of the previous phase of incessant growth of the world system. As we have discussed in the previous section, we are witnessing such deforestation levels today. Furthermore, the World Commission on

Forests and Sustainable Development (1999) has raised the alarm on the
ferocity of the deforestation globally, and others have also confirmed the
pace of cutting during the twentieth century (Chew 2001, Noble and Dirzo
1997, Marchak 1995, Tucker 2000, Williams 2003). Soil erosion, flooding,
and species endangerment, which are often the outcome of deforestation
that has occurred in previous Dark Ages, are also being signaled by scientists and environmentalists as dangers we are facing and will face in the
foreseeable future. At the level of the social system, in addition to what
was identified in the previous section, Grimes (1999) and McNeill (2000)
have documented for the contemporary period the various environmental
degradative outcomes from intensive and extensive resource extraction to
atmospheric pollution. For the latter, as indicated in *World Ecological Degradation,* atmospheric pollution was also occurring at the end the Greek
(First Dark Age) and Roman (Second Dark Age) eras and the medieval
period, and this was encountered as far away as Greenland.

With the recent reports on climatological changes by the Intergovernmental Panel on Climate Change and the United Nations Environment
Programme, anthropogenically induced climate change in terms of global
temperature increases are expected for this decade and beyond. Such
increases will have significant impact on socioeconomic life and water
supply, if it has not happened already. Similar climate changes have also
been reported during previous Dark Ages, and we have noted the impacts these changes had on the socioeconomic and political landscapes
of the social system then. In the World Disasters Report of 1999 by the
International Federation of Red Cross and Red Crescent, it was suggested
that global warming and climate change may have been responsible for
the harsher natural disasters and flooding that we have been experiencing. The contemporary changes in ocean temperature (the El Niño and
La Niña phenomena), which have also occurred in the past, have caused
severe hardship for the communities bordering the Pacific Ocean of the
Americas (Fagan 1999). Droughts triggered by El Niño have caused
huge forest fires in Brazil and Peru. Besides El Niño effects, in 1998, for
example, typhoons and floods killed 500 and affected 5 million in the
Philippines; floods killed 4,150 and affected 180 million people in China;
killed 400 and affected 200,000 in Korea; killed 1,000 and affected 25,000
in Pakistan; killed 1,400 and affected almost 340,000 in India. Monsoons
killed 1,300 and affected 31 million in Bangladesh, and killed 3,240 and
affected 36 million in northern India and Nepal. Two hurricanes killed a
total of 14,000 people and affected about 7 million people in the Carib-
bean and Central America. Economic costs alone are staggering. Losses
were $165 billion in Central America and the Caribbean, $2.5 billion in
Argentina, $868 million in Korea, $223 million in Bangladesh, and $150
million in Romania.

In view of the above, such contemporary ecological patterns tend to reflect the same trends and tendencies of previous Dark Ages in terms of ecological degradation and climate changes. The work of Modelski and Thompson (1999) with demarcated phases of concentration of the world economy with economic expansion, population growth, and urbanization, and so on, followed by phases of dispersion in which there are trade collapses, deurbanization, migration, and falls in population levels further dovetails with our analysis. In addition, Modelski (1999a) has noted a phase of dispersal (deurbanization, trade collapses, etc.) starting from A.D. 1850 or 1900 of the modern era that further reinforces our suggestion that perhaps we are now experiencing Dark Age conditions or heading into one.

SYSTEM TRANSFORMATION?

Let us use the patterns and tendencies of the past to be our guide. The recurring nature of these Dark Ages is troubling. It seems that over the course of world history, human communities have continued to repeat the materialistic practices of the past and have thus engendered ecologically stressful outcomes. Coupled with these circumstances, we find, over world history, movements to protect or conserve Nature along with attempts at recycling (Chew 2001). The current efforts to protect the environment need to be considered in view of these long-term dynamics of a historical system with its set of repetitive socioenvironmental practices. To this extent, what impact do such current environmental actions have in light of the dynamics and structures of the historical system? The impact of such activities does reduce and temper the intensity of our impact on Nature and might help to reduce the length of a Dark Age period should it occur.

Unlike past Dark Ages, the options today are limited in terms of the various paths for system recovery. In the previous Dark Age period, the world system was not as globalized and encompassing, and the system could expand in terms of the search for natural resources and labor, thereby enabling previously degraded and exploited areas to recover. At this stage of the globalization process, planet Earth is fully encompassed, and thus if ecological collapse (Dark Age) occurs there are few replacement areas for system expansion. Besides this, the level of connectivity of the world system in terms of production and reproduction processes means that the collapse will be felt globally, unlike previous Dark Ages in which not all the peripheral areas were impacted by the collapse.

The recovery path of incorporation of new geographic areas is no longer an option, as the world system is now globalized and connected, unless we consider tapping the aquatic resources following the melting of the Arctic ice cap or outer space planetary conquest as an opportunity for expanding the limits of the world system. Even if this latter option is considered, the path is fraught with difficulties in view of the current state of the global environment, the extent of globalization processes such as accumulation and urbanization, the size of the world's population, and the political imperative to pursue anthropocentric progress beyond the limits of the current planet. Terra forming has been broached in some circles, but this has not been declared the official policy of any legitimate core nation-state.

Thus the only choices left for recovery, if social progress and development are the goals, would be not to extensify the geospatial boundaries of the world system following the practices of the past, but instead to intensify the socioeconomic processes of the world system to meet the conditions of incessant accumulation, urbanization, and population growth; to develop new technologies that can deal with the scarcity of natural resources; or to totally reorganize the manner in which human societies have organized the reproduction of material life. However, before this can happen, and if we follow the trends of past Dark Ages, we can anticipate first reversals in socioeconomic growth, and disruptions and instability of political regimes along with climate changes and natural disturbances in view of the current environmental crisis. These are the characteristics and conditions we could face as we slide further into a devolutionary phase (Dark Age) of world system development. All indications suggest that the degradation of the environment will increasingly accelerate with the current economic globalizing forces all over the planet and especially with the ecologically impactful rapid industrialization and advanced technological developmental strategies of the People's Republic of China and India in the short to medium terms. Besides the incessant consumption of nation-states in the core zone, People's Republic of China and India pose major challenges for our planet's natural resource availability in view of their population sizes, and their potential megapollution sources. For example, China's oil consumption has risen from 230.1 million t in the year 2000 to 308.6 million t by the year 2004, which is a 35 percent increase over four years (*China Daily* 2005, 1). If the past is any indication, the Dark Age conditions will fortify and deepen in the short to medium terms.

Like previous Dark Ages, we will continue to see social, political, and economic turmoil, much like the Bronze Age crisis that occurred almost four thousand years ago. During those times, natural resource trade disruption and shortages led to the adoption of a new base metal. Economic scarcities and social constraints, such as population losses and deurbanization, led to the development of new political governance and political formation, such as the Greek polis, while other political entities such as Assyria, Babylonia, and Egypt continued their traditional political monarchical systems. Where sociopolitical changes occurred, traditional elites lost their economic and political dominance. In short, major socioeconomic and political restructuring took place then that led to a new path of political experimentation and different ideas of human governance and equality, that is, the promotion of authority being vested in the community and the sanctioning of individual human rights. All these occurred within an environment of natural resource constraints and ecological stress whereby these conditions induced the rethinking of the normal practices of governance of the past based on empire and kingship and the adoption and experimentation with different formulations, for example, the Greek polis.

In the late twentieth and twenty-first centuries, we are also witnessing numerous political unions, instabilities, and collapses in Africa, Asia, Latin America, and Europe. The formation of regional unions such as the European Community, the Association of Southeast Asian Nations, Economic Commission of West African States, and the African Union, for example, are political attempts to redefine political sovereignty and political rights. The collapse of the former Soviet Union and various other countries in Africa along socioeconomic lines are cases in point. By no means are these latter occurrences over—as the Dark Age crisis proceeds and deepens, more instability will appear.

The present levels of natural resources availability reflect similar tendencies to conditions over four thousand years ago during the Bronze Age crisis. It is clear we are seeing the increasing scarcity of fossil fuel availability as we have outlined in the previous section (Meadows et al. 2004, 90). The condition is critical especially when most of the world's industries and reproduction of social life is dependent on oil. Replacement base materials for commodity production will need to be determined and adopted. The trend tends toward carbon composites and silicon-based materials. The production of these base materials requires not only energy but also fresh water in abundant quantities. It is clear that these natural resources will increasingly be limited in terms of known sources and replacement sources or alternate forms of energy will be needed. It is not clear that the solution will be there. Some, like Rifkin (2002), have suggested a hydrogen-based economy, while others are stating and hoping that new technologies will save the human population or at least those in the core zone of the world system (e.g., see Ehrlich and Ehrlich 2004).

Beyond ecological devastation and the dwindling supply of natural resources for global consumption, we anticipate climate changes and natural disturbances as we have experienced in previous Dark Ages over world history. For example, in a recent study on the impact of climate change on the state of California, which has the fifth largest economy in the world system, the magnitude of the effects anticipated appears to be catastrophic (Hayhoe et al. 2004). It is projected that by the end of the century for California, under one scenario, heat waves and extreme heat will quadruple in frequency with heat-related mortality increased by two to three times, alpine and subalpine forests will be reduced by 50 to 75 percent, and the Sierra snow packs will be reduced by 30 to 70 percent. Another scenario with more elevated climate changes will further exacerbate the conditions delineated. The decrease in the Sierra snow packs will mean cascading impacts on reduced runoffs and stream flows, which will impact agricultural production in the central valley of California—a major agricultural production zone for the United States and the rest of the world.

Increasingly, evidence of tectonic shifts and El Niño have pervaded the latter half of the twentieth century, and most recently, the tsunami-related devastation in late December 2004 in Southeast Asia and the south Indian region are comparable to the tsunami event that impacted on Crete and the eastern Mediterranean during the late Bronze Age. Added to this is the most recent devastation on the southern coast of the United States by Hurricane Katrina. The World Disasters Report by the International Federation of Red Cross and Red Crescent that we cited earlier has documented the costs to economies and political systems. It has been suggested that global warming and climate change may have been responsible for the harsher natural disasters and flooding that we have been experiencing. The 2004 tsunami event in South Asia, Thailand, Indonesia, and Malaysia had devastating economic costs and loss of lives. This was then followed by the large-scale property damage caused by Hurricane Katrina in the southern part of the United States. The costs in terms of economies and human lives have not been realized fully for these recent natural disasters. If such natural disasters continue to surface in repetitions for the foreseeable future, the impact on the global economy will be extremely destabilizing.

Climate changes, landscape degradation, neocolonial exploitation via transnational operations, and indigenous elite domination have dislocated rural populations, which has led to large-scale migrations within and between nation-states. These migrations have occurred since the sixteenth century and will continue through the twenty-first century and beyond. Much like previous Dark Ages where we found evidence of movements across vast expanses of landmasses, we also see large-scale legal and illegal migrations on all continents of the world system today. The much-discussed illegal Mexican and Latin American migration into the southern United States is not a unique situation. Illegal and legal migrations have occurred everywhere in this globalized world since the sixteenth century. What is clear is that the movement has been from the periphery and semiperiphery to the core areas, and on occasions, from the core to the periphery during periods of expansion to extensify the boundaries of the world system.

Unlike previous Dark Ages, we have not yet witnessed the extensive deurbanization and population losses that we have evidence of in the previous Dark Ages. In the case of deurbanization, this development has started to manifest itself. We have witnessed signs of urban decay in the urban areas of the core zone with the closure of plants and factories in the late twentieth century, and the movement of the population out of the urban zones because of job losses, crime, environmental degradation, pollution, and contamination. There is also the call for urban renewal and the revitalization of the inner core of the cities. The urban renewal programs have had mixed success. In parts of Eastern Europe that were members of the former Soviet Bloc, there have been signs of urban "shrinkage" and population losses. The deurbanization of New Orleans because of a natural disaster should also be considered.

Deurbanization will occur further should energy shortages start to appear and climate warming begin, since urban living is the most intensive in terms of natural resource consumption, as everything has to be transported to an urbanized landscape to reproduce socioeconomic and political life (Chew 2001). The current architectural designs and infrastructures do not afford the opportunity to conform to temperature increases nor are they geared for living for long periods under conditions of energy shortages and high temperatures. Definitely, those living in the enclaves in the core zone will experience tremendous daily living challenges. Preliminary circumstances of this nature have occurred in West Africa in the 1980s, though not in the core zone, and in Europe during the summer of 2003.

Population losses have yet also to appear. It is anticipated that the global population will peak about 2035 to approximately 7.5 billion persons and then retreat to 7.4 billion by 2050 based on a low projection by the United Nations (Ehrlich and Ehrlich 2004). Furthermore, from 2000 to 2050, acquired immunodeficiency syndrome (AIDS) will reduce the population by 479 million. If a medium projection is used, the numbers come up higher, reaching 8.9 billion by 2050; if a high projection is used, the total by 2050 would be 10.6 billion. The latter would mean a doubling in just 25 years. There is no reason to believe that previous trends during prior Dark Ages of population losses will not be repeated. It is too early to suggest that population declines will not occur. Climate changes impacting crop harvest will generate famines; natural catastrophes, such as earthquakes, El Niño, and tsunamis, will take lives, and so will diseases and conflicts as a result of natural resource scarcity. We have already seen a glimpse of the effects of a tsunami in South Asia and Southeast Asia where over 200,000 lives were lost. Diseases such as AIDS have reduced populations as well. The United Nations has estimated that by 2050, the world population will be reduced by 200 million due to AIDS, and seven countries in Southern Africa will have little or no population growth (Ehrlich and Ehrlich 2004).

The above tendencies are likely to occur in the medium to long term and perhaps in the short term, if short means within this century. What is clear is that the global threats are the warming of the planet, the rapid deforestation of the world's forests, the loss of arable land and clean water, all of which form the basic material conditions for the reproduction of material human lives. Besides all the above trends and tendencies, Dark Ages are supposed also to be system transformative. What can we expect in terms of structural socioeconomic and political changes? Let us use what happened during the late Bronze Age as a guide to anticipating possible tendencies.

WHITHER SYSTEM TRANSFORMATION: THE FUTURE IS STILL OPEN[2]

Given that Dark Ages in world history are significant moments signaling system crisis and system reorganization, the final phase of the Bronze Age crisis led to ecological recovery, certain political-economic realignments and reorganization, and the transition to a new working metal—iron. The Dark Age crisis was *system transformative* for it led to fundamental social system changes evolving to a set of new patterns (Chew 2002b, Sheratt and Sheratt 1993).

The adoption of iron brought to an end centuries of bronze use that was in the control of palace economies and elites. Gordon Childe (1942) has suggested that cheap iron with its wide availability provided the opportunities for agriculture, industry, and even warfare with the adoption of iron as the base metal. With trade route disruption and copper scarcity, the adoption of iron use spread further, especially among the communities in Greece that were isolated as a consequence of Dark Age conditions, for iron was available locally. It led to the development of local iron-producing industries (Snodgrass 1971). The low cost of iron, because it was available locally, facilitated its widespread use in agriculture and industry (Childe 1942, McNeill and McNeill 2003).

All over Europe, the Mediterranean, and the Near East, cultivation was made easier with iron plowshares in heavy clay soils. This enabled the rural communities to participate further in the economy beyond subsistence, and in maintaining a class of miners, smelters, and metalsmiths fabricating the iron implements to reproduce material life. Such an explanation is also supported by Heichelheim (1968) and Polanyi (1977), who suggested that the widespread adoption of iron was the result of the opportunity for rural communities in south Russia, Italy, North Africa, Spain, Gaul, Germany, and Eurasia to work the heavy soils with iron implements, thus increasing their production levels. Production increases can be seen by the fluctuations in grain prices according to Heichelheim (1968). The consequence of such transformation is that the urban elites in the Near East who in the past controlled the grain and other commodities trade suffered losses as a consequence of changing prices and the falling demand in the copper, tin, and bronze trade, which they also controlled.

As a result of the above, the social structures were transformed with the formation of different regional centers in the periphery and in the Mediterranean. The opportunity for the farmers to farm in heavy clay soils utilizing cheap iron implements also provided the conditions for economic and system expansion following the end of the Dark Age where in the past these areas were not as productive. It enabled economic expansion and the move into newer areas for agriculture, as by this time some of the older settled areas were ecologically degraded and overworked.

As well, at the social system level, the Dark Age crisis thus ushered forth the dissociation of high-value commodities away from the control of the palace-state, for by the end of the Dark Age, the command palace economies in the eastern Mediterranean were dissolved. What emerged was the continued differentiation of commercial and economic structures from the political structures (Polanyi 1977). Instead of bureaucratic palace-centered trade, we see the development of mercantile city-states where merchant enterprise replaced the palace-controlled exchange. With this transformation, new forms of political powers and structures emerged. We have the emergence of a new political structure, the city-state (polis) in the Aegean, and the continuation of empire-type political structures where the rule was via direct political and military control.

The new political structure, the polis, as a social organization and political concept emerged in eighth-century Greece (Morris 1987, 1988b). As Morris (1988a, 752) has stated it was unique among ancient states for "its citizen body was actually the state." The rise of such a state form was a consequence of the collapse of the aristocratic society during the Greek Dark Ages. Other factors also precipitated its formation. Deurbanization and the loss of population in the urban areas resulted in the development of isolated communities during the Dark Age that engendered the structural conditions for the development of the polis. In addition, with the scarcity of resources and the abundance of poverty leading to less hierarchical social structures, the groundwork for the development of the polis was also put into place. The polis thus was one where all authority was divested to the community unlike previous political forms in Mycenaean Greece. Force, therefore, was located in the citizen body as a whole, and thus there was little need for a standing military. Individual natural rights were not sanctioned by a higher power and the highest authority was the polis, that is, the community. Such a political structure found expression in the Aegean. However, in other parts of the Near East, divine kingship was maintained with some minor modifications. According to Childe (1947), Assyria, Babylonia, and Egypt continued as Bronze Age states.

The above revealed what occurred in the past; there is no reason to consider that what happened will be repeated in similar fashion. The adoption of a new base metal during the late Bronze Age was systems transformative because it reduced the monopolization of bronze manufacturing of the palace-based monarchical systems and thus opened the opportunity for other communities to fabricate iron. According to Childe (1947), the manufacture of iron was made possible by traveling metalsmiths who when paid for their services, transmitted their knowledge. It has been stated that the shift to iron democratized the world system in terms of giving political entities room for expansion and thus jeopardized the traditional Bronze Age monarchical systems. Will we see this pattern of the resolution of natural resource scarcity for the current world system as it evolves into the future? That is hard to predict.

If we consider the advent of the computer (digital) revolution (age) as analogous to the adoption of iron production at the end of the Bronze Age, the predominance of computer-based systems in the current era with its decentralized production, design, and manufacturing becoming increasingly the norm, could be viewed as systems transformative. Clearly, the computer-oriented industries and their associated innovations and uses, such as the Internet, have provided the opportunities whereby others can participate and take advantage of the innovations besides those based in the core countries. Thus, the varied uses and innovations have also precipitated and opened up access to information and innovations for those that are dispossessed or are technologically deficient. It is still too early to evaluate the impacts of such developments to sociopolitical organizations. What is clear is that we are heading toward an ecological crisis of scarcity and degraded landscapes.

If this is the case, perhaps we will witness different political and economic trajectories for the world system. There will definitely be a continuance of the current economic and political systems (with authoritarian overtones) similar to what happened during the late Bronze Age. We project that continuation will be based on how structured the political and economic system was prior to the crisis and how much impact each entity experienced during the height of the Dark Age crisis. Those that persist will be those that were the most structured politically and economically (like Assyria, Babylonia, and Egypt at the end of the Bronze Age crisis) prior to the crisis or those that were impacted the least. They will have the least pressure to rethink and restructure. However, if history can be our guide, such systems will not continue in the very long term because they will be less innovative than those that had to proceed on other possible trajectories that are not resource intensive in terms of material production.

What possible trajectories are there? As human history is always an *open process,* there will be experimentation and adaptation based on the materialistic circumstances other social systems face. This we will discuss in detail in the forthcoming final volume of my exploration in ecological world system history. In a preliminary sense, I will however offer one possible trajectory as a conclusion to this volume.

If we assume the scenario that there is a tremendous scarcity of resources, deurbanization, and population losses, much like the Greek societies at the end of the Bronze Age, innovations will occur to adapt to the constricted natural environment. Furthermore, with scarcity of resources, such as energy, isolation also becomes an issue. In this case, isolation occurs because there is no energy available for transportation, and the current established political-economic systems based on a centralized and federalized configuration of command and control will be dysfunctional when communities are isolated from federated systems. In this context, a different type of political and economic structure will have to be considered and developed. With scarcity of natural resources, such isolated communities will need to rely on the immediate landscape for the reproduction of socioeconomic life. They will be isolated, community-governed social systems structured in conformity to the landscape and available natural resources to reproduce social life. Historically, the early Greek societies during the Dark Ages of 1200 B.C. are such historical occurrences. The other would be the monasteries that came into existence during the crisis of antiquity (chapters 4 and 5) that possessed the characteristics of self-sufficient entities that relied on their immediate ecological landscape for the reproduction of socioeconomic life in a decentralized political system.[3]

Such a shift in political economic structure requires a total rethinking of social, economic, and political structures and processes. By this time, there should be the realization of living in an interconnected natural-social world. It is very unlikely that if such a scenario occurs, the reorientation will be prompted by a voluntaristic human agency shift, but more likely it will be engendered by the structural conditions these communities faced in terms of ecological and natural resource scarcities as a consequence of Dark Age conditions. It will be just like what the Greeks faced during the end of the Bronze Age. From a social evolutionary point of view, this possible transformation might not be viewed as progressive from a modernist point of view, for we will encounter a sociocultural and sociopolitical lifestyle reconfiguration conditioned by a Dark Age whereby ecological sustainability is the basis of organization not by choice but by circumstances and necessity. If this is the case, production and exchange will probably be guided by very different rules, possibly via use value instead of exchange value, and as a result, the sociopolitical order is one that will be quite different from the past. If this is the case, this might be the system transition "progressive" scholars have been debating over the years.

Notwithstanding our brief argument given above, it is very difficult to project which political systems in the current configuration of the world system will propel along which trajectories. It is all dependent on the extent of their reliance on the ecosystem and the level of impact they sustain from Dark Age conditions. If history can guide us, there will be numerous trajectories just like what happened during the final Bronze Age crisis. What is clear is that with the level of globalization that we are witnessing today, almost all will be impacted tremendously. Such is the human nightmare we will face in the future. For some who eschew progress and modernity, Dark Ages conditions might not be viewed as a nightmare experience, but as a period that provides opportunities for Nature to recover, and for social systems to realign with the natural system: hence, a period of brightness. Notwithstanding this, for all of us, there is always hope. That hope is that our common future is still open!

NOTES

1. This is not to suggest that the current global environmental crisis is similar in terms of intensity and perhaps in nature as well. What is being asserted is that "global" environmental crisis is not a new phenomenon as various scholars have attributed, but one that has occurred in the past in the form of Dark Ages as we have suggested in the previous chapters.

2. A full detailed presentation of studies and information underlining the argument presented in this section including a discussion of the environmental movement and environmentalism will be made in the final forthcoming volume (entitled Ecological Futures: What Can History Tell Us) of my three-volume series on five thousand years of world ecological degradation.

3. Early Christian monasticism that started in Egypt in the fourth century was an attempt to live within the limits and boundaries of Nature. Work and agriculture was considered as the exploitation of Nature. Unmodified nature is what is important. An authority structure was rejected (Bergmann 1985).

Appendix 1

ARBOREAL
POLLEN INFLUXES

WESTERN EUROPE

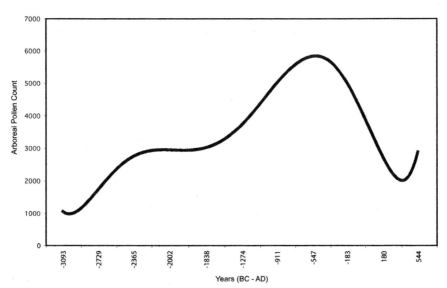

Figure A1.1.   Pollen Count, Belgium (Moerzeke)

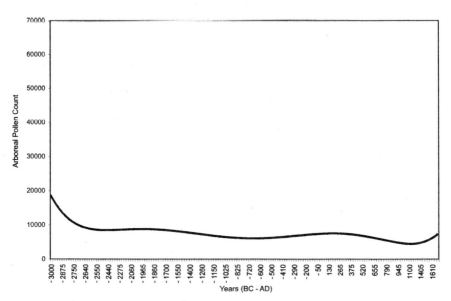

Figure A1.2.   Pollen Count, Germany 1 (Lake Constance)

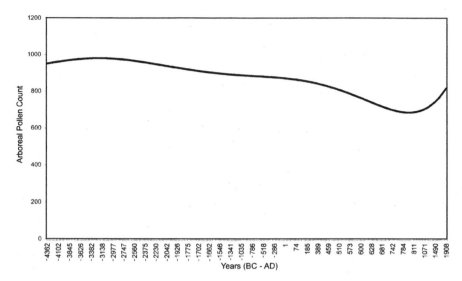

Figure A1.3.   Pollen Count, Germany 2 (Lake Steisslingen)

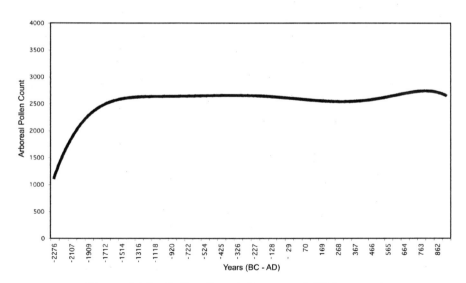

Figure A1.4.   Pollen Count, Germany 3 (Ahlenmoor)

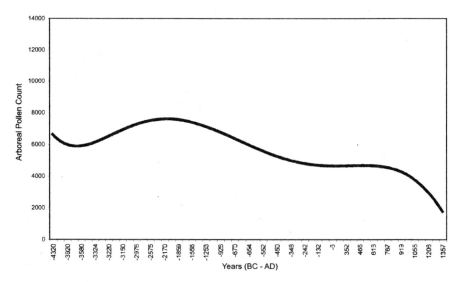

Figure A1.5.   Pollen Count, Switzerland (Lobsigensee)

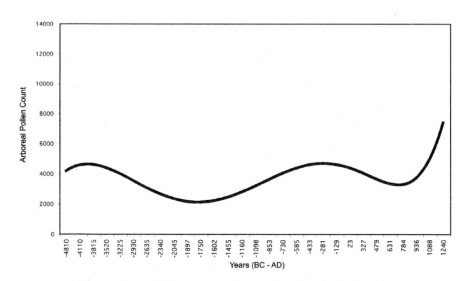

Figure A1.6.   Pollen Count, France (Le Marais St. Boetien)

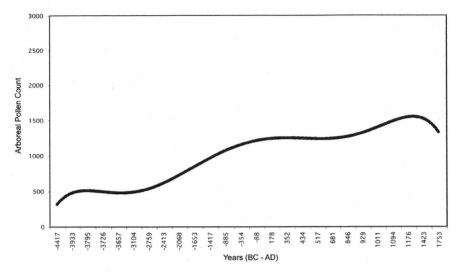

Figure A1.7. Pollen Count, Ireland (Arts Lough)

CENTRAL AND EASTERN EUROPE, RUSSIA

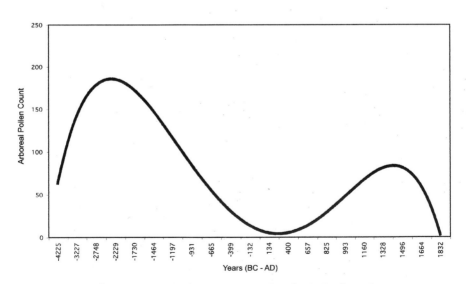

Figure A1.8. Pollen Count, Bulgaria 1 (Besbog 2)

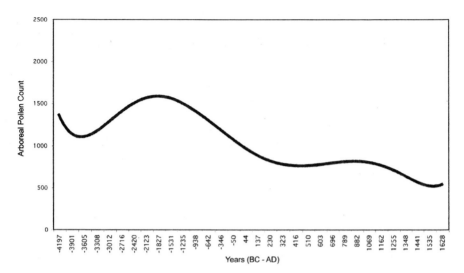

Figure A1.9.   Pollen Count, Bulgaria 2 (Mire Garvan)

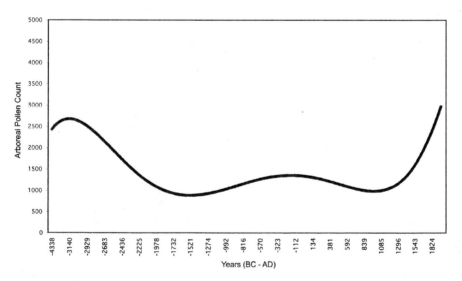

Figure A1.10.   Pollen Count, Hungary (Lake Balaton SW)

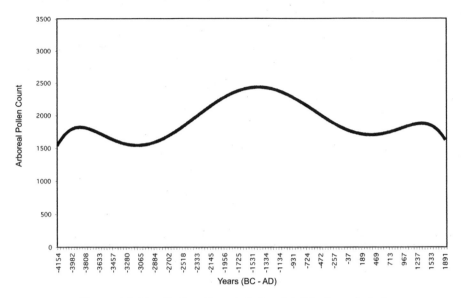

Figure A1.11.   Pollen Count, Poland 1 (Bledowo Lake)

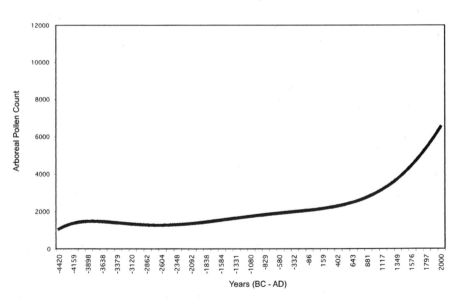

Figure A1.12.   Pollen Count, Poland 2 (Puscizna Rekowianska)

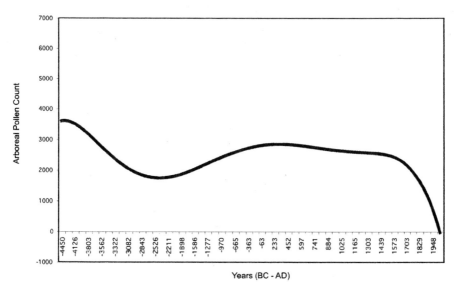

Figure A1.13.   Pollen Count, Poland 3 (Kluki)

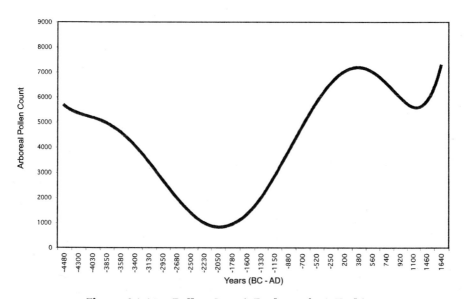

Figure A1.14.   Pollen Count, Byelorussia 1 (Dolgoe)

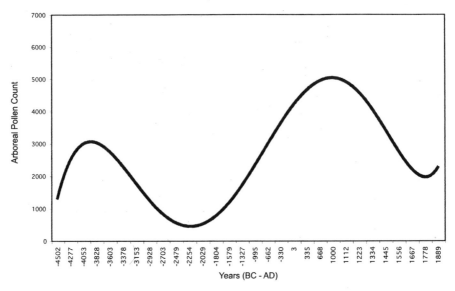

Figure A1.15.   Pollen Count, Byelorussia 2 (Osvea)

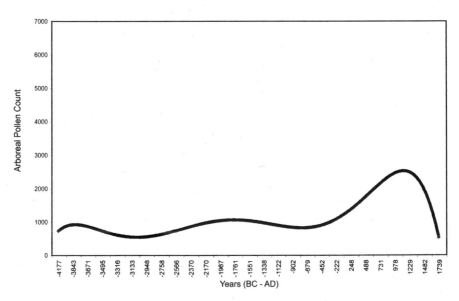

Figure A1.16.   Pollen Count, Ukraine 1 (Kardashinski Swamp)

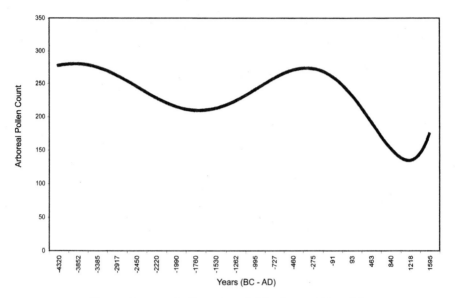

Figure A1.17.   Pollen Count, Ukraine 2 (Starniki)

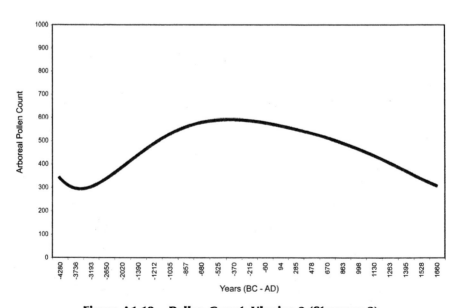

Figure A1.18.   Pollen Count, Ukraine 3 (Stoyanov 2)

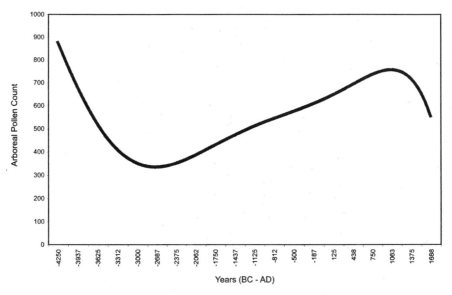

Figure A1.19.   Pollen Count, Ukraine 4 (Ivano-Frankovskoye)

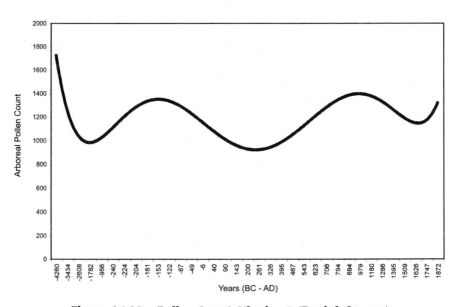

Figure A1.20.   Pollen Count, Ukraine 5 (Dovjok Swamp)

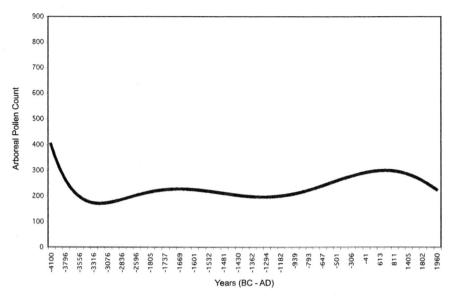

Figure A1.21.   Pollen Count, Russia (Chabada Lake)

NORTHERN EUROPE

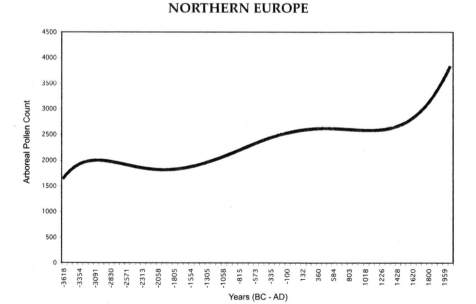

Figure A1.22.   Pollen Count, Sweden 1 (Ageröds Mosse)

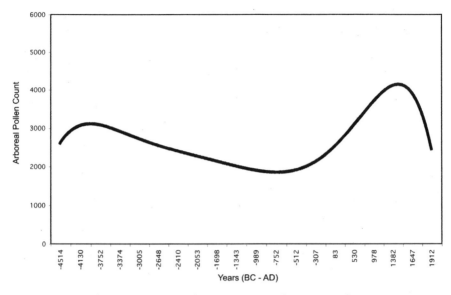

Figure A1.23.   Pollen Count, Sweden 2 (Kansjon)

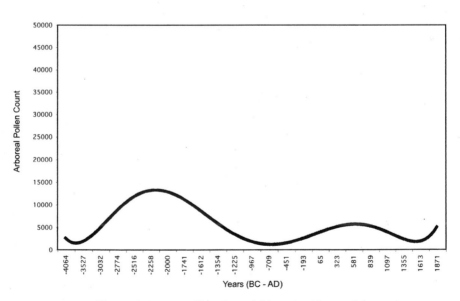

Figure A1.24.   Pollen Count, Norway (Grasvatn)

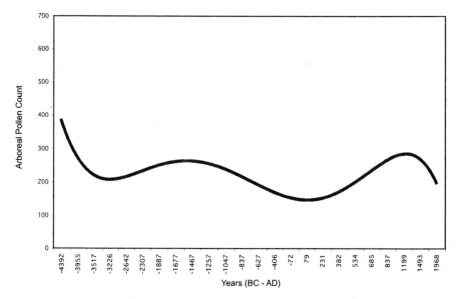

Figure A1.25.   Pollen Count, Latvia (Rudushskoe Lake)

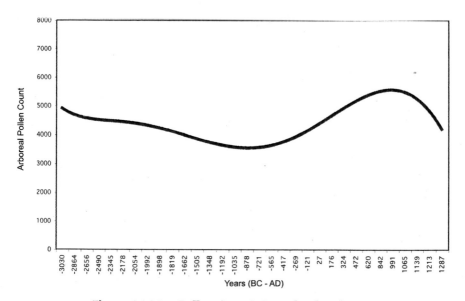

Figure A1.26.   Pollen Count, Greenland (Lake 31)

Appendix 1

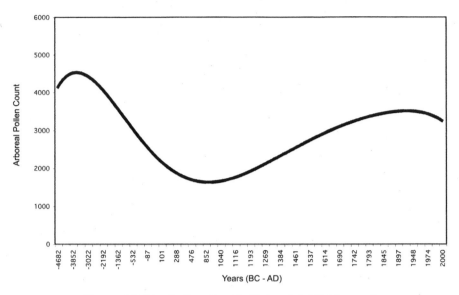

Figure A1.27.   Pollen Count, Finland 1 (Kirkkosaari)

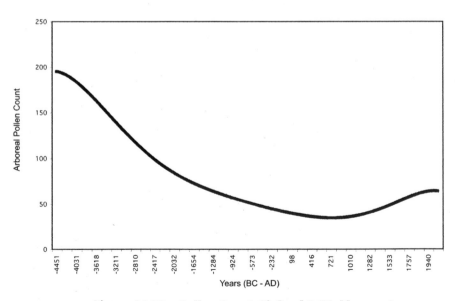

Figure A1.28.   Pollen Count, Finland 2 (Mukkavaara)

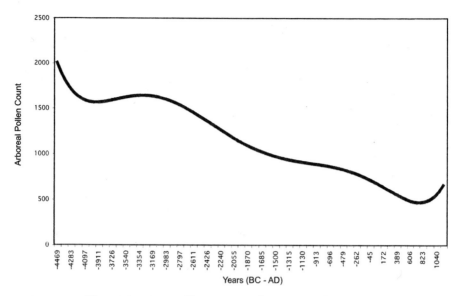

Figure A1.29.   Pollen Count, Finland 3 (Hirvilampi)

MEDITERRANEAN

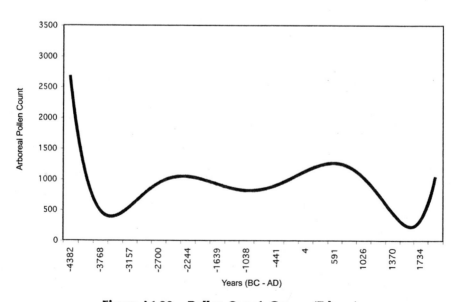

Figure A1.30.   Pollen Count, Greece (Edessa)

Appendix 1

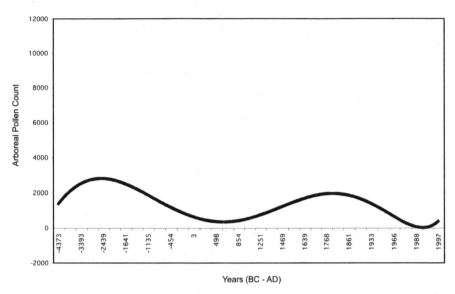

Figure A1.31. Pollen Count, Greece 2 (Khimaditis 1 B)

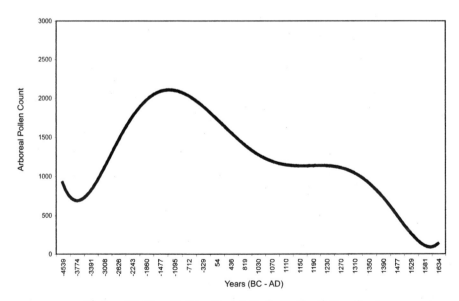

Figure A1.32. Pollen Count, Italy (Selle di Carnino)

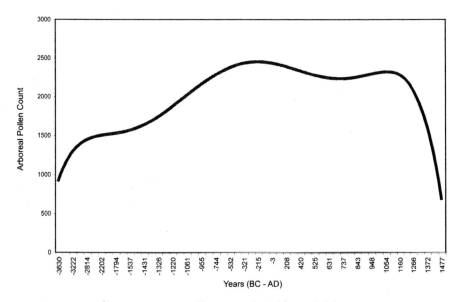

Figure A1.33. Pollen Count, Spain 1 (Saldropo)

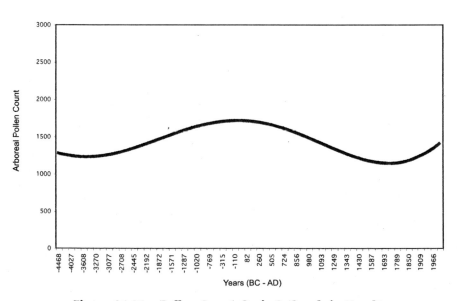

Figure A1.34. Pollen Count, Spain 2 (Sanabria Marsh)

Appendix 1

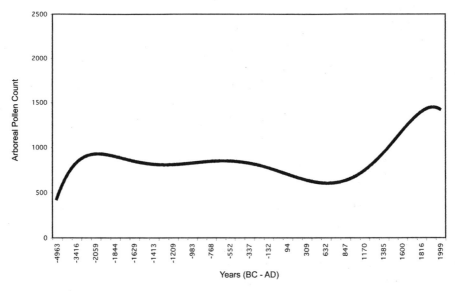

Figure A1.35.   Pollen Count, Spain 3 (Lago de Ajo)

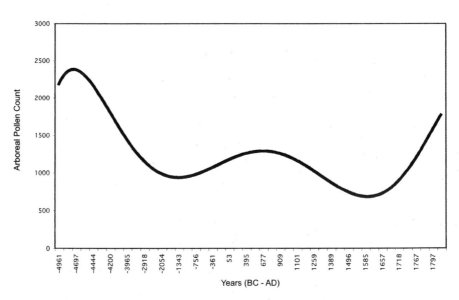

Figure A1.36.   Pollen Count, Spain 4 (Puerto de Los Tornos)

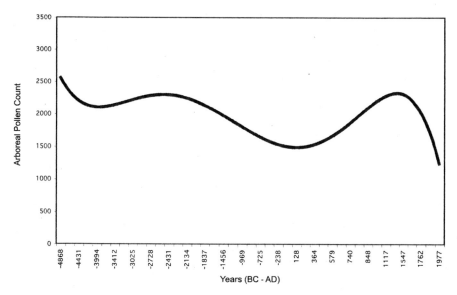

Figure A1.37. Pollen Count, Spain 5 (Laguna de la Roya)

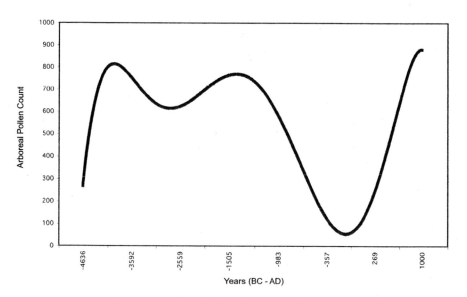

Figure A1.38. Pollen Count, Syria (Ghab)

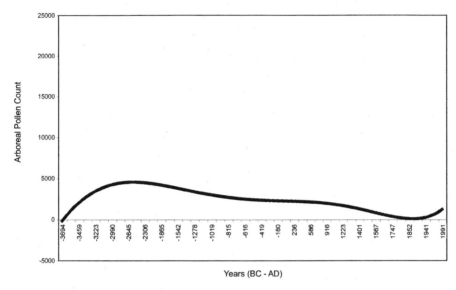

Figure A1.39. Pollen Count, Turkey 1 (Köycegiz Gölü)

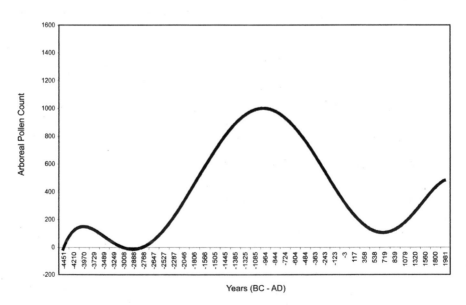

Figure A1.40. Pollen Count, Turkey 2 (Beysehir Gölü)

Appendix 2

PLANTAGO POLLEN INFLUXES

WESTERN EUROPE

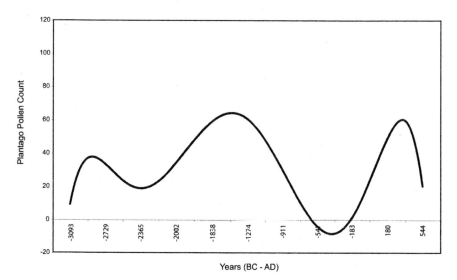

Figure A2.1.   Plantago Pollen Count, Belgium (Moerzeke)

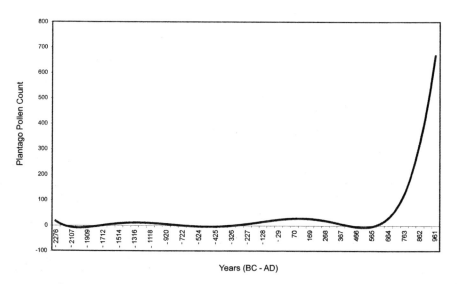

Figure A2.2.   Plantago Pollen Count, Germany 3 (Ahlenmoor)

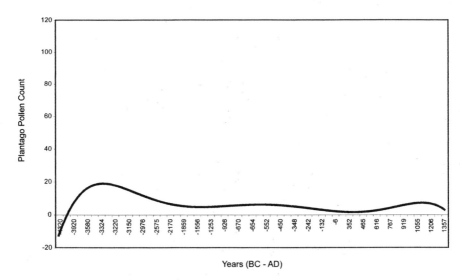

Figure A2.3.   Plantago Pollen Count, Switzerland (Lobsigensee)

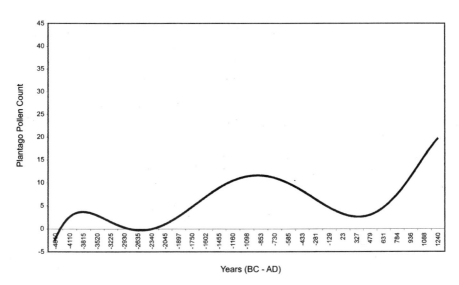

Figure A2.4.   Plantago Pollen Count, France (Le Marais St. Boetien)

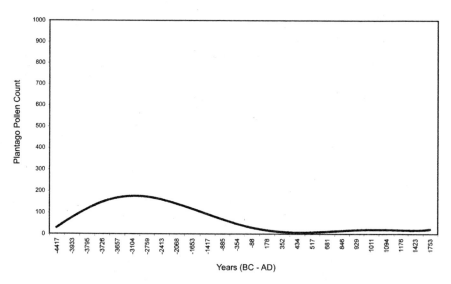

Figure A2.5. Plantago Pollen Count, Ireland (Arts Lough)

CENTRAL AND EASTERN EUROPE

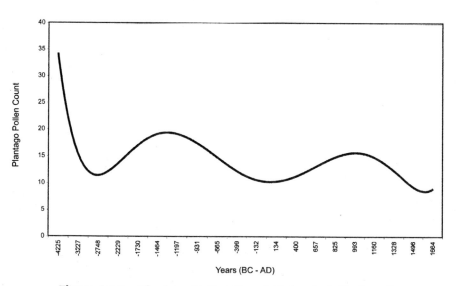

Figure A2.6. Plantago Pollen Count, Bulgaria 1 (Besbog 2)

Appendix 2

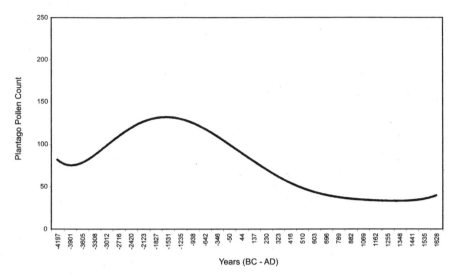

Figure A2.7. Plantago Pollen Count, Bulgaria 2 (Mire Garvan)

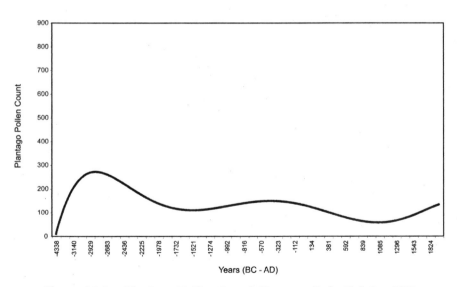

Figure A2.8. Plantago Pollen Count, Hungary (Lake Balaton SW)

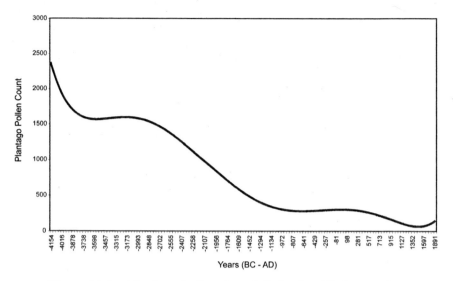

Figure A2.9.   Plantago Pollen Count, Poland 1 (Bledowo Lake)

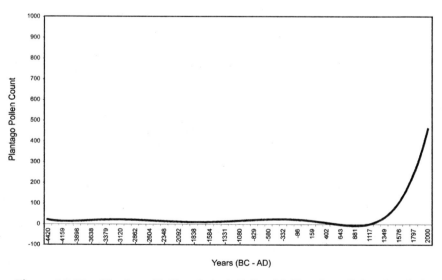

Figure A2.10.   Plantago Pollen Count, Poland 2 (Puscizna Rekowianska)

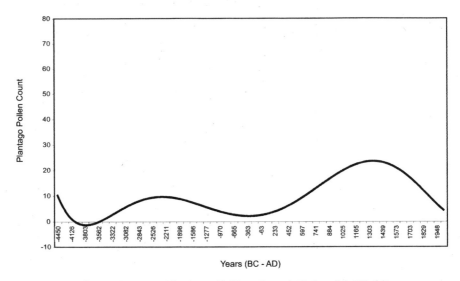

Figure A2.11.   Plantago Pollen Count, Poland 3 (Kluki)

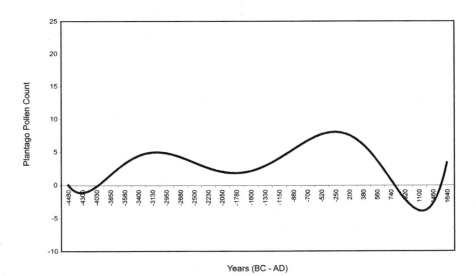

Figure A2.12.   Plantago Pollen Count, Byelorussia 1 (Dolgoe)

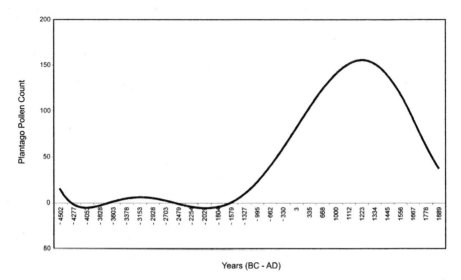

Figure A2.13.   Plantago Pollen Count, Byelorussia 2 (Osvea)

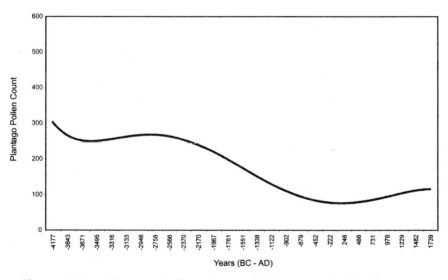

Figure A2.14.   Plantago Pollen Count, Ukraine 1 (Kardashinski Swamp)

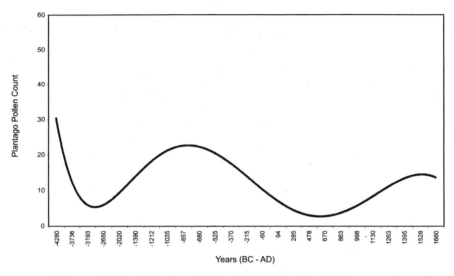

Figure A2.15. Plantago Pollen Count, Ukraine 3 (Stoyanov 2)

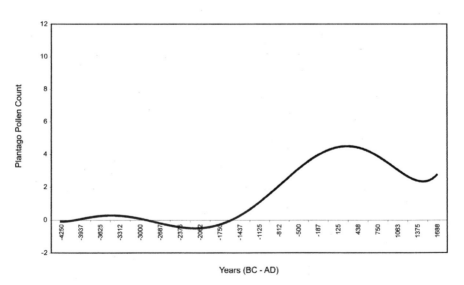

Figure A2.16. Plantago Pollen Count, Ukraine 4 (Ivano-Frankovskoye)

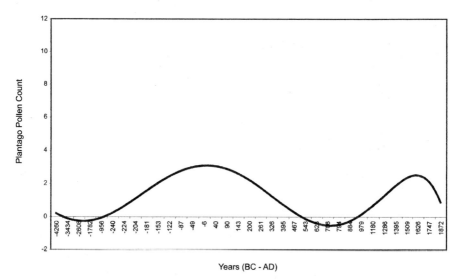

Figure A2.17.   Plantago Pollen Count, Ukraine 5 (Dovjok Swamp)

NORTHERN EUROPE

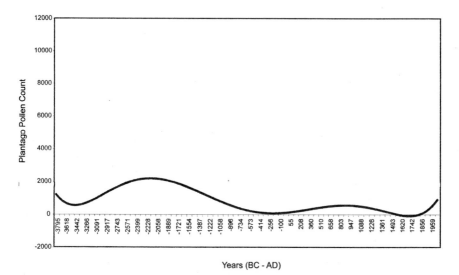

Figure A2.18.   Plantago Pollen Count, Sweden 1 (Ageröds Mosse)

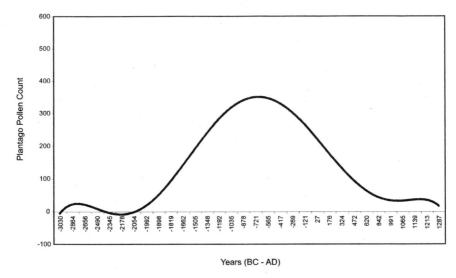

Figure A2.19.   Plantago Pollen Count, Greenland (Lake 31)

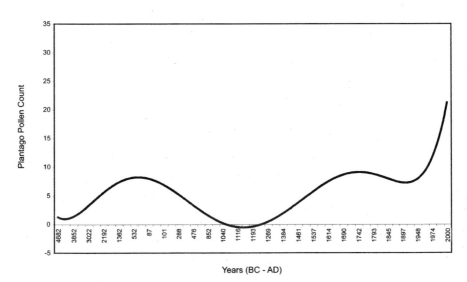

Figure A2.20.   Plantago Pollen Count, Finland 1 (Kirkkosaari)

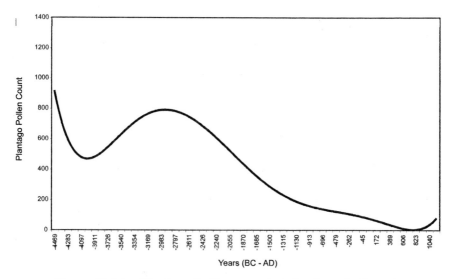

Figure A2.21.   Plantago Pollen Count, Finland 3 (Hirvilampi)

MEDITERRANEAN

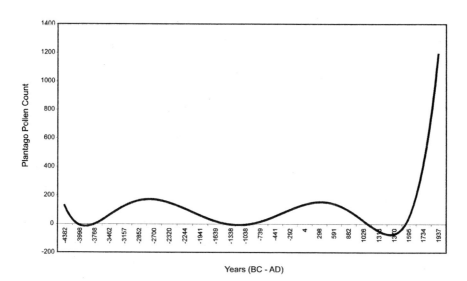

Figure A2.22.   Plantago Pollen Count, Greece (Edessa)

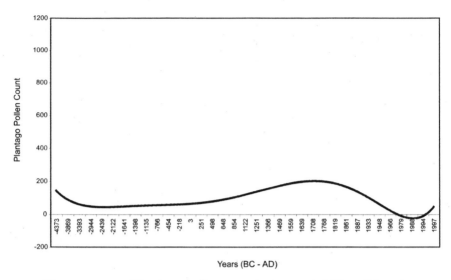

Figure A2.23.   Plantago Pollen Count, Greece 2 (Khimaditis 1 B)

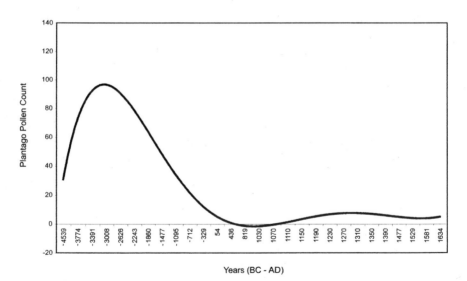

Figure A2.24.   Plantago Pollen Count, Italy (Selle di Carnino)

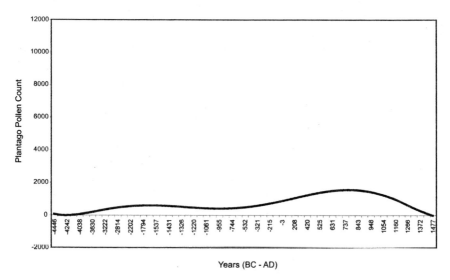

Figure A2.25. Plantago Pollen Count, Spain 1 (Saldropo)

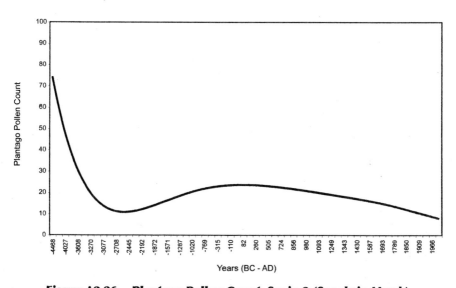

Figure A2.26. Plantago Pollen Count, Spain 2 (Sanabria Marsh)

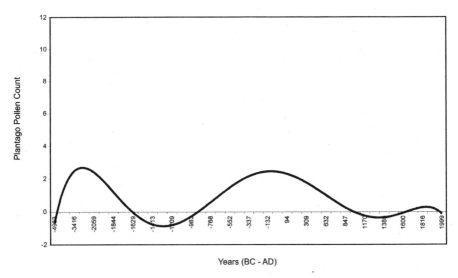

Figure A2.27.   Plantago Pollen Count, Spain 3 (Lago de Ajo)

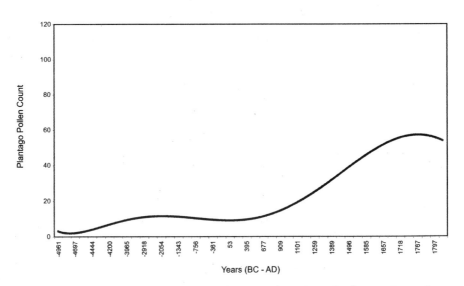

Figure A2.28.   Plantago Pollen Count, Spain 4 (Puerto de Los Tornos)

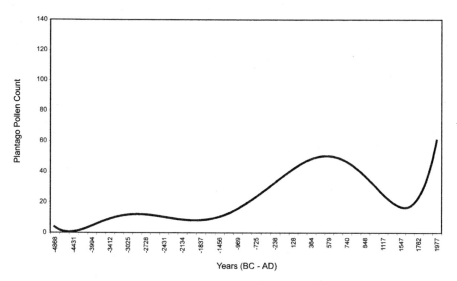

Figure A2.29. Plantago Pollen Count, Spain 5 (Laguna de la Roya)

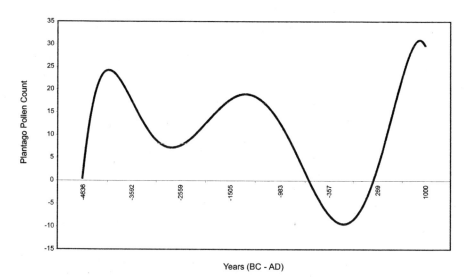

Figure A2.30. Plantago Pollen Count, Syria (Ghab)

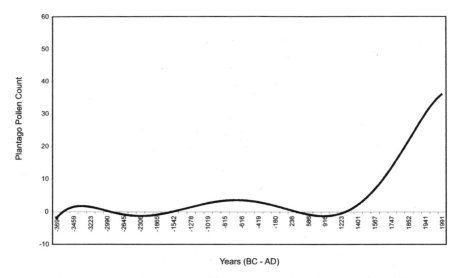

Figure A2.31. Plantago Pollen Count, Turkey 1 (Köycegiz Gölü)

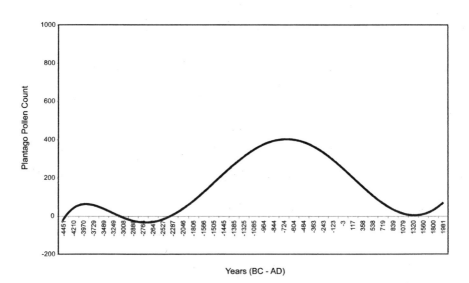

Figure A2.32. Plantago Pollen Count, Turkey 2 (Beysehir Gölü)

Appendix 3

ARBOREAL AND NONARBOREAL POLLEN INFLUXES PERCENTAGES

WESTERN EUROPE

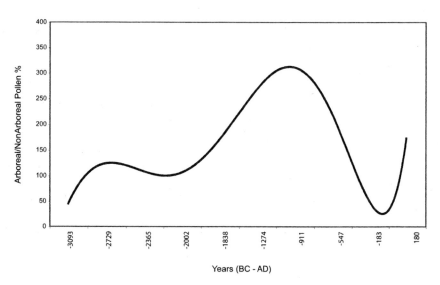

Figure A3.1. Arboreal/Nonarboreal Pollen %, Belgium (Moerzeke)

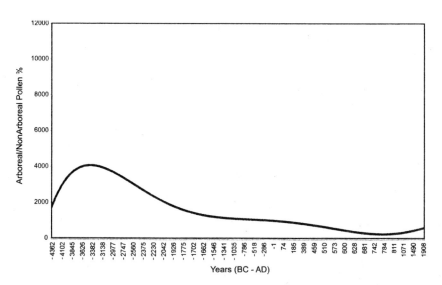

Figure A3.2. Arboreal/Nonarboreal Pollen %, Germany 2 (Lake Steisslingen)

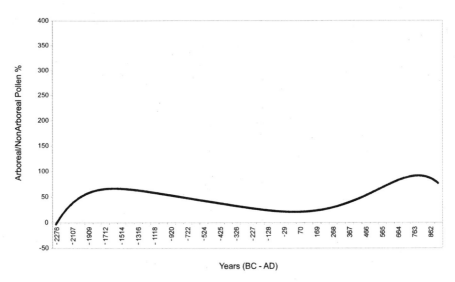

Figure A3.3.   Arboreal/Nonarboreal Pollen %, Germany 3 (Ahlenmoor)

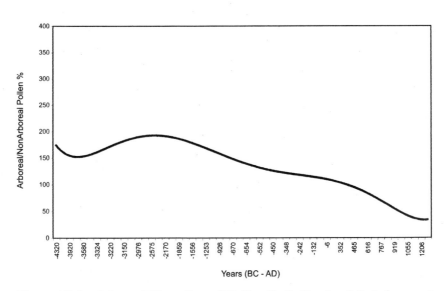

Figure A3.4.   Arboreal/Nonarboreal Pollen %, Switzerland (Lobsigensee)

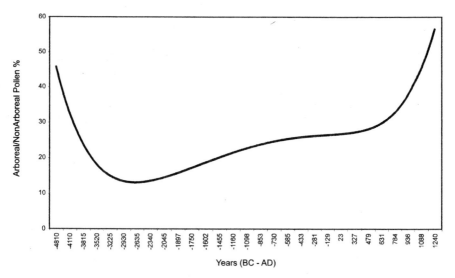

**Figure A3.5.   Arboreal/Nonarboreal Pollen %, France
(Le Marais St. Boetien)**

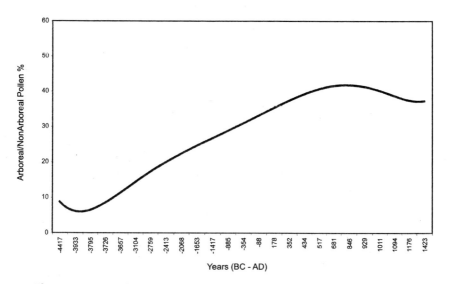

Figure A3.6.   Arboreal/Nonarboreal Pollen %, Ireland (Arts Lough)

Appendix 3

CENTRAL AND EASTERN EUROPE, RUSSIA

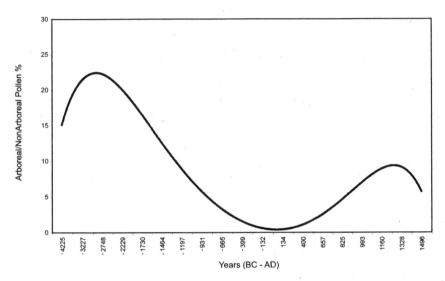

Figure A3.7.   Arboreal/Nonarboreal Pollen %, Bulgaria 1 (Besbog 2)

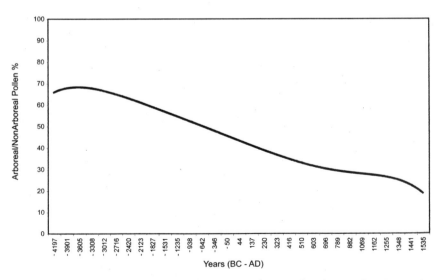

Figure A3.8.   Arboreal/Nonarboreal Pollen %, Bulgaria 2 (Mire Garvan)

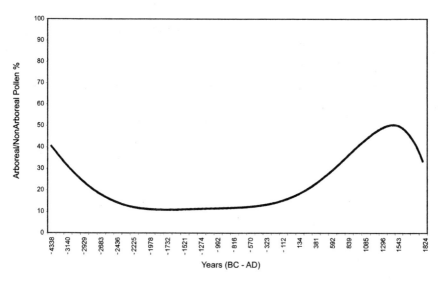

Figure A3.9.   Arboreal/Nonarboreal Pollen %, Hungary (Lake Balaton SW)

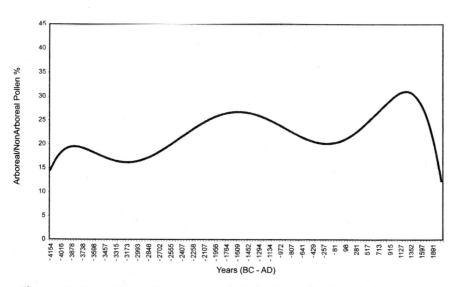

Figure A3.10.   Arboreal/Nonarboreal Pollen %, Poland 1 (Bledowo Lake)

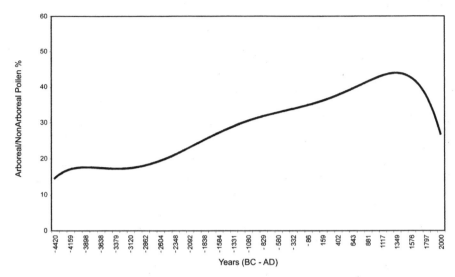

**Figure A3.11.   Arboreal/Nonarboreal Pollen %, Poland 2
(Puscizna Rekowianska)**

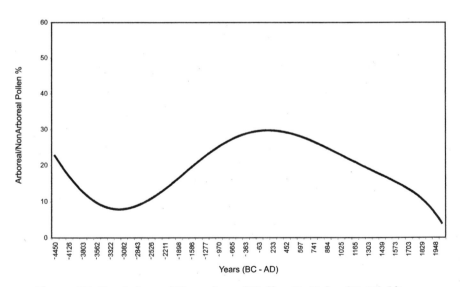

Figure A3.12.   Arboreal/Nonarboreal Pollen %, Poland 3 (Kluki)

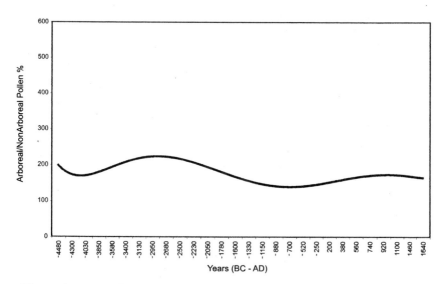

Figure A3.13.   **Arboreal/Nonarboreal Pollen %, Byelorussia 1 (Dolgoe)**

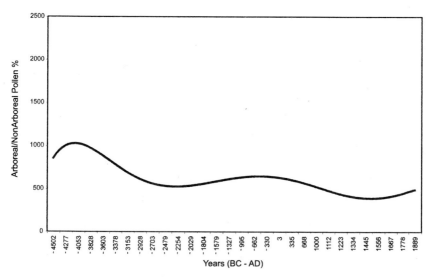

Figure A3.14.   **Arboreal/Nonarboreal Pollen %, Byelorussia 2 (Osvea)**

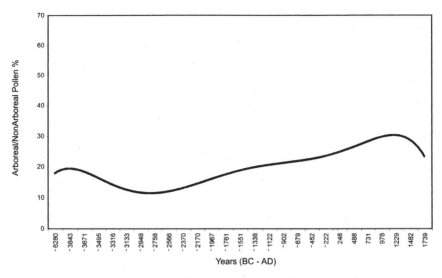

**Figure A3.15.   Arboreal/Nonarboreal Pollen %, Ukraine 1
(Kardashinski Swamp)**

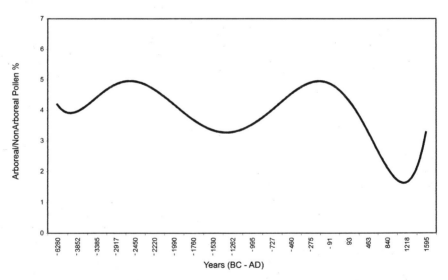

Figure A3.16.   Arboreal/Nonarboreal Pollen %, Ukraine 2 (Starniki)

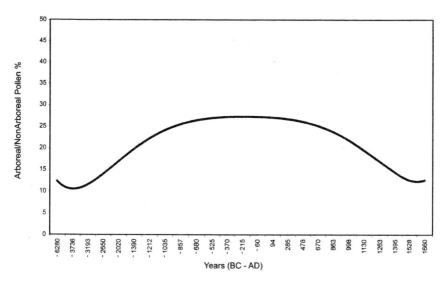

Figure A3.17.   Arboreal/Nonarboreal Pollen %, Ukraine 3 (Stoyanov 2)

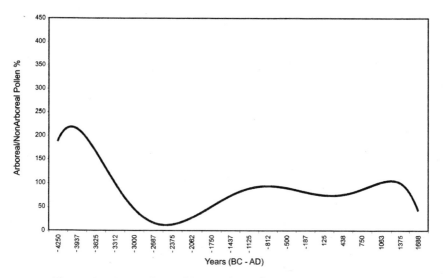

**Figure A3.18.   Arboreal/Nonarboreal Pollen %, Ukraine 4
(Ivano-Frankovskoye)**

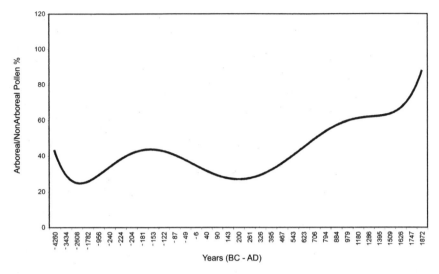

Figure A3.19. Arboreal/Nonarboreal Pollen %, Ukraine 5 (Dovjok Swamp)

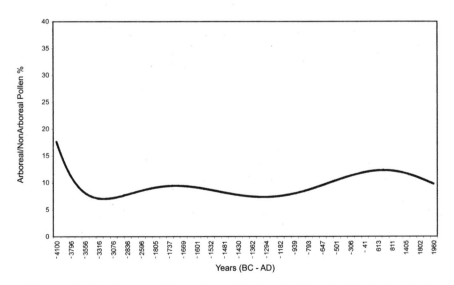

Figure A3.20. Arboreal/Nonarboreal Pollen %, Russia (Chabada Lake)

NORTHERN EUROPE

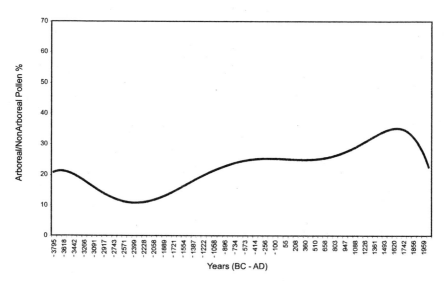

Figure A3.21.   Arboreal/Nonarboreal Pollen %, Sweden 1 (Ageröds Mosse)

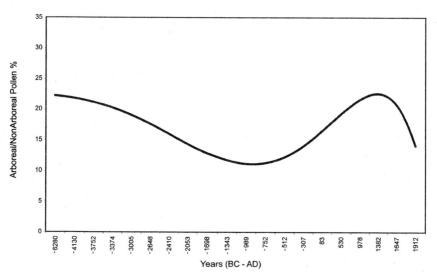

Figure A3.22.   Arboreal/Nonarboreal Pollen %, Sweden 2 (Kansjon)

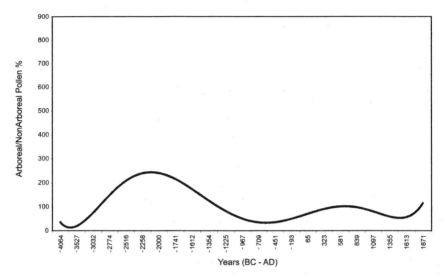

Figure A3.23. Arboreal/Nonarboreal Pollen %, Norway (Grasvatn)

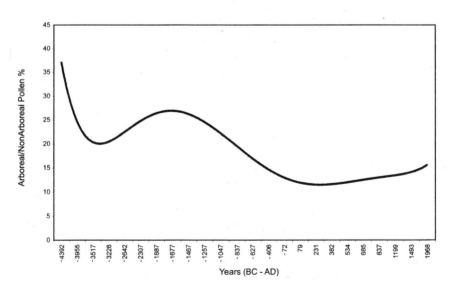

Figure A3.24. Arboreal/Nonarboreal Pollen %, Latvia (Rudushskoe Lake)

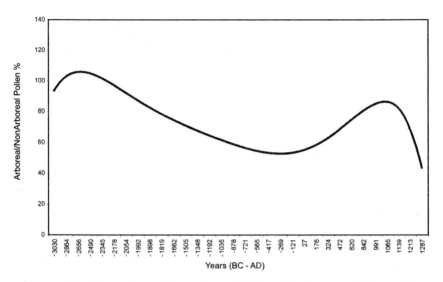

Figure A3.25. Arboreal/Nonarboreal Pollen %, Greenland (Lake 31)

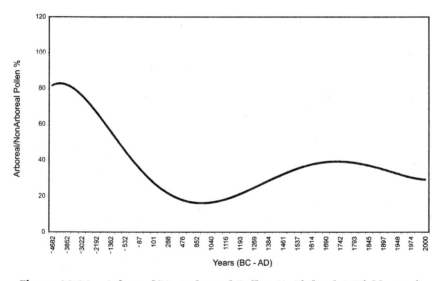

Figure A3.26. Arboreal/Nonarboreal Pollen %, Finland 1 (Kirkkosaari)

Appendix 3

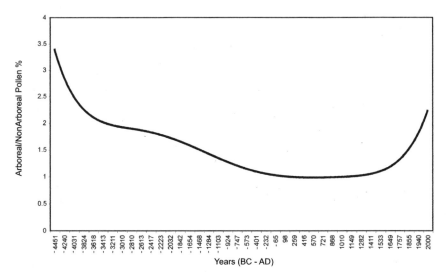

Figure A3.27. Arboreal/Nonarboreal Pollen %, Finland 2 (Mukkavaara)

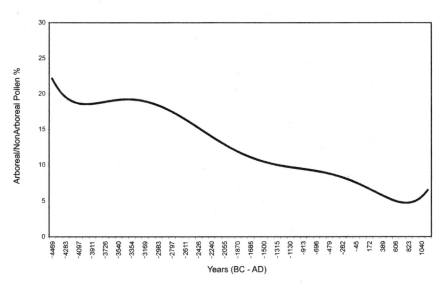

Figure A3.28. Arboreal/Nonarboreal Pollen %, Finland 3 (Hirvilampi)

MEDITERRANEAN

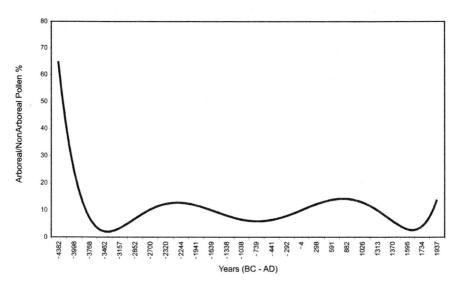

Figure A3.29.   Arboreal/Nonarboreal Pollen %, Greece (Edessa)

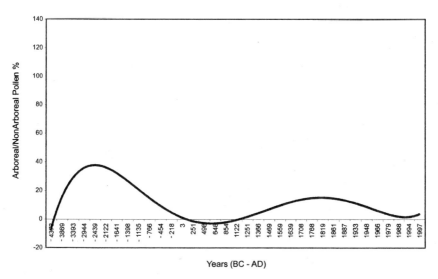

Figure A3.30.   Arboreal/Nonarboreal Pollen %, Greece 2 (Khimaditis 1 B)

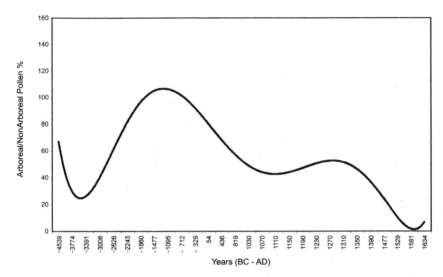

Figure A3.31.   Arboreal/Nonarboreal Pollen %, Italy (Selle di Carnino)

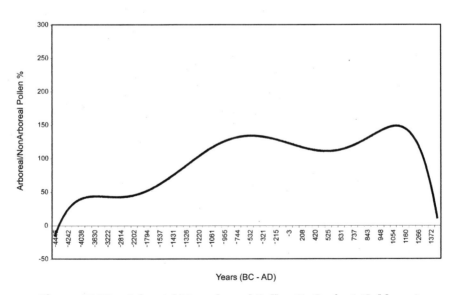

Figure A3.32.   Arboreal/Nonarboreal Pollen %, Spain 1 (Saldropo)

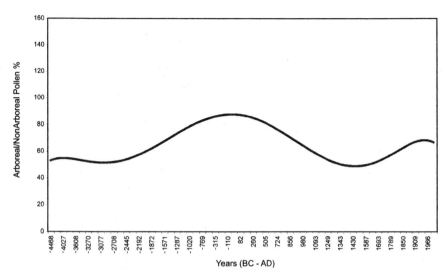

Figure A3.33.   Arboreal/Nonarboreal Pollen %, Spain 2 (Sanabria Marsh)

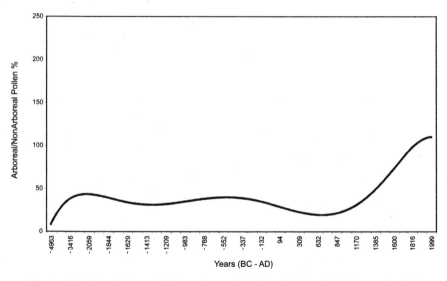

Figure A3.34.   Arboreal/Nonarboreal Pollen %, Spain 3 (Lago de Ajo)

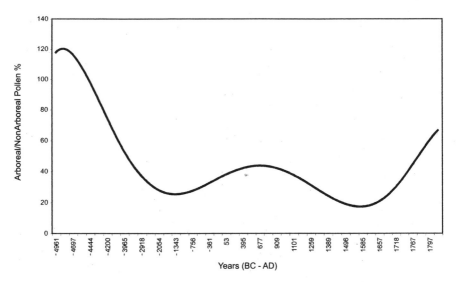

**Figure A3.35. Arboreal/Nonarboreal Pollen %, Spain 4
(Puerto de Los Tornos)**

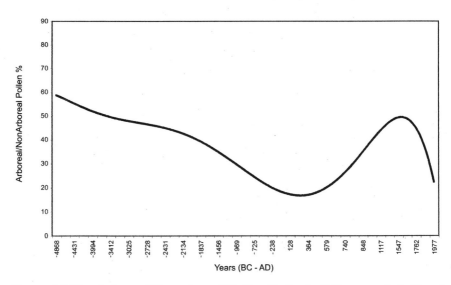

Figure A3.36. Arboreal/Nonarboreal Pollen %, Spain 5 (Laguna de la Roya)

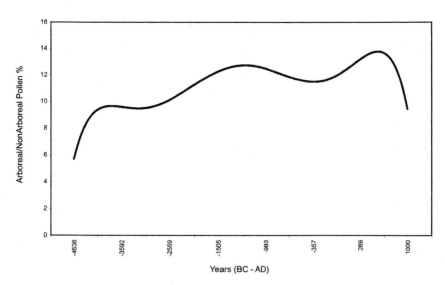

Figure A3.37.   Arboreal/Nonarboreal Pollen %, Syria (Ghab)

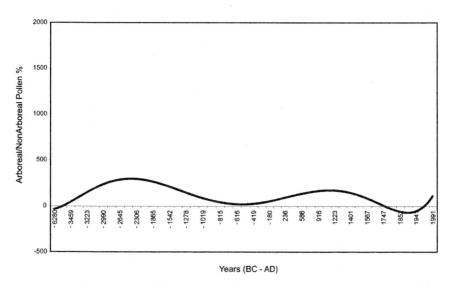

Figure A3.38.   Arboreal/Nonarboreal Pollen %, Turkey 1 (Köycegiz Gölü)

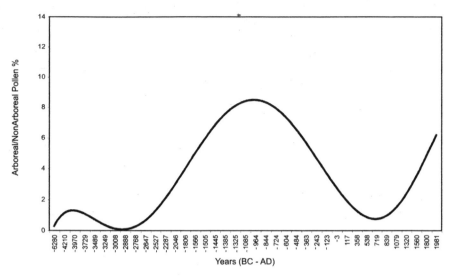

Figure A3.39. Arboreal/Nonarboreal Pollen %, Turkey 2 (Beysehir Gölü)

BIBLIOGRAPHY

Aaby, B. 1970. "Cyclic Change in Climate during 5,500 Years Reflected in Danish Bogs." In *Proceedings of the Nordic Symposium on Climate Changes and Related Problems,* edited by K. Frydendahl, 10–15. Copenhagen: The Danish Natural History Society and the Danish Meteorological Institute.

———. 1976. "Cyclic Climatic Variations in Climate over the Past 5,500 Years Reflected in the Raised Bogs." *Nature* 263: 5575–76.

Abbott, F. F., and A. H. Johnson. 1968. *Municipal Administration in the Roman Empire.* New York: Russell and Russell.

Abu-Lughod, J. 1989. *Before European Hegemony.* New York: Oxford University Press.

Adam, Barbara. 1988. "Social vs. Natural Time, a Traditional Distinction Re-Examined." In *The Rhythms of Society,* edited by M. Young and T. Schuller. London: Routledge.

———. 1997. "Time for the Environment: The Tutzing Project Time Ecology." *Time and Society* 6 (1): 73–84.

———. 1998. *Timescapes of Modernity.* London: Routledge.

Adams, Robert McC. 1981. *Heartland of the Cities.* Chicago: University of Chicago Press.

Agrawal, D. P., and R. K. Sood. 1982. "Ecological Factors and the Harappan Civilization." In *Harappan Civilization: Contemporary Perspective,* edited by G. Possehl, 223–31. New Delhi: Oxford University Press.

Albright, W. F. 1956. "Northeast Mediterranean Dark Ages and the Early Iron Age Art of Syria." In *The Aegean and the Near East: Studies Presented to Hetty Goldman,* edited by S. S. Weinberg, 144–64. Locust Valley: Augustic.

Algaze, Guillermo. 1989. "The Uruk Expansion: Cross-Cultural Exchange in Early Mesopotamia." *Current Anthropology* 30 (5): 571–608.

———. 1993a. *The Uruk World System.* Chicago: University of Chicago Press.

———. 1993b. Expansionary Dynamics of Some Early Pristine States. *American Anthropologist* 95 (2): 304–33.

———. 2001. "Research at Titris Hoyuk in Southeastern Turkey: The 1999 Season." *Anatolica* 27: 23–106.

Allen, J. R. M., B. Hientley, and W. A. Watts. 1996. "The Vegetation and Climate of the Northwest Iberia over the Last 14,000 years." *Journal of Quaternary Science* 11: 125–47.

Amin, Samir et al. 1982. *Dynamics of Global Crisis.* New York: Monthly Review Press.

Amman, B. 1985. Lobsingensee-Late Glacial and Holocene Environments of a Lake on the Central Swiss Plateau. *Disertationes. Botanicae* 87: 127–34.

Anderson, Perry. 1974. *Passages from Antiquity to Feudalism.* London: New Left Books.

Asouti, E. 2003. "Wood Charcoal from Santorini: New Evidence for Climate Vegetation and Timber Imports in the Aegean Bronze Age." *Antiquity* 77 (297): 471–84.

Asthana, Shashi. 1982. Harappan Trade in Metals and Minerals: A Regional Approach. In *Harrapan Civilization,* edited by G. Possehl. New Delhi: Oxford University Press.

Astrom, Paul. 1985. "The Sea Peoples in the Light of New Excavations." *Centre d'Etudes chypriotes* 3: 3–17.

Badian, E. 1968. *Roman Imperialism in the Late Republic.* Oxford: Oxford University Press.

Baillie, M. 1982. *Tree Ring Dating and Archaeology.* London: Croom Helm.

———. 1994. "Dendrochronology Raises Questions about the Nature of A.D. 536 Dust-Veil Event." *The Holocene* 4 (2): 212–17.

———. 1995. *A Slice through Time.* London: Routledge.

———. 1996. " Extreme Environmental Events and the Linking of the Tree-Ring and Ice-Core Records." In *Proceedings of the International Conference,* edited by J. S. Dean, D. M. Mekr, and T. W. Sivetnam. Tucson, AZ: University of Arizona Press.

———. 1998. "Hints that Cometary Debris Played Some Role in Several Tree-Ring Dated Environmental Downturns in the Bronze Age." *Cambridge BAR International Series* 728: 109–16.

———. 1999a. *Exodus to Arthur: Catastrophic Encounters with Comets.* London: Batsford.

———. 1999b. "A View from Outside: Recognizing the Big Picture." *Quaternary Proceedings* 7: 625–35.

Balcer, Jack Martin. 1974. "The Mycenaean Dam at Tiryns." *American Journal of Archaeology* 78 (2): 77–149.

Bao, Y. et al. 2002. "General Characteristics of Temperature Variations in China During the Last Two Millennia." *Geophysical Research Letters* 29 (9): 1324–28.

Barker, G., and J. H. Allen. 1981. *The Sahara, Ecological Change and Early Economic History.* Outwell, Cambridgeshire, UK: Middle East and North African Studies Press.

Bar-Mathews, M., and A. Avalon. 1997. Late Quaternary Paleoclimate in the Eastern Mediterranean Region from Stable Isotope Analysis of Speleothems at Soreq Cave, Israel. *Quaternary Research* 47: 155–68.

———. et al. 1998. A Middle to Late Holocene Paleoclimate in the Eastern Mediterranean Region. In *Water, Environment and Society in Times of Climate Change*, edited by A. S. Issar and N. Brown, 203–14. Amsterdam: Kluwer.

———. et al. 1999. The Eastern Mediterranean Paleoclimate as a Reflection of Regional Events; Soreq Cave, Israel. *Earth and Planetary Science Letters* 166: 85–95.

Barnes, Harry Elmer. 1965. *An Intellectual and Cultural History of the Western World*. New York: Dover Publications.

Barnett, R. D. 1975. *The Sea Peoples*. Cambridge Ancient History II, Part 2. Cambridge: Cambridge University Press.

Barry, R. and Richard Chorley. 1992. *Atmosphere, Weather, and Climate*. New York: Routledge.

Bass, G. F. et al. 1989. The Bronze Age Shipwreck at Ulu Burna: 1986 Campaign." *American Journal of Archaeology* 93: 1–29.

Baynes, N. H. 1943. "The Decline of the Roman Empire in Western Europe: Some Modern Explanations." *Journal of Roman Studies* 33: 29–35.

Behre, Karl Ernst. 1990. "Some Reflections on Anthropogenic Indicators and the Record of Prehistoric Occupation Phases in Pollen Diagrams." In *Man's Role in the Shaping of the Eastern Mediterranean Landscape*, edited by S. Bottema, G. Entjesbieburg, and W. Van Zeist, 219–30. Rotterdam, The Netherlands: Balkema.

Behre, K. E., A. Brande, H. Küster, and M. Rösch. 1996. "Germany." In *Palaeoecological Events During the Last 15,000 Years: Regional Syntheses of Palaeoecological Studies of Lakes and Mires in Europe*, edited by Bjorn Berglund et al., 507–51. New York: John Wiley and Sons

Behre, K. E., and D. Kucan. 1986. Die Reflektion archäologisch bekannter in Pollendiagrammen verschiedener Entfernung. In *Anthropogenic Indicators in Pollen Diagrams*, edited by K. E. Behre, 95–114. Rotterdam, The Netherlands: Belkema.

Bell, Barbara. 1971. "The Dark Ages in Ancient History I: The First Dark Age in Egypt." *American Journal of Archaeology*. 75: 1–20.

———. 1975. "Climate and History of Egypt." *American Journal of Archaeology* 79: 223–79.

Bentaleb, I. et al. 1997. "Monsoon Regime Variations During the Late Holocene in Southwestern India." In *Third Millennium B.C. Climate Change and Collapse*, edited by H. Dalfes and G. Kukla, 193–44. Berlin: Springer-Verlag.

Berglund, Bjorn. 1969. "Vegetation and Human Influences in South Scandinavia During Prehistoric Time." *Oikos Supplement* 12: 9–28.

———. 2003. "Human Impact and Climate Changes—Synchronous Events and a Causal Link?" *Quaternary International* 105: 7–12.

Bergmann, Werner. 1985. "Das Frühe Mönchtum als soziale Bewegung." In *Kölner Zeitschrift für Soziologie und Sozialpsychologie*. 37 (1): 30–59.

Bezusko, L. G. 1987. "The Oak Forest of Maloye Polessie in the Late Post Glacial Period." *Ukrayins'kyi Botanichnyi Zhurnal* 71: 4–8.

——— et al. 1985. "Paleobotanical and Radiological Studies of Deposit from Bog Starniki." *Ukrayins'kyi Botanichnyi Zhurnal* 42: 27–30.

Bietak, M. 1996. *Avaris, The Capital of the Hyksos: Recent Excavations at Tel el-Dab'a*. London: British Museum Publications.

Binford, Michael W. et al. 1997. "Climate Variation and the Rise and Fall of Andean Civilization." *Quaternary Research* 47: 235–48.

Binka, K. et al. 1988. "Bledowo Lake: History of Vegetation and Lake Development During the Last 12 Kyr." *Bulletin Academie Polonaise des Sciences* 36 (2): 147–58.

Bintliff, J. 1982. "A Climate Change, Archaeology and Quaternary Science in the Eastern Mediterranean Region." In *Climate Change in Later Prehistory,* edited by A. F. Harding, 143–61. Edinburgh: Edinburgh University Press.

———. 1984. "Iron Age in the Context of Social Evolution from the Bronze Age through to Historic Times." In *European Social Evolution: Archaeological Perspectives,* edited by J. Bintliff. Bradford, UK: University of Bradford.

———. 1992. "Erosion in the Mediterranean Lands: Reconsideration of Pattern, Process, and Methodology." In *Past and Present Soil Erosion,* edited by M. Bell and J. Boardman. Oxford: Oxbow.

———. 2004. "Dark Age Greece." In *Encyclopedia of the Barbarian World,* edited by Peter Bogucki and Pam J. Crabtree, Vol. 1, 312–18. New York: Thomson Gale.

Biraben, Joean-Noel. 1980. "Essai sur l'evolution du nombre des homes." *Population* 1: 13–25.

Blegen, Carl et al. 1950. *Troy.* 4 vols. Princeton, NJ: Princeton University Press.

Bolin, S. 1958. *State and Currency in the Roman Empire to AD 300.* Stockholm: Almquist and Wiksell.

Bondyrev, I. V. 2003. "Colonization of the Black Sea by the Ancient Greeks and Its *Consequences" Webfestschrift Marshak Transoxiana.* www.transoxiana.com .ar/Eran/Articles/bondyrev.html.

Bookman, R., Yehouda Enzel, Amotz Agnon, and Mordechai Stein. 2004. "Late Holocene Lake Levels of the Dead Sea." *Bulletin of the Geological Society of America* 116 (5/6): 555–71.

Bottema, S. 1974. "Late Quaternary Vegetation History of Northwestern Greece." Ph.D. diss., Groningen University.

———. 1994. "The Prehistoric Environment of Greece: A Review of Palynological Record." In *Beyond the Site,* edited by Nick Kardulias, 45–68. Lanham, Maryland: University Press of America.

———. 1997. "Third Millennium Climate in the Near East Based upon Pollen Evidence." In *Third Millennium BC Climate Change and Old World Collapse,* edited by H. Dalfes et al., 488–515. Heidelberg: Springer-Verlag.

Bottema, S., and H. Woldring. 1990. "Anthropogenic Indicators in the Pollen Record of the Eastern Mediterranean." In *Man's Role in the Shaping of the Eastern Mediterranean Landscape,* edited by S. Bottema, G. Entjes Niebourg, and W. Van Zeist, 231–64. Rotterdam, The Netherlands: Balkema.

Bottema, S., and W. Van Zeist, 1982. "Eastern Mediterranean and the Near East during the Last 20,000 Years." In *Paleoclimate, Paleoenvironment, and Human Communities in the Eastern Mediterranean Region in Later Prehistory,* edited by J. L Bintliff and W. Van Zeist, BAR International Series, 277–321. Oxford: Archeopress.

Bosworth, Andrew. 1995. "World Cities and World Economic Cycles." In *Civilizations and World Systems,* edited by Stephen Sanderson. Walnut Creek, CA: AltaMira Press.

Bouzek, J. 1969. "Homerische Griechenland im Lichte der archaologischen Quellen." *Acta Universitatis Carolinae Philosophica et Historica* 29: 245–51.

———. 1982. "Climate Change and Central Europe." In *Climate Change in Later Prehistory,* edited by A. F. Harding, 162–78. Edinburgh: Edinburgh University Press.

Bovarski, Edward. 1998. "First Intermediate Period Private Tombs." In *Encyclopedia of Ancient Egypt,* edited by K. Bard, 316–19. New York: Routledge.

Bradshaw, R. H. W. et al. 1988. "The Extent and Time Course of Mountain Blanket Peat Erosion in Ireland." *New Phytologist* 108: 219–24.

Branigan, K. 1981. "Minoan Civilization." *Annual of the British School at Athens* 76: 23–33.

———. 1984. "Minoan Community Colonies in the Aegean." In *The Minoan Thalassocracy: Myth and Reality,* edited by Robin Haag and Nanno Marinatos. Stockholm: Paul Astroms Forlag.

———. 1989. "Minoan Foreign Relations in Transition." *Aegaeum* 3: 65–71.

Braudel, Fernand. 1972. *The Mediterranean and the Mediterranean World in the Age of Philip II.* Vol. 1. London: Fontana.

———. 1980. *On History.* Chicago: University of Chicago Press.

———. 1981. *The Structure of Everyday Life.* Vol. 1. New York: Harper and Row.

———. 1982. *The Wheels of Commerce.* Vol. 2. New York: Harper and Row.

———. 1984. *The Perspective of the World.* Vol. 3. New York: Harper and Row.

———. 1989. *The Identity of France.* 2 vols. New York: Harper and Row.

———. 2001. *Memory and the Mediterranean.* New York: Alfred Knopf.

Briffa, K. 1999. "Analysis of Dendrochronological Variability and Associated Natural Climates in Eurasia the Last 10,000 Years." *PAGES Newsletter* 7 (1): 6–8.

Brinkman, J. A. 1968. "Ur: The Kassite Period and the Period of Assyrian Kings." *Orientalis* 38: 310–48.

Broecker, Wallace S. 2001. "Was the Medieval Warm Period Global?" *Science,* February 23, 1497–99.

Brogan, Olwen. 1936. "Trade between the Roman Empire and the Free Germans." *Journal of Roman Studies* 26: 196–223.

Brown, N. 1995. "The Impact of Climate Change: Some Indications from History A.D. 250–1250." Oxford Centre for the Environment, Ethics and Society Research Papers.

———. 2001. *History and Climate Change: A Eurocentric Perspective.* London: Routledge.

Brown, Peter. 1971. *The World of Late Antiquity.* London: Harcourt Brace.

Brunt, P. A. 1971. *Italian Manpower 225 B.C.–A.D. 14.* Oxford: Oxford University Press.

Bryce, Trevor. 1999. *The Kingdom of the Hittites.* Oxford: Oxford University Press.

———. 2002. *Life and Society in the Hittite World.* Oxford: Oxford University Press.

Bryson, R., and T. Swain. 1981. "Holocene Variations of Monsoon Rainfall in Rajasthan." *Quaternary Research* 16: 135–45.

Bryson, R. A., H. H. Lamb, and David L. Donley. 1974. "Drought and the Decline of Mycenae." *Antiquity* 48 (189): 46–50.

Bryson, R. A., and C. Padoch. 1980. "On Climates of History." *Journal of Interdisciplinary History* 10 (4): 583–97.

Bryson, Robert, and Reid Bryson. 1998. "Application of a Global Volcanicity Time Series on High Resolution Paleoclimatic Modeling of the Eastern Mediterranean." In *Water, Environment and Society in Times of Change,* edited by A. Issar and N. Brown, 1–19. Dordrecht, The Netherlands: Kluwer.

Buckland, P. C., A. J. Dugmore, and K. J. Edward. 1997. "Bronze Age Myths? Volcanic Activity and Human Response in the Mediterranean and North Atlantic Regions." *Antiquity* 71: 581–93.

Burgess, C. 1989. "Volcanoes, Catastrophe, and Global Crisis of the Late 2nd Millennium B.C." *Current Anthropology* 10 (10): 325–29.

Burroughs, William J. 2005. *Climate Change in Prehistory.* Cambridge: Cambridge University Press.

Bury, J. B. 1913. *A History of Greece.* London: Croom Helm.

Butzer, K.W. 1976. *Early Hydraulic Civilization in Egypt.* Chicago: University of Chicago Press.

———. 1980. "Adaptation to Global Environmental Change." *Professional Geographer* 32: 269–78.

———. 1983. "Long Term Nile Flood Variation and Political Discontinuities in Pharaonic Egypt." In *From Hunters to Farmers,* edited by J. D. Clark and S. Brandt, 102–12. Berkeley: University of California Press.

———. 1995. "Environmental Change in the Near East and Human Impact on the Land." In *Civilizations of the Ancient Near East,* edited by J. M. Sasson, 123–51. New York: Scribners.

———. 1997. "Socio Political Discontinuity in the Near East c. 2200 B.C.E. Scenarios from Palestine and Egypt." In *Third Millennium B.C. Climate Change and Old World Collapse,* edited by H. Dalfes et al., 245–96. Heidelberg: Springer-Verlag.

———. 2005. "Environmental History in the Mediterranean World: Cross-Disciplinary Investigation of Cause-and-Effect for Degradation and Soil Erosion." *Journal of Archaeological Sciences* 32: 1773–1800.

Cadogan, G. 1983. "Early Minoan and Middle Minoan Chronology." *American Journal of Archaeology* 87: 507–18.

———. 1984. "A Minoan Thalassocracy." In *The Minoan Thalassocracy: Myth or Reality,* edited by Robin Hagg and Nanno Marinatos. Stockholm: Paul Astroms Forlag.

Cantor, Norman F. 1993. *The Civilization of the Middle Ages.* New York: Harper.

Carcopino, J. B. 1940. *Daily Life in Ancient Rome.* New Haven: Yale University Press.

Carpenter, Rhys. 1968. *Discontinuity in Greek Civilization.* Cambridge: Cambridge University Press.

Carswell, John. 1991. "The Port of Mantai, Sri Lanka." In *Rome and India,* edited by V. Begley and D. L. Puma, 197–203. Madison: University of Wisconsin Press.

Carter, Vernon, and Tom Dale. 1974. *Topsoil and Civilization.* Norman: University of Oklahoma Press.

Caselgrove, Colin. 1987. "Culture Process on the Periphery." In *Centre and Periphery in the Ancient World,* edited by Michael Rowlands et al., 104–24. Cambridge: Cambridge University Press.

Casson, Lionel. 1954. "Trade in the Ancient World." *Scientific American* 191 (5): 98–104.

Chadwick, J. 1972. "Life in Mycenaean Greece." *Scientific American* 227 (4): 36–44.

———. 1976. *The Mycenaean World.* New York: Cambridge University Press.

Chandler, T. 1974. *Three Thousand Years of Urban Growth.* New York: Academic Press.

———. 1987. *Four Thousand Years of Urban Growth.* Lewiston, NJ: Edwin Mellen Press.

Chase-Dunn, C., and T. Hall. 1997. *Rise and Demise: Comparing World-Systems.* Boulder, CO: Westview Press.

Chernykh, E. N. 1992. *Ancient Metallurgy in the U.S.S.R.: The Early Metal Age.* Cambridge: Cambridge University Press.

Chew, Sing C. 1992. *Logs for Capital: The Timber Industry and Capitalist Enterprise in the Nineteenth Century.* Westport, CT: Greenwood Press.

———. 1995a. "Environmental Transformations: Accumulation, Ecological Crisis, and Social Movements." In *A New World Order? Global Transformation in the Late Twentieth Century,* edited by Jozsef Borocz and David A. Smith. Westport, CT: Praeger.

———. 1995b. "Environmental Imperatives and Development Strategies: Challenges for Southeast Asia." In *Asia: Who Pays for Growth?* edited by Jayant Lele. London: Dartmouth.

———. 1997a. "Accumulation, Deforestation, and World Ecological Degradation 2500 B.C. to A.D. 1990." *Advances in Human Ecology.* Vol. 6. Westport, CT: JAI Press.

———. 1997b. "For Nature: Deep Greening World Systems Analysis for the Twenty-First Century." *Journal of World-Systems Research* 3 (3): 381–402.

———. 1999. "Ecological Relations and the Decline of Civilizations in the Bronze Age World System: Mesopotamia and Harappa 2500 B.C.–1700 B.C." In *Ecology and the World System,* edited by W. Goldfrank et al. Greenwich, CT: Greenwood Press.

———. 2001. *World Ecological Degradation: Accumulation, Urbanization, and Deforestation.* Lanham, MD: AltaMira Press/Rowman & Littlefield Publishers.

———. 2002a. Globalization, Dark Ages, and Ecological Degradation. *Global Society* 16 (4): 333–56.

———. 2002b. "Ecology in Command." In *Structure, Culture, and History. Recent Issues in Social Theory,* edited by Sing C. Chew and J. David Knottnerus, 217–30. Lanham, MD: Rowman & Littlefield Publishers.

———. 2005a. "From Mycenae to Mesopotamia and Egypt to Mycenae: Dark Ages, Political Economic Declines, and Environmental/Climatic Changes 2200 B.C.–700 B.C." In *The Historical Evolution of World-Systems,* edited by Christopher Chase-Dunn and E. N. Anderson, 52–74. London: Palgrave MacMillan.

———. 2005b. "Dark Ages over World History: Ecological Crisis and System Changes." Paper presented at International Symposium on Environment and Society in Chinese History, Nankai University, Tianjin, People's Republic of China, August 17–19, 2005.

———. 2006. "Dark Ages." In *Globalization and Global History,* edited by Barry K. Gills and William R. Thompson, 163–202. London: Routledge.

Childe, Gordon. 1942. *What Happened in History.* Harmondsworth, UK: Penguin.

———. 1950. "The Urban Revolution." *Town Planning Review* 21: 3–17.

———. 1952. *New Light on the Most Ancient East.* London: Routledge.

———. 1957. "The Bronze Age." *Past and Present* 12: 2–15.

———. 1969. *Prehistoric Migrations in Europe.* Oosterhout, The Netherlands: Anthropology Publications.

China Daily. 2005. "Oil Change." August 22–28, 2005, 1.

Cipolla, Carlo, ed. 1970. *The Economic Declines of Empires.* London: Methuen.

Cline, E. H. 1994. *Sailing the Wine-Dark Sea. International Trade and the Late Aegean Bronze Age.* Oxford: Oxford University Press.

Cohen, Joel E. 1995. *How Many People Can the Earth Support?* New York: W. W. Norton.

Coldstream, J. N. 1977. *Geometric Greece.* London: Routledge.

Collis, J. 1984. *The European Iron Age.* London: Batsford.

Connah, Graham. 1996. *Three Thousand Years in Africa.* Cambridge: Cambridge University Press.

Connolly, Peter. 1981. *Greece and Rome at War.* Englewood Cliffs, NJ: Prentice Hall.

Crawley, Thomas J. 2003. "When Did Global Warming Start?" *Climate Change* 61 (3): 259–60.

Crutzen, P. I. and E. F. Stoermer. 2000. "The 'Anthropocene.'" *IGBP Newsletter* no. 41: 2–3.

Curry, C. J. 1928. "Climate and Migrations." *Antiquity* 2: 292–307.

Curtin, Philip. 2000. *The World and the West.* London: Cambridge University Press.

Dales, G. F. 1977. "Shifting Trade Patterns between Iranian Plateau and the Indus Valley." In *Le Plateau Iranien et l'Asie Centrale,* edited by J. Deshayes, 67–78. Paris: CNRS.

———. 1979. "The Decline of the Harappans." In *Ancient Cities of the Indus,* edited by G. Possehl, 307–12. New Delhi: Vikas.

Davies, Roy W. 1969. "Social and Economic Aspects." In *The Roman Villa in Britain.* A. L. Rivet, 173–216. London: Routledge.

Davis, J., ed. 1998. *Sandy Pylos.* Austin: University of Texas Press.

Davis, M. and Shaw R. 2001. "Range Shifts and Adaptive Responses to Quaternary Climate Change." *Science,* April 27, 667–73.

Deger-Jalkotzy, Sigrid. 1998. "The Last Mycenaean and their Successors Updated." In *Mediterranean Peoples in Transition,* edited by Seymour Gitin et al., 114–28. Jerusalem: Israel Exploration Society.

DeMenocal, Peter B. 2001. "Cultural Response to Climate Change during the Late Holocene." *Science,* April 27, 667–72.

Denemark, R. et al., eds. 2000. *World System History: The Social Science of Long-Term Change.* London: Routledge.

Deo, S. B. 1991. "Roman Trade: Recent Archaeological Discoveries in Western India." In *Rome and India,* edited by V. Begley and R. DePuma, 39–45. Madison: University of Wisconsin Press.

Desborough, V. R. 1972. *The Greek Dark Ages.* London: Ernest Benn.

————. 1975. "The End of Mycenaean Civilization and the Dark Age." In *Cambridge Ancient History,* edited by I. E. S. Edwards et al., 658–77. Cambridge: Cambridge University Press.

Dever, William G. 1998. "Social Structure in Palestine in the Iron II Period on the Eve of Destruction." In *The Archaeology of Society in the Holy Land,* edited by T. E. Levy, 416–31. London: Leicester University.

Diakonoff, I. M. 1991a. "The City States of Sumer." In *Early Antiquity,* edited by I.. Diakonoff, 67–83. Chicago: University of Chicago Press.

————. 1991b. "Early Despotisms in Mesopotamia." In *Early Antiquity,* edited by I. M. Diakonoff, 84–97. Chicago: University of Chicago Press.

Dickinson, O. T. 1977. *The Origins of Mycenaean Civilization.* Goteborg, Sweden: SIMA.

————. 1994. *The Aegean Bronze Age.* Cambridge: Cambridge University Press.

Dornborg, John. 1992. "Battle of the Teutoborg Forest." *Archaeology* 45. (5): 26–33.

Downey, Glanville. 1969. *The Late Roman Empire.* New York: Holt, Rinehart, and Winston.

Drews, R. 1993. *The End of the Bronze Age.* Princeton, NJ: Princeton University Press.

Driessen, Jan, and C. Macdonald. 2000. "The Eruption of the Santorini Volcano and Its Effects on Minoan Crete." In *The Archaeology of Geological Catastrophe,* edited by W. J. McGuire et al., 81–93. London: Geological Society.

Drummond, Steven, and Lynn H. Nelson. 1994. *The Western Frontiers of Imperial Rome.* Armonk, NY: M. E. Sharpe.

Dubowski, Y., J. Erez, and M. Stiller. 2003. "Isotopic Paleolimnology of Lake Kinneret." *Limnology and Oceanography* 48 (1): 68–78.

Duncan-Jones, Richard. 1990. *Structure and Scale in the Roman Economy.* Cambridge: Cambridge University Press.

Earle, T. 2002. *Bronze Age Economics.* Boulder, CO: Westview.

Eder, Klaus. 1999. "Societies Learn and Yet the World Is Hard to Change." *European Journal of Social Theory* 2 (2): 195–215.

Ehrlich, Paul, and Anne Ehrlich. 2004. *One with Nineveh.* Washington D.C.: Island Press.

Eisenstadt, S., and W. Schluchter. 1998. "Introduction: Paths to Early Modernities." *Daedalus* 127 (3): 1–18.

Eisner, W. R. et al. 1995. "Paleoecological Studies of a Holocene Lacustine Record from the Kangerlussnaq." *Quaternary Research* 43: 55–66.

Elkington, H. D. H. 1976. "The Mendip Lead Industry." In *The Roman West Country,* edited by Keith Branigan and P. J. Fowler, 123–45. London: David and Charles.

Elvin, Mark. 1993. "Three Thousand Years of Unsustainable Growth: China's Environment from Archaic Times to the Present." *East Asian History* 6: 7–46.

————. 2004. *The Retreat of the Elephants.* New Haven: Yale University Press.

Enzel, Y. et al. 1999. "High Resolution Holocene Environmental Changes in the Thar Desert, Northwestern India." *Science,* April 2, 125–28.

Eronen, M., and Hyvrinen, H. 1982. "Subfossil Dates and Pollen Diagrams from Northern Fennoscandia." *Geologis Frem* 103: 437–55.

Esse, Douglas. 1991. *Subsistence, Trade, and Social Change in Early Bronze Age Palestine.* Chicago: University of Chicago Press.

Evans, Arthur. 1921. *The Palace of Minos*. London: MacMillan.

Fagan, Brian. 1999. *Floods, Famines, and Emperors El Nino and the Fate of Civilizations*. New York: Basic Books.

———. 2004. *The Long Summer*. New York: Basic Books.

Fairbridge, R. O. et al. 1997. "Background to Mid-Holocene Climate Change in Anatolia and Adjacent Regions." In *Third Millennium BC Climate Change and Old World Collapse*, edited by H. Dalfes et al. Heidelberg: Springer-Verlag.

Fairservis, Walter. 1979a. "The Harappan Civilization: New Evidence and More Theory." In *Ancient Cities of the Indus*, edited by G. Possehl, 50–65. New Delhi: Vikas.

———. 1979b. "The Origin, Character, and Decline of an Early Civilization." In *Ancient Cities of the Indus*, edited by G. Possehl, 66–89. New Delhi: Vikas.

Faulkner, R. 1940. "Egyptian Seagoing Ships." *Journal of Egyptian Archaeology* 26: 3–9.

———. 1975. "Egypt from the Inception of the 19th Century to the Death of Ramasses III." In *Cambridge Ancient History*. vol. 2, part 2, 217–51. Cambridge: Cambridge University Press.

Finkelstein, Israel, and Ram Gophna. 1993. "Settlement, Demographic, and Economic Patterns in the Highlands of Palestine in the Chalcolithic and Early Bronze Periods and the Beginning of Urbanization." *Bulletin of the American School of Oriental Research* 289: 1–22.

Finley, M. I. 1965. "Technical Innovations and Economic Progress in the Ancient World." *Economic History Review* 18: 217–25.

———. 1973. *The Ancient Economy*. London: Penguin.

———. 1977. "The Ancient City: From Fustel de Coulanges to Max Weber and Beyond." *Comparative Studies in Society and History* 19 (3): 305–27.

Fischer, Ulrich. 1961. "Frankfurt-Heddernheim: A Roman Frontier Town beyond the Rhine." *Archaeology* 14: 36–37.

Flotz, Richard C. 2003. "Does Nature Have Historical Agency? World History and Environmental History and How Histories Can Help to Save the Planet." *The History Teacher* 37 (1): 9–28.

Frank, Andre Gunder. 1980. *Crisis in the World Economy*. New York: Holmes and Meier.

———. 1991. "Transitional Ideological Modes: Feudalism, Capitalism, and Socialism." *Critique of Anthropology* 11 (2): 171–88.

———. 1993. "Bronze Age World System Cycles." *Current Anthropology* 34 (4): 383–429.

———. 1998. *ReOrient: Global Economy in the Asian Age*. Berkeley, CA: University of California Press.

Frank, Andre Gunder, and B. K. Gills. 1992. "World System Cycles, Crises, and Hegemonial Shifts." *Review* 15 (4): 621–88.

Frank, Tenny. 1927. *An Economic History of Rome*. Baltimore: Johns Hopkins Press.

Frankenstein, S. 1979. "The Phoenicians in the Far West: A Function of Neo-Assyrian Imperialism." In *Power and Propaganda*, edited by M. T. Larsen, 24–56. Copenhagen: Akademisk Forlag.

Frankenstein, S., and M. Rowlands. 1978. "The Internal Structure and Regional Context of Early Iron Age Society in S.W. Germany." *Bulletin of the Institute of Archaeology* 15: 73–112.

Frere, Sheppard. 1967. *Britania: A History of Roman Britain.* Cambridge, MA: Harvard University Press.

Friedman, Harriet. 2000. "What on Earth is the Modern World-System? Food Getting and Territory in the Modern Era and Beyond." *Journal of World Systems Research* 6: 480–515.

Friedman, Jonathan. 1982. "Catastrophe and Continuity in Social Evolution." In *Theory and Explanation in Archaeology,* edited by Colin Renfrew et al., 56–79. London: Academic Press.

Friedman, Jonathan, and Michael Rowlands. 1977. "Notes toward an Epigenetic Model of the Evolution of Civilization." In *The Evolution of Social System,* edited by M. J. Rowlands and J. Friedman, 201–76. London: Academic Press.

Friedman, Kajsa. 2003. "Structure, Dynamics, and the Final Collapse of Bronze Age Civilizations in the Second Millennium." Paper presented at Political Economy of World-Systems Conference, University of California, Riverside. March 23–25, 2002.

Friedrich, Walter L. et al. 2006. "Santorini Eruption Radiocarbon Dated to 1627–1600 B.C." *Science* 312: 548.

Fulford, Michael. 1992. "Territorial Expansion and the Roman Empire." *World Archaeology* 23 (3): 294–305.

Gale, N. H., ed. 1991. *Bronze Age Trade in the Mediterranean.* Gothenburg, Sweden: Jonsered.

Gardiner, A. 1961. *Egypt of the Pharoahs.* Oxford: Oxford University Press.

Garnsey, Peter. 1970. "Septimus Severus and the Marriage of Roman Soldiers." *California Studies in Classical Antiquity* 3: 45–55.

Garnsey, Peter, and Richard Saller. 1987. *The Roman Empire.* Berkeley: University of California Press.

Gasse, F. 2000. "Hydrological Changes in the African Tropics since the Last Glacial Maximum." *Quaternary Science Review* 19: 189–212.

Ge, Q. et al. 2003. "Winter Half-Year Temperature Reconstruction for the Middle and Lower Reaches of the Yellow River and Yangtze River, China During the Past 2000 Years." *Holocene* 13 (6): 933–40.

Gelb, I. J. 1973. "Prisoners of War in Early Mesopotamia." *Journal of Near Eastern Studies* 32: 70–98.

Gelburd, Diane E. 1985. "Managing Salinity: Lessons from the Past." *Journal of Soil and Water Conservation* 40 (4): 329–31.

Geselowitz, M. 1988. "Technology and Social Change: Ironworking in the Rise of Social Complexity in Iron Age Europe." In *Tribe and Polity in Late Prehistoric Europe. Demography, Production, and Exchange in the Evolution of Complex Social Systems,* B. Gibson and M. Geselowitz, 204–34. New York: Plenum Press.

Giardino, Claudio. 2000. "Sicilian Hoards and Protohistoric Metal Trade in Central West Mediterranean." In *Metals Make the World Go Round,* edited by C. Pare, 99–107. Oxford: Oxbow Books.

Gibbon, Edward. 1966. *The Decline and Fall of the Roman Empire.* New York: E. P. Dutton.

Gibson, McGuire. 1970. "Violation of Fallow and Engineered Disaster in Mesopotamian Civilization." In *Irrigation's Impact on Society,* edited by T. Downing and M. Gibson. Tucson: University of Arizona Press.

———. 1973. "A Population Shift and the Rise of Mesopotamian Civilization." In *The Explanation of Culture Change: Models in Prehistory*, edited by Colin Renfrew, 447–63. London: Duckworth.

Gill, R. B. 2000. *The Great Mayan Droughts: Water, Life, and Death*. Albuquerque: University of New Mexico Press.

Gills, Barry K., and A. G. Frank. 1990. "The Cumulation of Accumulation: Theses and Research Agenda for Five Thousand Years of World System History." *Dialectical Anthropology* 15: 19–42.

———. 1991. "Five Thousand Years of World System History: The Cumulation of Accumulation." In *Core-Periphery Relations in the Pre-Capitalist World*, edited by C. Chase-Dunn and T. Hall. Boulder, CO: Westview Press.

———. 1992. World System Cycles, Crises, and Hegemonial Shifts 1700 B.C. to 1700 A.D. *Review* 15 (4): 621–87.

———. 2002. "A Structural Theory of the 5,000 Year Old System." In *Structure, Culture and History*, edited by Sing C. Chew and David Knottnerus, 151–76. Lanham, MD: Rowman & Littlefield.

Goetze, A. 1975. "The Hittite and Syria (1300–1200 B.C.)." In *The Cambridge Ancient History II*, edited by I. E. S. Edward, C. J. Gadd, N. G. L. Hammond, and E. Sollberger, 2 vols., 3rd ed., 275–314. Cambridge: Cambridge University Press.

Goffart, W. 1974. *Caput and Colonate: Towards a History of Late Roman Taxation*. Toronto: University of Toronto Press.

———. 1980. *Barbarians and Romans A.D. 418–584*. Princeton, NJ: Princeton University Press.

Goldsmith, E. et al. 1990. *Imperiled Planet*. Cambridge: Cambridge University Press.

Goldstone, J. 1991. *Revolution and Rebellion in the Early Modern World*. Berkeley: University of California Press.

Goodfriend, Glenn. 1991. "Holocene Trends in ^{18}O in Land Snail Shells from the Negev Desert and Their Implications for Changes in Rainfall Source Areas." *Quaternary Research* 35: 417–26.

Gophna, Ram, and Juval Portugali. 1988. "Settlement and Demographic Processes in Israel's Coastal Plain from the Chalcolithic to the Middle Bronze Age." *Bulletin of the American School of Oriental Research* 269: 11–28.

Gorny, Ronald L. 1989. "Environment, Archaeology, and History in Hittite Anatolia." *Biblical Archaeologist* 52 (2–3): 78–96.

Grimes, Peter. 1999. "The Horsemen and the Killing Fields: The Final Contradiction of Capitalism." In *Ecology and the World System*, edited by Walter Goldfrank et al., 13–42. Westport, CT: Greenwood Press.

Grove, A. T., and O. Rockham. 2001. *The Nature of Mediterranean Europe: An Ecological History*. New Haven: Yale University Press.

Grove, J. M. 1988. *The Little Ice Age*. New York: Methuen.

Gurney, O. R. 1990. *The Hittites*. London: Penguin.

Gunn, Joel, ed. 2000. *The Years Without Summer: Tracing A.D. 536 and its Aftermath*. Oxford: Archaeopress.

Haggis, Donald C. 1991. "Survey at Kavousi Crete: The Iron Age Settlements." *American Journal of Archaeology* 95: 291–98.

Haldon, J. F. 1990. *Byzantium in the 7th Century.* Cambridge: Cambridge University Press.

Halstead, Paul, and C. Frederick, eds. 2000. *Landscape and Land Use in Post Glacial Greece.* Sheffield, UK: Sheffield University Press.

Hammer, C. H., H. B. Clausen, and W. Dansgaard. 1980. "Greenland Ice Sheet Evidence of Post Glacial Volcanism and its Climatic Impact." *Nature* 288: 230–35.

———. 1987. "The Minoan Eruption of Santorini in Greece dated in 1645 B.C." *Nature* 328: 517–19.

Hansen, B. C. S., et al. 1984. "Pollen Studies in the Junin Area, Central Peruvian Andies." *Bulletin of the Geological Society of America* 95 (12): 1454–65.

Harding, A., ed. 1982. *Climatic Change in Later Prehistory* Edinburgh: Edinburgh University Press.

———. 1984. *The Mycenaeans and Europe.* London: Academic Press.

———. 1987. *European Societies in the Bronze Age.* Cambridge: Cambridge University Press.

Harrison, Anne B., and Nigel Spencer. 1998. "After the Palace: The Early History of Messinia." In *Sandy Pylos,* edited by Jack Davis, 147–66. Austin: University of Texas Press.

Harrison, R. J. 1988. *Spain at the Dawn of History: Iberians, Phoenicians, and Greeks.* London: Thames and Hudson.

Harrison, Robert Pogue. 1992. *Forests: The Shadow of Civilization.* Chicago: University of Chicago Press.

Harrison, Timothy. 1997. "Shifting Patterns of Settlement in the Highlands of Central Jordan during the Early Bronze Age." *Bulletin of the American School Oriental Research* 306: 1–38.

Hassan, Fekri. 1986. "Holocene Lakes and Prehistoric Settlements of the Western Fayum." *Journal of Archaeological Science* 13: 483–501.

———. 1988. The Predynasty of Egypt. *Journal of World Prehistory* 2: 135–85.

———. 1997. "Nile Floods and Political Disorder in Early Egypt." In *Third Millennium B.C. Climate Change and Old World Collapse,* edited by H. Dalfes et al., 1–23. Heidelberg: Springer-Verlag.

Hayhoe, Katherine et al. 2004. "Emissions Pathways, Climate Change and Impacts on California." *Proceedings of National Academy of Sciences* 101 (34): 12422–27.

Hedeager, Lotte. 1987. "Empire, Frontier and Barbarian Hinterland: Rome and Northern Europe from A.D. 1–400." In *Centre and Periphery in the Ancient World,* edited by M. Rowlands et al., 125–40. Cambridge: Cambridge University Press.

———. 1992. *Iron Age Societies: From Tribe to State 500 B.C. to A.D. 700.* Oxford: Blackwell.

Heichelheim, Fritz M. 1968. *An Ancient Economic History.* Vol. 1. Leiden, The Netherlands: A. W. Sijthoff.

Herlihy, David. 1974. "Ecological Conditions and Demographic Change." In *One Thousand Years,* edited by Richard Demolen, 3–34. Boston: Houghton Mifflin and Co.

Hiebert, Fredrik. 2000. "Bronze Age Central Eurasian Cultures in their Steppe and Desert Environments." In *Environmental Disaster and the Archaeology of Human Response,* edited by G. Bawden and R. Reycraft, 51–62. Albuquerque: University of New Mexico Press.

Hodges, Richard. 1989. *Dark Age Economics: The Origins of Towns and Trade A.D. 600–1000*. London: Duckworth.

Hodgett, G. 1972. *A Social and Economic History of Medieval Europe*. London: Methuen.

Hogarth, D. G. 1926. "The Hittites of Asia Minor." In *The Cambridge Ancient History II*, edited by J. B. Bury, S. A. Cook, and F. E. Adcock, 252–74. New York: MacMillan.

Hole, Frank. 1997. "Evidence for Mid-Holocene Environmental Change in the Western Khabur Drainage, Northeastern Syria." In *Third Millennium B.C. Climate Change*, edited by H. Dalfes et al., 41–65. Berlin: Springer-Verlag.

Honey, W. B. 1948. *Korean Pottery*. New York: Nostrand.

Hooker, J. T. 1976. *Mycenaean Greece*. London: Routledge.

Hope Simpson, R., and O. T. P. Dickinson. 1979. *A Gazetteer of Aegean Civilization in the Bronze Age*, Vol. 1. Göteborg: Åström.

Hopkins, Keith. 1977. "Economic Growth and Towns in Classical Antiquity." In *Towns in Societies: Essays in Economic History and Historical Sociology*, edited by P. Abrams and E. A. Wrigley, 165–86. Cambridge: Cambridge University Press.

———. 1980. "Taxes and Trade in the Roman Empire 200 B.C.—A.D. 400." *Journal of Roman Studies* 70: 137–56.

———. 1988. "Roman Trade, Industry, and Labor." In *Civilization of the Ancient Mediterranean: Greece and Rome*. Vol. 2, edited by P. Kitzinger, 753–78. New York: Charles Scribner and Sons.

Horden, Peregrine, and Nicholas Purcell. 2000. *The Corrupting Sea: A Study of Mediterranean History*. Oxford: Blackwell.

Howgego, Christopher. 1992. "The Supply and Use of Money in the Roman World 200 B.C. to A.D. 300." *Journal of Roman Studies* 82: 1–31.

Hughes, J. Donald. 1975. *Ecology in Ancient Civilizations*. Albuquerque: University of New Mexico Press.

———. 1994. *Pan's Travail*. Baltimore: Johns Hopkins University Press.

———. 2001. *Environmental History of the World*. London: Routledge.

Hughes, J. Donald, and J. V. Thirgood. 1982. "Deforestation, Erosion, and Forest Management in Ancient Greece and Rome." *Journal of Forest History* 26 (2): 60–75.

Huntington, Ellsworth. 1917a. "Climatic Changes and Agricultural Decline as Factors in the Fall of Rome." *The Quarterly Journal of Economics* 31: 173–208.

———. 1917b. *World Power and Evolution*. New Haven, CT: Yale University Press.

———. 1924. *Civilization and Climate*. New Haven, CT: Yale University Press.

Huntington, Ellsworth, and Sargent Fisher. 1978. *Climatic Changes: Their Nature and Causes*. New York: AMS Press.

Huntley, B., and H. J. B. Birks. 1983. *An Atlas of Past and Present Pollen Maps for Europe 0–13,000 Years Ago*. Cambridge: Cambridge University Press.

Hutchinson, G. E., R. Patrick, and E. S. Deevey. 1956. "Sediments of Lake Patzcuaro, Michoacan Mexico." *Bulletin of the Geological Society of America*, pp. 1491–504.

Huth, Christopher. 2000. "Metal Circulation, Communication and Traditions of Craftsmanship in Late Bronze Age and Early Iron Age Europe." In *Metals Make the World Go Round*, edited by C. Pare, 176–93. Oxford: Oxbow Press.

Iakovides, S. 1977. "The Present State of Research at the Citadel of Mycenae." *Bulletin of the Institute of Archaeology* no. 14, 99–141.

Immerwahr, Sara A. 1960. "Mycenaean Trade and Colonization." *Archaeology* 13 (1): 4–13.

Intergovernmental Panel on Climate Change. 2001. "Climate Change 2001: Impacts, Adaptation, and Vulnerability." Report of the Sixth Session. Geneva.

Issar, Arie. 1998. "Climate Change and History during the Holocene in the Eastern Mediterranean Region." In *Water, Environment, and Society in Times of Climatic Change*, edited by A. Issar and N. Brown, 113–28. Hague: Kluwer.

Jacobsen, T. 1970. "On the Textile Industry at Ur under Ibbi-Sin." In *Toward the Image of Tammuz*, edited by W. L. Moran. Cambridge: Cambridge University Press.

Jacobsen, T., and R. M. Adams. 1958. "Salt and Silt in Ancient Mesopotamian Agriculture." *Science* 128: 1251–58.

Jacomet, Stefanie. 1990. "Veranderungen von Wirtschaft und Umwelt wahrend des Spatneolithi kums im westlichen Bodenseegebietes." In *Siedlungsarchaologie im Alpenvorland*. Vol. II, 295–324. Stuggart: Konrad Theiss.

Jameson, Michael et al. 1994. *A Greek Countryside: The Southern Argolid from Prehistory to the Present Day*. Stanford, CA: Stanford University Press.

Janes, P. J. 1991. *Centuries of Darkness: A Challenge to the Conventional Chronology of Old World Archaeology*. London: Jonathan Cape.

Jennison, George. 1937. *Animals for Show and Pleasure in Ancient Rome*. New York: Barnes and Noble.

Johnson, T. C., and E. O. Odada, eds. 1996. *The Liminology, Climatology, and Paleoclimatology of the East African Lakes*. New York: Gordon and Breach.

Jones, A. H. M. 1959a. "Over Taxation and Decline of the Roman Empire." *Antiquity* 33: 24–56.

———. 1959b. *The Later Roman Empire*. 2 vols. Norman: University of Oklahoma Press.

———. 1966. *The Decline of the Ancient World*. London: Longman.

———. 1974. *The Roman Economy*. Totowa, NJ: Rowman & Littlefield.

Kagan, Donald. 1992. *The End of the Roman Empire*. Lexington, MA: D. C. Heath.

Kantor, H. 1992. "The Relative Chronology of Egypt and Its Foreign Correlations before the First Intermediate Period." In *Chronologies in Old World Archaeology*, edited by Robert W. Ehrlich, Vol. 1. Chicago: University of Chicago Press.

Karageorghis, V. 1992. "The Crisis Years: Cyprus." In *The Crisis Years: The 12th Century B.C.*, edited by W. Ward and M. Joukowsky, 79–86. Dubuque, IA: Kendall Hunt.

Katz, Solomon. 1961. *The Decline of Rome and the Rise of Medieval Europe*. Ithaca, NY: Cornell University Press.

Kay, P. A., and D. L. Johnson. 1981. "Estimation of Tigris-Euphrates Stream Flow from Regional Paleoenvironmental Proxy Data." *Climate Change* 3: 251–63.

Kemp, Barry. 1989. *Ancient Egypt: Anatomy of a Civilization*. New York: Routledge.

Kempter, H., M. Gorres, and B. Frenzel. 1997. "Ti and Pb Concentration in Rainwater Fed Bogs in Europe as Indicators of past Anthropogenic Activities." *Water, Air and Soil Pollution* 100: 367–77.

Keys, David. 1999. *Catastrophe*. New York: Ballantine Books.

Khomutova, V. et al. 1994. "Lake Status Records from the Former Soviet Union and Mongolian Database." Paleoclimatology Publication Report 2, World Data Center for Paleoclimatology, 86–88.

Knapp, A. Bernard. 1993. "Thalassocracies in the Bronze Age Eastern Mediterranean Trade: Making and Breaking a Myth World." *World Archaeology* 24 (3): 332–47.

Kohl, Philip. 1978. "The Balance of Trade in Southwestern Asia in the Mid-Third Millennium." *Current Anthropology* 193: 480–81.

———. 1987a. "The Ancient Economy, Transferable Technologies, and the Bronze Age World System: A View from the Northeastern Frontiers of the Ancient Near East." In *Centre and Periphery in the Ancient World,* edited by M. Rowlands, Mogens Larsen, and Kristian Kristiansen. Cambridge: Cambridge University Press.

———. 1987b. "Sumer and Indus Valley Civilization Compared: Towards an Historical Understanding of the Evolution of Early States." *Perspectives in U.S. Marxist Anthropology,* edited by D. Hakken and H. Lessinger. London: Westview Press.

Kraft, John, Stanley Aschenbrenner, and George Rapp. 1977. "Paleographic Reconstructions of Coastal Aegean Archaeological Sites." *Science* 195 (4282): 941–47.

Krementski, Constantin. 1997. "The Late Holocene Environmental and Climate Shift in Russia and Surrounding Lands." In *Third Millennium B.C. Climate Change and Old World Collapse,* edited by H. Dalfes et al., 351–70. Heidelberg: Springer-Verlag.

Kristiansen, Kristian. 1993. "The Emergence of the European World System in the Bronze Age: Divergence, Convergence, and Social Evolution during the First and Second Millennia B.C. in Europe." Sheffield Archaeological Monographs no. 6.

———. 1998a. "The Construction of a Bronze Age Landscape, Cosmology, Economy, and Social Organization in Thy, Northwestern Jutland." In *Mensch und Umwelt in der Bronzezeit Europas,* edited by Bernhard Hansel, 281–92. Kiel, Germany: Oetker-Vosges-Verlag.

———. 1998b. *Europe before History.* Cambridge: Cambridge University Press.

———. 2005. "What Language did Neolithic Pots Speak? Colin Renfrew's European Farming-Language-Dispersal Model Challenged." *Antiquity* 79: 679–91.

Kristiansen, Kristian, and Thomas Larsson. 2005. *The Rise of Bronze Age Society Travels, Transmission, and Transformation.* Cambridge: Cambridge University Press.

Kuniholm, P. I., and C. L. Striker. 1987. "Dendochronological Investigations in the Aegean and Neighboring Regions 1983–1986." *Journal of Field Archaeology* 14: 385–98.

———. 1992. "Dendochronological Wood from Anatolia and Environs." In *Trees and Timber in Mesopotamia,* edited by N. Postgate and T. Powell. Bulletin on Sumerian Agriculture 6. Cambridge: Cambridge University.

——— et al. 1996. "Anatolian Tree Rings and the Absolute Chronology of the Eastern Mediterranean 2220 B.C.–718 B.C." *Nature* 381: 780–83.

Ladurie, L. 1971. *Times of Feast and Times of Famines.* New York: Doubleday.

Lal, B. B. 1993. "A Glimpse of the Social Stratification and Political Set-Up of the Indus Civilization." In *Harappan Studies*, edited by G. Possehl and M. Tosi, Vol. 1. New Delhi: Oxford University Press.

———. 1997. *The Earliest Civilization of South Asia: Rise, Maturity, and Decline.* New Delhi: Aryan Books International.

Lamb, H. 1967. "R. Carpenter's Discontinuity in Greek Civilization." *Antiquity* 41: 233–34.

———. 1968. *The Changing Climate.* London: Methuen.

———. 1981. "Climate and Its Impact on Human Affairs." In *Climate and History*, edited by T. M. Wigley et al., 289–90. Cambridge: Cambridge University Press.

———. 1982a. *Climate, History, and the Modern World.* London: Methuen.

———. 1982b. "Reconstruction of the Course of Postglacial Climate over the World." In *Climate Change in Later Pre-History*, edited by Anthony Harding. Edinburgh: Edinburgh University Press.

Lamberg-Karlovsky, C. C. 1975. "Third Millennium Exchange and Production." In *Ancient Civilization and Trade*, edited by Jeremy Sabloff and C. C. Lamberg-Karlovsky. Albuquerque: University of New Mexico Press.

———. 1979. "Trade Mechanisms in Indus-Mesopotamian Interrelations." In *Ancient Cities of the Indus*, edited by G. Possehl. New Delhi: Vikas.

———. 1986. "Third-Millennium Structure and Process: From the Euphrates to the Indus and the Oxus to the Indian Ocean." *Oriens Antiquvvs* 25: 189–219.

Lambrick, H. T. 1967. "The Indus Flood Plain and the 'Indus' Civilization." *The Geographical Journal* 133 (4): 483–89.

Larsen, Mogens Trolle. 1987. "Commercial Network in the Ancient Near East." In *Centre and Periphery in the Ancient World*, edited by Michael Rowlands et al., 47–56. Cambridge: Cambridge University Press.

Latouche, Robert. 1961. *The Birth of the Western Economy.* London: Methuen.

Lazarova, M. 1995. "Human Impact on the Natural Vegetation in the Region of Lake Srebarna and Mire Girvan." In *Advances in Holocene Paleoecology in Bulgaria*, edited by T. Bozilova, 47–67. Sofia, Russia: Pensoft Publication.

Leemans, W. F. 1960. *Foreign Trade in the Old Babylonian Period as Revealed by Texts from Southern Mesopotamia.* Leiden, The Netherlands: Brill.

Lemcke, G. et al. 2000. "Holocene Climate Change in the New East: The Perspectives from Lake Van." *Climate Change* 28: 234–55.

Lemcke, G., and M. Sturm. 1997. "d18O and Trace Element Measurement as Proxy for the Reconstruction of Climatic Changes at Lake Van." In *Third Millennium BC Climate Change and Old World Collapse*, edited by H. Dalfes et al., 653–78. Heidelberg: Springer-Verlag.

Lentz, D., ed. 2000. *Imperfect Balance: Landscape Transformations in the Precolumbian Americas.* New York: Columbia University Press.

Lieberman, Victor. 2003. *Strange Parallels Integration on the Mainland: Southeast Asia in Global Context C800–1830.* Vol. 1. Cambridge: Cambridge University Press.

Liverani, Mario. 1987. "The Collapse of the Near Eastern Regional System at the End of the Bronze Age: The Case of Syria." In *Centre and Periphery in the Ancient World*, edited by Michael Rowlands et al., 66–73. Cambridge: Cambridge University Press.

Luttwak, Edward N. 1976. *The Grand Strategy of the Roman Empire.* Baltimore: Johns Hopkins University Press.

MacMullen, R. 1984. "The Legion as a Society." *Historia* 33: 440–56.

———. 1997. "The Roman Empire." In *Ancient History: Recent Works and New Directions,* edited by S. Burstein et al., 79–104. Claremont, CA: Regina Books.

MacQueen, J. G. 1986. *The Hittites and Their Contemporaries in Asia Minor.* London: Thames and Hudson.

Mann, Michael. 1986. *The Sources of Social Power.* Vol. 1. Cambridge: Cambridge University Press.

Manning, S. 1988. "The Bronze Age Eruption of Thera: Absolute Dating, Aegean Chronology and Mediterranean Cultural Interrelations." *Journal of Mediterranean Archaeology* 1 (1): 17–82.

Manning, S., et al. 2002. "New Evidence for an Early Date for the Aegean Late Bronze Age and Thera Eruption." *Antiquity* 76 (293): 733–44.

Manning, S., and Bernhard Weninger. 1992. "A Light in the Dark: Archaeological Wiggle Matching and the Absolute Chronology of the Close of the Aegean Late Bronze Age." *Antiquity* 66: 636–63.

Manning, Sturt W. 1994. "The Emergence of Divergence: Development and Decline in Bronze Age Crete and the Cyclades." In *Development and Decline in the Mediterranean Bronze Age,* edited by C. Mathers and S. Stoddatm, 221–70. Sheffield: J. R. Collins.

Manning, Sturt W., et al. 2006. "Chronology for the Aegean Late Bronze Age 1700–1400 b.c." *Science* 312: 565–69.

Marchak, Pat. 1995. *Logging the Globe.* Kingston: Queen's University Press.

Marfoe, Leon. 1987. "Cedar Forests to Silver Mountains: Social Change and Development of Long Distance Trade in Early Near Eastern Societies." In *Centre and Periphery in the Ancient World,* edited by Michael Rowlands et al., 25–35. Cambridge: Cambridge University Press.

Marinatos, S. 1939. "The Volcanic Eruption of Minoan Crete." *Antiquity* 13: 425–39.

Martino, Stefano. 2004. "A Tentative Chronology of the Kingdom of Mittani from Its Rise to the Reign of Tusratta." In *Mesopotamian Dark Age Revisited,* edited by H. Hunger and R. Pruzsinsky, 35–42. Wien, Austria: Verlag der Osterreichischen Akademie Der Wissenschaften.

Matthews, R. 2002. "Zebu: Harbinger of Doom in Bronze Age Western Asia." *Antiquity* 76: 438–46.

———. 2003. *The Archaeology of Mesopotamia Theories and Approaches.* London: Routledge.

McCormick, Michael. 2001. *Origins of the European Economy.* Cambridge: Cambridge University Press.

McDonald, W. A., and G. Rapp. 1972. *The Minnesota-Messenia Expedition: Reconstructing a Bronze-Age Environment.* Minneapolis: University of Minnesota Press.

McEvedy, Colin, and Sarah McEvedy. 1972. *Dark Ages.* London: Macmillan.

McGovern, P. 1987. "Central TransJordan in Late Bronze Age and Early Iron Ages: An Alternative Hypothesis of SocioEconomic Collapse." In *Studies in the History and Archaeology of Jordan 3,* edited by A. Hadidi, 267–73. London: Routledge and Kegan Paul.

McIntosh, Jane. 2001. *A Peaceful Realm*. Boulder, CO: Westview Press.

McIntosh, R. et al., eds. 2000. *The Way the Wind Blows: Climate, History, and Human Action*. New York: Columbia University Press.

McNeill, J. R. 1998. "China's Environmental History." In *Sediments of Time*, edited by Mark Elvin. Cambridge: Cambridge University Press.

———. 2000. *Something New Under the Sun*. New York: W. W. Norton.

McNeill, J. R., and W. McNeill, 2003. *The Human Web*. New York: Norton.

McNeill, William. 1963. *The Rise of the West*. Chicago: University of Chicago Press.

———. 1974. *Venice: The Hinge of Europe 1081–1797*. Chicago: University of Chicago Press.

———. 1976. *Plagues and Peoples*. New York: Anchor Books.

———. 1990. "The Rise of the West after Twenty-Five Years." *Journal of World History* 1: 1–21.

———. 1992. *The Global Condition*. Princeton, NJ: Princeton University Press.

Meadows, D. et al. 1972. *Limits to Growth*. New York: New American Library.

———. 1992. *Beyond the Limits*. Post Mills, VT: Chelsea Green

———. 2004. *Limits to Growth: The 30-Year Update*. White River Junction, VT: Chelsea Green.

Mellink, Machfeld. 1986. "The Early Bronze Age in Western Anatolia: Aegean and Asiatic Correlations." In *End of the Early Bronze Age in the Aegean*, edited by G. Cadogan, 139–52. Leiden, The Netherlands: Brill.

Mertens, J. 1983. "The Military Origins of Some Roman Settlements in Belgium." In *The Towns of Roman Britain*, edited by Brian Hartley and John Wacher, 155–68. Gloucester, UK: Alan Sutton.

Mesarovic, M. and E. Pestel. 1974. *Mankind at the Turning Point*. New York: E. P. Dutton.

Millar, F. 1981. *The Roman Empire and Its Neighbors*. New York: Holmes and Meier.

Miller, Innes. 1969. *The Spice Trade of the Roman Empire*. Oxford: Oxford University Press.

Mocsy, Andres. 1974. *Pannonia and Upper Moesia: A History of the Middle Danube Provinces of the Roman Empire*. London: Routledge.

Modelski, George. 1997. "Early World Cities." Paper presented at International Studies Association Meeting. Toronto.

———. 1999a. "Ancient World Cities 4000–1000 B.C.: Center/Hinterland in the World System." *Global Society*. 13 (4): 383–92.

———. 1999b. "Classical World Cities: 1200 B.C. to A.D. 1000." In *Human Ecology*, edited by K. Watt. London: Routledge.

———. 2003. *World Cities*. Washington, DC: Faros.

Modelski, George, and W. Thompson. 1999. "The Evolutionary Pulse of the World System: Hinterland Incursion and Migrations 4000 B.C. to A.D. 1500." In *World System Theory in Practice*, edited by Nick Kardulias, 241–74. Lanham, MD: Rowman & Littlefield.

———. 2001. "Evolutionary Pulsations in the World System." In *Structure, Culture, and History*, edited by Sing Chew and David Knottnerus. Lanham, MD: Rowman & Littlefield.

Moorey, P. R. S. 1987. "On Tracking Cultural Transfers in Prehistory: The Case of Egypt and Lower Mesopotamia in the 4th Millennium B.C." In *Centre and Periphery in the Ancient World,* edited by M. Rowlands et al., 36–46. Cambridge: Cambridge University Press.

———.1994. *Ancient Mesopotamian Materials and Industries.* Oxford: Clarendon Press.

Morris, Ian. 1987. *Burial and Ancient Society: The Rise of the Greek City-State.* Cambridge: Cambridge University Press.

———. 1988a. "Tomb Cult and the Greek Renaissance: The Past in the Present 8th Century BC." *Antiquity* 62 (237): 750–61.

———. 1988b. "Changing Perceptions of the Past: The Bronze Age: A Case Study." In *Extracting Meaning from the Past,* edited by J. Bintliff, 213–33. Oxford: Oxbow Books.

———. 1989. "Circulation, Deposition and the Formation of the Greek Dark Age." *Man* 24 (3): 78–85.

———. 1997a. "Homer and the Iron Age." In *A New Companion to Homer,* edited by Ian Morris and Barry Powell, 535–59. Leiden, The Netherlands: Brill.

———. 1997b. "An Archaeology of Equalities? The Greek City-States." In *The Archaeology of City-States: Cross-Cultural Approaches,* edited by D. L. Nichols and T. H. Charlton. Washington, DC: Smithsonian Institution Press.

———. 2000. *Archaeology as Cultural History: Words and Things in Iron Age Greece.* Malden, MA: Blackwell.

Muhly, J. D. 1973. "Tin Trade Routes of the Bronze Age." *American Scientist* 61 (4): 404–13.

———. 1980. "The Bronze Age Setting." In *The Coming of the Iron Age,* edited by T. Wertime and J. Muhly, 25–67. New Haven, CT: Yale University Press.

———. 1984. "The Role of the Sea People in Cyprus during the LC III Period." In *Cyprus at the Close of the Late Bronze Age,* edited by V. Karageorghis and J. Muhly, 39–56. Nicosia, Cyprus: Zavallis.

———. 1998. "Metallic Ores as an Incentive for Foreign Expansion." In *Mediterranean Peoples in Transition 13th to 10th BCE,* edited by S. Gitin et al., 314–29. Jerusalem: Israel Exploration Society.

Munro, Dana Carleton, and Raymond James Sontag. 1928. *The Middle Ages 395–1500.* London: The Century.

Murray, G. 1907. *The Rise of the Greek Epic.* Oxford: Oxford University Press.

Murray, O. 1980. *Early Greece.* Oxford: Blackwell.

Mylonas, George. 1966. *Mycenae and the Mycenaean Age.* Princeton, NJ: Princeton University Press

Nash, D. 1985. "Celtic Territorial Expansion and the Mediterranean World." In *Settlement and Society: Aspects of West European Prehistory in the First Millennium BC,* edited by T. C. Champion and J. V. S. Megaw, 134–45. Leicester, UK: Leicester University Press.

———. 1987. "Imperial Expansion under the Roman Empire." In *Centre and Periphery in the Ancient World,* Michael Rowland, 87–103. Cambridge: Cambridge University Press.

Needham, Joseph. 1959. *Science and Civilization in China.* Vol. 3. Cambridge: Cambridge University Press.

Needham, S. 2000. "Power Pulses across a Cultural Divide: Cosmologically Driven Acquisition between Armorica and Wessex." *Proceedings of the Prehistoric Society* 66: 151–207.

Neev, David, N. Bakler, and K. O. Emery. 1987. *Mediterranean Coasts of Israel and Sinai: Holocene Tectionism, Geology, Geophysics, and Archaeology.* London: Taylor and Francis.

Neumann, J., and S. Parpola. 1987. "Climatic Change and 11–10th Century Eclipse of Assyria and Babylonia." *Journal of Near Eastern Studies* 46: 161–82.

Neumann, J., and R. Sigrist. 1978. "Harvest Dates in Ancient Mesopotamia as Possible Indicators of Climatic Variations." *Climate Change* 1: 239–52.

Newman, Lucile, ed. 1990. *Hunger and History.* Oxford: Basil Blackwell.

Noble, Ian, and Rodolfo Dirzo. 1997. "Forests as Human-Dominated Ecosystems." *Science* 277: 522–25.

Obidowicz, A. 1989. "Type Region P-a: Inner West Carpathians Nowy Targ Basin." *Acta Paleobotanica* 29 (2): 11–15.

O'Connor, D. 1974. "Political Systems and Archaeological Data in Egypt 2600—1700 B.C." *World Archaeology* 6: 15–38.

———. 1983. "New Kingdom and the Third Intermediate Period, 1552–664 B.C." In *Ancient Egypt: A Social History,* edited by B. G. Trigger et al. Cambridge: Cambridge University Press.

Orejas, Almudena and F. Javies Sanchez-Palencia. 2002. "Mines, Territorial Organization and Social Structure in Roman Iberia: Carthago Nona, and the Peninsular Northwest." *American Journal of Archaeology* 106: 581–99.

Page, D. L. 1963. *History and the Homeric Iliad.* Berkeley: University of California Press.

Pang, K. D. 1987. "Extraordinary Floods in Early Chinese History and their Absolute Dates." *Journal of Hydrology* 96: 139–55.

———. 1991. "The Legacies of Eruption." *The Sciences* 31 (1): 30–33.

Pang, K. D. and H. Chou. 1985. "Three Very Large Volcanic Eruptions in Antiquity and Their Effects on the Climate of the Ancient World." *EOS Transactions, American Geophysical Union* 66: 816.

Pang, K. D. et al. 1987. "Climate Anomalies of Late 3rd Century B.C.: Correlation with Volcanism, Solar Activity and Planetary Alignment." *EOS Transactions, American Geophysical Union* 68: 1234.

———. 1988. "Climate Impacts of Past Volcanic Eruptions: Inferences from Ice Core, Tree-Ring and Historical Data." *EOS Transactions, American Geophysical Union* 69: 1062.

———. 1989. "Climatic and Hydrologic Extremes in Early Chinese History: Possible Causes and Dates." *EOS, Transactions, American Geophysical Union* 70: 1095.

Pare, C. 2000. "Bronze and Bronze Age." In *Metals Make the World Go Round,* edited by C. Pare, 1–38. Oxford: Oxbow Press.

Parker, H. M. D. 1958. *The Roman Legions.* Cambridge: W. Heffer and Sons.

Penalba, M. C. 1994. "The History of the Holocene Vegetation in Northern Spain from Pollen Analysis." *Journal of Ecology* 82: 815–32.

Perlin, John. 1989. *A Forest Journey.* Cambridge: Harvard University Press.

Polanyi, Karl. 1957. *The Great Transformation.* Boston: Beacon Press.

———. 1977. *The Livelihood of Man.* New York: Academic Press.

Polybius. 1979. *The Rise of the Roman Empire.* London: Penguin.

Pomeranz, K. 2000. *The Great Divergence: Europe China and the Making of the Modern World.* Princeton, NJ: Princeton University Press.

Ponting, Clive. 1991. *A Green History of the World.* London: Penguin.

Possehl, G. 1979. *Ancient Cities of the Indus.* New Delhi: Vikas.

———. 1982. "The Harappan Civilization: A Contemporary Perspective." In *Harappan Civilization,* edited by G. Possehl. New Delhi: Oxford University Press.

———., ed. 1993. *Harappan Civilization.* New Delhi: Oxford University Press.

———. 1996. "Meluhha." In *The Indian Ocean in Antiquity,* edited by Julian Reade. London: Kegan and Paul.

———. 1997. "Climate and the Eclipse of the Ancient Cities of the Indus." In *Third Millennium B.C. Climate Change and Old World Collapse,* edited by H. Nuzhet Dalfes, George Kukla, and Harvey Weiss. Heidelberg: Springer-Verlag.

———. 2000. "The Drying Up of the Saravati." In *Environmental Disaster and the Archaeology of Human Response,* edited by G. Bawden and R. Reycraft, 63–74. Albuquerque: University of New Mexico Press.

———. 2002. *The Indus Civilization.* Walnut Creek, CA: AltaMira Press.

Possehl, G., and M. Raval. 1989. *Harappan Civilization and the Rojdi.* New Delhi: Oxford.

Possehl, G., and M. Tosi, eds. 1993. *Harappan Studies.* New Delhi: Oxford University Press.

Rackham, Oliver, and J. Moody. 1996. *The Making of the Cretan Landscape.* Manchester: Manchester University Press.

Raikes, Robert. 1964. The End of the Ancient Cities of the Indus. *American Anthropologist* 66 (2): 284–299.

———. 1984. *Water, Weather, and Prehistory.* Atlantic Highlands, NJ: Humanities Press.

Raikes, Robert, and G. F. Dales. 1977. "The Mohenjo-Daro Floods Reconsidered." *Journal of the Palaeontological Society of India* 20: 251–60.

Raikes, Robert, and R. Dyson. 1961. "The Prehistoric Climate of Baluchistan and the Indus Valley." *American Anthropologist* 63 (2): 265–81.

Randers-Pehrson, Justine Davis. 1983. *Barbarians and Romans.* Norman: University of Oklahoma Press.

Randsborg, Klav. 1991. *The First Millennium AD in Europe and the Mediterranean.* Cambridge: Cambridge University Press.

Rankama, T., and I. Vuorela. 1988. "Memo. Soc. Fauna Flora." *Fennica* 64: 25–34.

Ratnagar, Shereen. 1981. *Encounters: The Westerly Trade of the Harappan Civilization.* New Delhi: Oxford University Press.

———. 1986. "An Aspect of Harappan Agricultural Production." *Studies in History* 2: 137–53.

———. 1991. *Enquiries into the Political Organization of the Harappan Society.* Pune: Ravish.

———. 1994. Harappan Trade in Its World Context. *Man and Environment* 19 (1–2): 115–27.

Redman, Charles. 1978. *The Rise of Civilization.* San Francisco: W. H. Freeman.

Redman, C. L. 1999. *Human Impact on Ancient Environments.* Tucson: University of Arizona Press.

———. and A. P. Kinzig. 2003. "Resilience of Past Landscapes Resilience Theory, Society, and the Longue Durée." *Conservation Ecology* 7: 14–17.

Ren, G., and H. J. Beng. 2002. "Mapping Holocene Pollen and Vegetation of China." *Quaternary Science Review* 21: 1395–97.

Renfrew, Colin. 1972. *The Emergence of Civilization.* London: Collins.

———. 1979. "Systems Collapse as Social Transformation: Catastrophe and Anastrophe in Early State Society." In *Transformations: Mathematical Approaches to Cultural Change,* edited by C. Renfrew and K. L. Cooke, 481–506. New York: Academic Press.

———. 1982. "Post Collapse Resurgence: Culture Process in the Dark Ages." In *Ranking, Resource and Exchanges: Aspects of the Archaeology of Early European Society,* edited by Colin Renfrew and S. Shennan, 113–16. Cambridge: Cambridge University Press.

Renfrew, Colin, and Paul Bahn. 2000. *Archaeology: Theories, Methods, and Practice.* London: Thames and Hudson.

Richardson, J. S. 1986. *Hispaniae: Spain and the Development of Roman Imperialism.* Cambridge: Cambridge University Press.

Ricketts, R. C., and T. G. Johnson. 1996. "Climate Change in Turkana Basin as Deduced from a 4000 Year-Long d18O Record." *Earth and Planetary Science Letters* 142: 7–17.

Rifkin, Jeremy. 2002. *The Hydrogen Economy.* New York: Putnam.

Robbins, Manuel. 2001. *Collapse of the Bronze Age.* New York: Author's Choice Press.

Robertshaw, Peter. 2004. "Famine, Climate, and Crisis in Western Uganda." In *Past Climate Variability through Europe and Africa,* edited by R. W. Battarbee et al., 535–49. Dordrecht, The Netherlands: Springer.

Rockham, O. J., and J. A. Moody. 1996. *The Making of the Cretan Landscape.* Manchester, UK: University of Manchester Press.

Rosch, Manfred. 1990. Vegetationsgechichtliche Untersuchungen im Durchenbergried. In *Siedlungsarchaologie im Alpenvorland II,* edited by Andre Billamboz et al. Stuttgart, Germany: Konrad Theiss.

———. 1996. "New Approaches to Prehistoric Land-Use Reconstruction in Southwestern Germany." *Vegetation History and Archaeobotany* 5(1/2): 45–57.

———. 1998. "The History of Crops and Crop Weeds in Southwestern Germany from the Neolithic Period to Modern Times as Shown by Archaeological Evidence." *Vegetation History and Archaeobotany* 7 (2): 65–78.

Rostovtzeff, M. 1930. The Decay of the Ancient World and Its Economic Explanations. *Economic History Review* 2 (2): 197–214.

———. 1957. *The Social and Economic History of the Roman Empire.* Oxford: Clarendon Press.

Rowton, M. B. 1967. "The Woodlands of Ancient Western Asia." *Journal of Near Eastern Studies* 26: 261–77.

Ruddiman, W. F., and J. S. Thomson. 2001. "The Case for Human Causes of Increased Atmospheric Methane over Last 5,000 Years." *Quaternary Science Review* 20: 1769–75.

Ruddiman, William. 2003. "The Anthropogenic Greenhouse Era Began Thousands of Years Ago." *Climate Change* 61 (3): 261–93.

———. 2005. *Plows, Plagues, and Petroleum*. Princeton, NJ: Princeton University Press.

Runnels, Curtis N. 1995. "Environmental Degradation in Ancient Greece." *Scientific American* 272 (3): 96–99.

Russell, J. C. 1971. "Population in Europe A.D. 500–1500." In *The Fontana Economic History of Europe*, edited by Carlo Cipolla, Vol. 1, 5–71. London: Collins.

Rutter, Jeremy. 1989. "Cultural Novelties in the Post Palatial Aegean World: Indices of Vitality or Decline." In *The Crisis Years: The 12th Century B.C.*, edited by W. Ward and M. Joukowsky, 61–78. Dubuque, IA: Kendall Hunt.

Saggs, H. W. F. 1962. *The Greatness that Was Babylon*. New York: Hawthorn Books.

———. 1989. *Civilization before Greece and Rome*. New Haven: Yale University Press.

Sahni, M. R. 1956. "Biogeological Evidence Bearing on the Decline of the Indus Valley Civilization." *Journal of the Palaeontological Society of India* 1 (1): 101–7.

Salgado, L. 1988. "Sequence of Colonization by Plants in the Venezuelan Andes after the Last Pleistocene Glaciation." *Journal of Palynology* 23/24: 189–204.

Sallares, Robert. 1991. *The Ecology of the Ancient Greek World*. Ithaca, NY: Cornell University Press.

Salway, Peter. 1965. *The Frontier Region of Roman Britain*. Cambridge: Cambridge University Press.

Sanders, W. T., and D. Webster. 1978. "Unilinealism, Multilinealism, and the Evolution of Complex Societies." In *Social Archaeology: Beyond Subsistence and Dating*, C. L. Redman et al., 164–97. New York: Academic Press.

Sarabia, Daniel. 2004. "Dark Age Phases as Periods of Ecological Crisis: An Analysis of the Interplay between Economy, Nature, and Culture in East Asia." PhD diss., Oklahoma State University.

Schaeffer, C. F. A. 1948. "Stratigraphie comparee et chronologie de l'Asie occidentale (III et II millenaire)." *Economics and Social History of the Orient* 5: 279–308.

———. 1968. "Commentaires sur les letters et documents trouvés dans les bibliothèques privées d'Ugarit." *Ugaritica* 5: 607–768.

Schwartz, G. 1988. "Excavation at Karatut Mevkii and Perspective on the Uruk/Jemdet Nasr Expansion." *Akkadica* 56: 1–42.

Seger, Joe D. 1989. "Some Provisional Correlations in Eb Iii Stratigraphy in Southern Palestine." In *L'urbanisation De La Palestine À L'âge Du Bronze Ancien: Bilan Et Perspectives Des Recherches Actuelles: Actes Du Colloque D'emmaüs 6*, edited by P. de Miroschedji, BAR International Series no. 527, 117–35. Oxford: Archeopress.

Shaffer, J. 1982. "Harappan Culture: A Reconsideration." In *Harappan Civilization*, edited by G. Possehl. New Delhi: Oxford University Press.

Shaw, B. 1981. "Climate, Environment, and History: The Case of Roman North Africa." In *Climate and History*, edited by T. M. L. Wigley, M. J. Ingram, and G. Farmer. Cambridge: Cambridge University Press.

———. 1995. *Environment and Society in Roman North Africa*. Brookfield, MA: Variorum.

Shaw, Ian, ed. 2000. *The Oxford History of Ancient Egypt*. Oxford: Oxford University Press.

Sheratt, Andrew. 1981. "Plough and Pastoralism: Aspects of the Secondary Products Revolution." In *Pattern of the Past,* edited by Ian Hodder et al., 261–306. Cambridge: Cambridge University Press.

———. 1997. *Economy and Society in Prehistoric Europe: Changing Perspectives.* Princeton, NJ: Princeton University Press.

Sheratt, Susan, and Andrew Sheratt. 1993. "The Growth of the Mediterranean Economy in the Early First Millennium B.c." *World Archaeology* 24 (3): 361–78.

Sheratt, Susan. 1998. "Sea Peoples and the Economic Structure of the late 2nd Millennium in the Eastern Mediterranean." In *Mediterranean Peoples in Transition: 13th to Early 10th Century B.C.E.,* edited by S. Gitin, A. Mazar, and E. Sternleds, 292–313. Jerusalem: Jerusalem Archaeological Society.

———. 2000. "Circulation of Metals and the End of the Bronze Age in the Eastern Mediterranean." In *Metals Make the World Go Round,* edited by C. Pare, 82–98. Oxford: Oxbow Books.

Sidebotham, Steven. 1991. "Parts of the Red Sea and the Arabia-India Trade." In *Rome and India: The Ancient Sea Trade,* edited by V. Begley and R. DePuma, 12–38. Madison: University of Wisconsin Press.

Simkhovitch, V. 1916. "Rome's Fall Reconsidered." *Political Science Quarterly* 31: 201–43.

Singh, G. 1971. "The Indus Valley Culture Seen in the Context of Post Glacial and Ecological Studies in Northwest India." *Archaeology and Physical Anthropology in Oceania* 6 (2): 177–89.

———. et al. 1974. "Late Quaternary History of Vegetation and Climate of Rajasthan Desert India." *Philosophical Transactions of the Royal Society of London, B, Biological Sciences* 267 (889): 467–501.

———. 1990. "Vegetational and Seasonal Climatic Changes Since the Last Full Glacial in the Thar Desert, Northwestern India." *Review of Paleobotany and Palynology* 64: 351–58.

Slack, Paul, ed. 1999. *Environments and Historical Change.* Oxford: Oxford University Press.

Small, D. 1990. "Handmade Burnished Ware and Prehistoric Aegean Economics." *Journal of Mediterranean Archaeology* 3: 3–25.

Smith, R. E. 1972. "The Army Reforms of Septimius Severus." *Historica* 21: 481–90.

Smith, W. S. 1971. "The Old Kingdom in Egypt and the Beginning of the First Intermediate Period." In *The Cambridge Ancient History 1,* edited by I. E. S. Edwards, C. J. Gadd, and N. G. L. Hammond, 2 vols., 3rd ed., 145–207. Cambridge: Cambridge University Press.

Snodgrass, A. M. 1971. *The Dark Age of Greece.* Edinburgh: Edinburgh University Press.

———. 1980. *Archaic Greece.* London: MacMillan.

———. 1987. *An Archaeology of Greece.* Berkeley: University of California Press.

———. 1989. "The Coming of the Iron Age in Greece: Europe's Earliest Bronze/Iron Transition." In *The Bronze-Iron Age Transition in Europe,* edited by M. L. S. Sorensen and R. Thomas, BAR International Series no. 483. Oxford: Archeopress.

Sorensen, M. L. S. and R. Thomas, eds. 1989. *The Bronze Age-Iron Age Transition in Europe: Aspects of Continuity and Change in European Societies c 1200 to 500 B.C.* BAR International Series 483. Oxford: Archeopress.

Speth, James Gustave. 2004. *Red Sky at Morning*. New Haven, CT: Yale University Press.

Stager, L. 1992. "The Periodization of Palestine from Neolithic to Early Bronze Times." In *Chronologies in Old World Archaeology*, edited by R. Ehrich, 3rd ed., 22–41. Chicago: University of Chicago Press.

Stanislawski, D. 1973. "Dark Age Contributions to the Mediterranean Way of Life." *Annals of the Association of American Geographers* 63 (4): 397–410.

Stefanova, I. 1995. "Studies on the Holocene History of Vegetation in the Northern Pirin Mountains." In *Advances in Holocene Paleoecology in Bulgaria*, edited by T. Bozilova, 9–37. Sofia, Bulgaria: Tonkov.

Stein, Burton. 1998. *A History of India*. London: Blackwell.

Stein, Gils. 1999. *Rethinking World-Systems: Diaspora, Colonies, and Interaction in Uruk Mesopotamia*. Tucson: University of Arizona Press.

Steinberg, Ted. 2002. "Down to Earth: Nature, Agency, and Power in History." *American Historical Review* 107 (3): 798–820.

Stern, M. 1991. "Early Roman Export Glass in India." In *Rome and India*, edited by V. Begley and L. DePuma. Madison: University of Wisconsin Press.

Steward, Julian. 1955. *Cultural Causality and Law: A Trial Formulation of the Development of Early Civilizations*. Urbana: University of Illinois Press.

Strange, John. 1987. "The Transition from the Bronze Age to the Iron Age in the Eastern Mediterranean and the Emergence of the Israelite State." *Scandinavian Journal of the Old Testament* 2: 1–19.

Sürenhagen, D. 1986. "The Dry Farming Belt: The Uruk Period and Subsequent Development." In *The Origins of Cities in Dry Farming Syria and Mesopotamia in the Third Millennium B.C.*, edited by H. Weiss, 7–43. Guilford, CT: Four Quarters Publishing.

Symes, R. 1960. *The Roman Revolution*. Oxford: Oxford University Press.

Tacitus, Cornelius. 1925. *Histories Vol. 2*. Cambridge, MA: Harvard University Press.

Tainter, Joseph. 1988. *The Collapse of Complex Societies*. Cambridge: Cambridge University Press.

———. 1999. "Post Collapse Societies." In *Common Encyclopedia of Archaeology*, edited by G. Barker, 988–1039. London: Routledge.

———. 2000. "Problem Solving: Complexity, History, Sustainability." *Population and Environment* 22 (1): 3–41.

Tan, Ming, and Tungsheng Liu. et al. 2003. "Cyclic Rapid Warming on Centennial-Scale Revealed by a 2650-Year Stalagmite Record on Warm Season Temperature." *Geophysical Research Letters* 30 (12): 1617–20.

Tarasov, P. E. et al. 1994. "Lake Status Records from the Former Soviet Union and Mongolia: Data Base Documentation." Paleoclimatology Publication Series Report no. 2, World Data Center for Paleoclimatology, 86–88.

Teggart, F. 1969. *Rome and China*. Berkeley: University of California Press.

Thayer, Robert L. 2003. *Life-place: Bioregional Thought and Practice*. Berkeley: University of California Press.

Thompson, William R. 2000. "C-Waves, Center-Hinterland Contact and Regime Change in the Ancient Near East: Early Impacts of Globalization." Paper presented at International Studies Association Annual Meetings, Los Angeles. March 23–26.

———. 2001. "Trade Pulsations, Collapse, and Reorientation in the Ancient World." Paper presented at International Studies Association Annual Meetings, Chicago. March 24–27.

———. 2004. "Complexity, Diminishing Marginal Return and Serial Mesopotamia Fragmentation." Paper presented to the Working Group on Analyzing Complex Microsystems as Dynamic Networks, Santa Fe Institute, Santa Fe, New Mexico, April 28–May 2, 2004.

Tierney, Brian, and Sidney Painter. 1992. *Western Europe in the Middle Ages 300–1475.* New York: McGraw Hill.

Tilly, Charles. 1992. *Coercion, Capital, and European States A.D. 990–1992.* Oxford: Blackwell.

Tosi, Mauricio. 1982. "The Harappan Civilization: Beyond the Indian SubContinent." In *Harappan Civilization,* edited by G. Possehl, 64–79. New Delhi: Oxford University Press.

Toynbee, A. J. 1939. *A Study of History IV and V.* Oxford: Oxford University Press.

Treadgold, W. 1988. *The Byzantine Revival 780–842.* Stanford, CA: Stanford University Press.

———. 1995. *Byzantium and Its Army 284–1081.* Stanford, CA: Stanford University Press.

———. 1997. *A History of the Byzantine State and Society.* Stanford, CA: Stanford University Press.

Trigger, Bruce et al. 1983. *Ancient Egypt: A Social History.* Cambridge: Cambridge University Press.

———. 1985. *Early Civilizations: Ancient Egypt in Context.* Cairo: American University in Cairo Press.

———. 2003. *Understanding Early Civilizations: A Comparative Approach.* Cambridge: Cambridge University Press.

Tucker, Richard. 2000. *Insatiable Appetite: The United States and the Ecological Degradation of the Tropical World.* Berkeley: University of California Press.

United Nations Conference on Environment and Development. 1992. *Earth Summit '92.* London: The Regency Press.

United Nations Environment Programme. 2002. *World Environment Outlook.* Vol. 3. Nairobi: UNEP.

Van Andel, T., C. Runnels, and O. Pope. 1986. "Five Thousand Years of Land Use and Abuse in the Southern Argolid Greece." *Hesperia* Vol. 55 no. 1: 103–28.

Van Andel, T., and C. Runnels. 1987. *Beyond the Acropolis: A Rural Greek Past.* Stanford, CA: Stanford University Press.

———.1988. "An Essay on the Emergence of Civilization in the Aegean World." *Antiquity* 62 (235): 234–47.

Van Andel, T., and E. Zangger. 1990. "Landscape Stability and Destabilization in the Prehistory of Greece." In *Man's Role in the Shaping of the Eastern Mediterranean Landscape,* edited by S. Bottema and G. Entjes-Nieborg. The Hague: Elsevier.

————. and A. Demitrack. 1990. "Land Use and Soil Erosion in Prehistoric and Historical Greece." *Journal of Field Archaeology* 17 (4): 379–96.

Van De Mieroop, Marc. 1992. "Wood in Old Babylonian Texts from Southern Babylonia." In *Trees and Timber in Mesopotamia,* edited by J. N. Postgate and M. A. Powell. Bulletin on Sumerian Agriculture 6. Cambridge: Cambridge University.

————. 2004. *A History of the Ancient Near East.* Oxford: Blackwell Publishing.

Van Zeist, W. et al. 1980. "A Palynological Study of the Late-Glacial and the Postglacial in the Paris Basin." *Paleohistoria* 22: 67–109.

Velikovsky, Immanuel. 2003. *Ages in Chaos.* New York: Amereon Ltd.

Verbruggen, C. et al. 1997. "Paleoecological Events in Belgium during the Last 13,000 Years." In *Paleoecological Events in Europe during the Last 15,000 Years. Patterns, Processes, and Problems,* edited by C. Verbruggen, 67–94. Chichester, UK: J. Wiley.

Vermeule, Emily. 1960. "The Fall of the Mycenaean Empire." *Archaeology* 13 (1): 66–75.

Veschuren, D. 2004. "Decadal and Century-Scale Climate Variability in Tropical Africa during the Past 2000 Years." In *Past Climate Variability through Europe and Africa,* edited by R. W. Battarbee et al., 139–58. Dordrecht, The Netherlands: Springer.

Waldbaum, Jane. 1978. *From Bronze to Iron: The Transition from the Bronze Age to the Iron Age in the Eastern Mediterranean.* Goteborg, Sweden: Åströms.

————. 1980. "The First Archaeological Appearance of Iron." In *The Coming Age of Iron,* edited by T. A. Wertime and J. Muhly, 69–98. New Haven, CT: Yale University Press.

Wallerstein, I. 1974–1980. *The Modern World-System.* Vols. 1–3. New York: Academic Press.

————. 1979. "Kondratieff Up or Down." *Review* 2, (4): 663–73.

Ward, W. A., and Joukowsky, M.S. 1992. *The Crisis Years: The 12ᵗʰ Century B.C. from Beyond the Danube to the Tigris.* Dubuque, IA: Kendall Hunt.

Warren, Peter M. 1985. "Minoan Palaces." *Scientific American* 253 (1): 94–103.

Watrous, L. Vance. 1994. "Review of Aegean Prehistory III: Crete from Earliest Prehistory through the Protopalatial Period." *American Journal of Archaeology* 98: 695–753.

Watts, W. A. et al. 1996. "The Vegetation and Climate of Northwest Iberia over the Last 14,000 Years." *Journal of Quaternary Science* 11: 125–47.

Webster, Graham. 1985. *The Roman Imperial Army of the 1ˢᵗ and 2ⁿᵈ Centuries.* London: A. C. Black.

Webster, Leslie, and Michelle Brown, eds. 1997. *Transformation of the Roman World A.D. 400–900.* Berkeley: University of California Press.

Weinstein, James. 1989. "The Collapse of the Egyptian Empire in the Southern Levant." In *The Crisis Years,* edited by W. Ward and M. Joukowsky, 142–50. Dubuque, IA: Kendall Hunt.

Weiss, H. 1982. "The Decline of Late Bronze Age Civilization as a Possible Response to Climate Change." *Climate Change* 4: 173–98.

————. 2000. "Beyond the Younger Drayas." In *Environmental Disaster and the Archaeology of Human Response,* edited by G. Bawden and R. Reycraft, 75–98. Albuquerque: University of New Mexico Press.

————. et al. 1993. "The Genesis and Collapse of Third Millennium Northern Mesopotamian Civilization." *Science,* August 20, 995–1004.

Weiss, H., and R. Bradley. 2001. "Archaeology: What Drives Societal Collapse?" *Science* January 26, 609–10.

Wells, Peter. 1980. *Culture Contact and Culture Change: Early Iron Age Central Europe and the Mediterranean World.* Cambridge: Cambridge University Press.

————. 1984. *Farms, Villages, and Cities. Commerce and Urban Origins of Late Prehistoric Europe.* Ithaca, NY: Cornell University Press.

————. 1989. "Intensification, Entrepreneurship, and Cognitive Change in the Bronze-Iron Age Transition." In *The Bronze-Iron Age Transition in Europe,* edited by R. Thomas, BAR International Series no. 48, 355–64. Oxford: Archeopress.

————. 1999a. *Barbarians Speak: How Conquered People Shaped Roman Europe.* Princeton, NJ: Princeton University Press.

————. 1999b. "Production Within and Beyond Imperial Boundaries: Goods Exchange and Power in Roman Europe." In *World Systems Theory in Practice,* edited by Nick Kardulias, 85–102. London: Rowman & Littlefield.

Wertime, Theodore A. 1980. "The Pyrotechnologic Background." In *The Coming of the Age of Iron,* edited by T. Wertime and J. Muhly, 1–24. New Haven, CT: Yale University Press.

————. 1983. "The Furnace vs. the Goat: The Pyrotechnologie Industries and Mediterranean Deforestation in Antiquity." *Journal of Field Archaeology* 10: 445–52.

West, Louis C. 1935. *Roman Gaul: The Objects of Trade.* Oxford: Blackwell.

Wheeler, R. E. M. 1968. *The Indus Civilization.* Cambridge: Cambridge University Press.

White, Lynne. 1963. "What Accelerated Technological Progress in the Western Middle Ages." In *Scientific Change,* edited by A. C. Crombie, 272–91. London: Macmillan.

Whitley, James. 1991. *Style and Society in Dark Age Greece: The Changing Face of a Pre-Literate Society 1100–700 B.C.* Cambridge: Cambridge University Press.

Whittaker, C. R. 1994. *Frontiers of the Roman Empire.* Baltimore: Johns Hopkins University Press.

Widgren, Mats. 1983. *Settlement and Framing Systems in the Early Iron Age. A Study of Fossil Agrarian Landscapes, Östergötland, Sweden.* Stockholm: Almquist and Wiksell.

Wilkinson, David. 1991. "Cores, Peripheries, Civilizations." In *Core-Periphery Relations in Pre-Capitalist Worlds,* edited by C. Chase-Dunn and T. Hall. Boulder, CO: Westview Press.

————. 1995. "Civilizations Are World Systems!" In *Civilizations and World Systems,* edited by Stephen Sanderson. Walnut Creek, CA: AltaMira Press.

Wilkinson, T. J. 1990. *Town and Country in Southeastern Anatolia.* Chicago: Oriental Institute.

————. 1997. "Environmental Fluctuations, Agricultural Production, and Collapse: A View from Bronze Age Upper Mesopotamia." In *Third Millennium BC Climate Change and Old World Collapse,* H. Dalfes et al., 67–105. Berlin: Springer-Verlag.

Willcox, G. H. 1974. "A History of Deforestation as Indicated by Charcoal Analysis of Four Sites in Eastern Anatolia." *Anatolian Studies* 24: 116–33.

———. 1992. "Timber and Trees: Ancient Exploitation in the Middle East." In *Trees and Timber in Mesopotamia,* edited by J. N. Postgate and M. A. Powell. Bulletin on Sumerian Agriculture 6. Cambridge: Cambridge University.

Williams, L. D. and T. M. L. Wigley. 1983. "A Comparison of Evidence for Late Holocene Summer Temperature Variations in the Northern Hemisphere." *Quaternary Research* 20: 286–307.

Williams, Michael. 1990. "Forests." In *The Earth as Transformed by Human Action,* edited by B. L. Turner, William C. Clark, Robert W. Kates, John Richards, Jessica Mathews, and William B. Meyer. Cambridge: Cambridge University Press.

———. 1997. "Imperialism and Deforestation." In *Ecology and Empire,* edited by Tom Griffiths and Robin Coles Libby. Seattle: University of Washington Press.

———. 2000. "Dark Ages and Dark Areas: Global Deforestation in the Deep Past." *Journal of Historical Geography* 26 (1): 28–46.

———. 2003. *Deforesting the Earth: From Prehistory to Global Crisis.* Chicago: University of Chicago Press.

Wilson, E. O. 2002. *The Future of Life.* New York: Alfred Knopf.

Wolf, Eric. 1982. *Europe and the People without History.* Berkeley: University of California Press.

Wolfram, Herwig. 1990. *The Roman Empire and Its Germanic Peoples.* Berkeley: University of California Press.

Wood, Michael. 1991. *In Search of Dark Ages.* London: BBC Books.

Woolley, Leonard. 1953. *A Forgotten Kingdom.* Harmondsworth, UK: Penguin.

World Commission on Environment and Development. 1987. *Our Common Future.* Oxford: Oxford University Press.

World Commission on Forests and Sustainable Development. 1999. *Our Forests Our Future.* Cambridge: Cambridge University Press.

Wright, H. E. 1968. "Climate Change in Mycenaen Greece." *Antiquity* 42: 123–27.

———. 1972. "Vegetation History." In *The Minnesota Messinia Expedition,* edited by W. A. MacDonald and G. R. Rapp, 188–99. Minneapolis: University of Minnesota Press.

Yasuda, Yoshinori et al. 2000. "The Earliest Record of Major Anthropogenic Deforestation in the Ghab Valley, Northwest Syria: A Palynological Study." *Quaternary International* 73/74: 127–36.

Yoffee, Norman. 1988. "The Collapse of Ancient Mesopotamian States and Civilization." In *The Collapse of Ancient States and Civilizations,* edited by N. Yoffee and G. Cowgill, 44–68. Tucson: University of Arizona Press.

Yon, Marguerite. 1989. "The End of the Kingdom of Ugarit." In *The Crisis Years,* edited by W. Ward and M. Joukowsky, 111–22. Dubuque, IA: Kendall Hunt.

Zaccagnini, C. 1986. "Aspects of Copper Trade in the Eastern Mediterranean during the Late Bronze Age." In *Traffici micenei Mediterraneo,* edited by M. Marazzi, S. Tusa, and L. Vagnetti, 413–24. Rome: Taranto.

———. 1990. "The Transition from Bronze to Iron in the Near East and in the Levant: Marginal Notes." *Journal of American Oriental Society* 110: 493–502.

Zangger, E. 1993. "Neolithic to Present Soil Erosion in Greece." In *Past and Present Soil Erosion,* edited by M. Bell and J. Boardman, 133–47. Oxford: Oxbow Press.

————. 1998. "The Environmental Setting." In *Sandy Pylos*, edited by Jack Davis, 1–9. Austin: University of Texas Press.

Zohary, D., and M. Hopf. 1993. *Domestication of Plants in the Old World*. Oxford: Oxford University Press.

Index

About the Author

Sing C. Chew is senior research scientist in the Department of Urban and Environmental Sociology, Helmholtz Centre for Environmental Research—UFZ, Leipzig, Germany, and professor of Sociology at Humboldt State University, Arcata, California. He is the founding editor of the interdisciplinary journal *Nature and Culture*. This book is the second volume of a three-volume series on Nature-Culture relations over world history of which the first volume, *World Ecological Degradation: Accumulation, Urbanization, and Deforestation 3000 B.C.–A.D. 2000* has been published. He is presently completing the third volume, entitled *Ecological Futures: What Can History Tell Us*.